Other Books by James Garbarino

Children and Families in the Social Environment
(with associates)

Troubled Youth, Troubled Families
(with C. Schellenbach, J. Sebes, and associates)

The Psychologically Battered Child:
Strategies for Identification, Assessment, and Intervention
(with E. Guttmann and J. W. Seeley)

What Children Can Tell Us
(with F. Stott and associates)

No Place to Be a Child:
Growing Up in a War Zone
(with K. Kostelny and N. Dubrow)

Children in Danger:
Coping with the Consequences of Community Violence
(with N. Dubrow, K. Kostelny, and C. Pardo)

Raising Children in a Socially Toxic Environment

Understanding Abusive Families
(with J. Eckenrode and associates)

Lost Boys

Why Our Sons Turn Violent and
How We Can Save Them

JAMES GARBARINO, Ph.D.

THE FREE PRESS

THE FREE PRESS
A Division of Simon & Schuster Inc.
1230 Avenue of the Americas
New York, NY 10020

THE FREE PRESS and colophon are trademarks
of Simon & Schuster Inc.

Designed by Carla Bolte

Manufactured in the United States of America

10   9   8   7   6   5   4

Library of Congress Cataloging-in-Publication Data

Garbarino, James.
    Lost boys: why our sons turn violent and how we can save them/
James Garbarino.
        p.   cm.
    Includes bibliographical references.
    1. Youth and violence—United States.   2. Violence—United States—
Prevention.   I. Title
HQ799.2.V56G37   1999   99-19897   CIP
303.6'0835—dc21

ISBN 0-684-85908-4

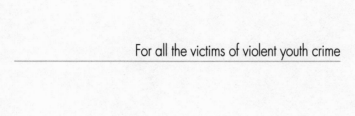

For all the victims of violent youth crime

Contents

Preface

Youth violence is spreading across America. Until recently, acts of lethal youth violence were mostly confined to certain parts of the United States, most notably the war zone neighborhoods of New York, Chicago, Detroit, Los Angeles, Houston, and other big cities. As a society we have become numb or indifferent to this fact of life. But when young boys in Pearl, Mississippi, Paducah, Kentucky, Jonesboro, Arkansas, and Springfield, Oregon, went on shooting sprees aimed at their classmates in 1998, they made headlines across the country and around the world. These dramatic acts of violence provoked anger and dismay across the United States, in part because while we have grown accustomed to lethal violence among inner-city, impoverished minority youth, we are stunned to see it happen in the heartland of America, where such killings seem particularly senseless. People want to know why this tragedy is happening and what they can do to stop it from happening to their kids or the kids in their community.

Whether or not your child has an easy temperament and is peaceful and nonviolent, he or she has peers who are angry and sad—and capable of lethal violence. Whether or not you or your neighbor maltreats, rejects, ignores, or abandons children, virtually all parents send their kids to school with children who *are* maltreated, rejected, ignored, or abandoned, and who thus are at special risk for becoming violent.

This book is my effort to make sense of senseless youth violence. In writing it I have listened to the words of violent youth themselves and have attempted to make sense of what they have to say through the lens of the latest child development research. But I don't stop there: I go on to use that understanding as the basis for proposing strategies to prevent youth violence, when possible, and to rehabilitate violent teenagers when prevention fails, as it sometimes does no matter how much we invest in efforts to teach nonviolence to our children.

For more than twenty-five years I have been studying violence and its impact on children and youth in the United States and around the world. I relied on these early years of study to prepare in 1994 for a segment on NBC's *Dateline* in which correspondent Stone Phillips and I visited a youth prison in North Carolina to interview three boys serving time for violent crimes. One had shot a cop, another had fatally shot his stepfather, and the third had murdered a friend of his family. Despite my years of studying violence, I left that prison knowing my expertise was incomplete. I realized that I had to learn more about youth violence from the perspective of the kids who kill.

This desire to know more intensified when I was asked to serve as an expert witness in several youth homicide trials in Colorado, Illinois, Wisconsin, Washington, New York, and Florida. I realized that neither I nor my colleagues active in this area know enough to do what needs to be done to help kids and protect society.

In the wake of those trials I teamed up with my colleague Claire Bedard to interview kids who had committed acts of lethal violence and were in jail serving out their sentences or awaiting trial. Claire came from a background in human rights education and international work with street children. She brought a keen insight into how to approach troubled boys in a way that would open up channels of communication. Together we assembled a small team of professionals and students at Cornell University's Family Life Development Center, a unit of the College of Human Ecology, where I am the co-director and a professor of human development.

I interviewed each boy one-on-one over a period of weeks to hear him out. This was not the first time these boys had talked to adults about their lives and their crimes, of course; they had all been interrogated and evaluated numerous times. But virtually every boy said that he had never before told his *whole* story to anyone.

I have seen and heard a lot about violence in my work in the last twenty-five years. As a representative of UNICEF, I interviewed Kuwaiti children in the wake of the Gulf War in 1991 and heard about the Iraqi atrocities they witnessed. In the Middle East during the late 1980s, I listened to Palestinian kids talk about how the street soldiers in the Intifada threw rocks at Israeli soldiers and how they all had to deal with the rubber bullets and tear gas that came back at them. But the litany of violent experiences I hear from some boys in America still staggers me. They have participated in drug-related kidnappings, both as victim and as perpetrator; they have been the target of drive-by shootings, and they have retaliated with drive-by shootings of their own. Some of them have committed numerous armed robberies. Many of them have scars on their bodies from beatings administered by mothers, fathers, uncles, stepfathers, drug bosses, and neighborhood rivals. Some of them have been beaten up by the police.

In this book I introduce some of the boys I came to know. I rely upon my knowledge of child and adolescent development as a psychologist to provide a context for their first-person accounts, which come from face-to-face interviews conducted from fall 1996 to fall 1998. I have changed the boys' names and enough details of their stories to protect their identities without altering the meaning and significance of their accounts.

As a father and stepfather of boys myself, I was able to recognize both the everydayness of the interviewed boys' self-doubts and concerns (e.g., about popularity and image) and the differentness of the challenges they faced: handling humiliation and rejection at home and at school, earning respect as a drug dealer, encountering lethal violence on every corner, making do without sufficient adult monitoring.

Sitting behind closed doors week after week with boys who have nowhere to go, I gained a new appreciation for the value and the power of reflection, introspection, reading, and an open heart—on both the part of the boy and the therapist—in the process of human growth and development. I came to understand better than ever before the power of one's story, the value of one's personal narrative in making sense of experience, no matter how dark that experience may have been. And I came to appreciate as never before the critical importance of taking time, of being given time, and of feeling included. In no case did I condone the violent acts committed by the boy sitting before me. But I did come to understand that making sense of a horrible act without judging the person who committed it is possible when you start from a basic respect for the humanness of the perpetrator and refuse to give in to the temptation to demonize him, regardless of what he has done.

Because I believe that understanding without acting is irresponsible,

I want to share some conclusions I have reached about what it will take to make a difference in these young lives, including how schools can do a better job of preventing violent acts and how the youth prison system can provide violent youth with a first opportunity to learn alternative models for living and being. I consider the power of personal and spiritual development to be a vital resource in healing the traumatized child inside the teenager who kills. I search for ways to offer these teens less toxic alternatives to the communities that spawned them. For me, these insights are the key to helping people understand what is happening and what we all can do to stop it, the key to recovering the lost boys and preventing another generation of boys from becoming lost in the first place.

There are many people who contributed to the writing of this book, and I offer them my thanks and appreciation. Claire Bedard is first on the list. Her influence is felt throughout this book. The staff at the MacCormick Secure Center and the Gossett Center were extremely helpful, particularly Joe Impicciatore, Alvin Lollie, Reuben Reyes, Brenda Aulbach, and Puck Wullenweber. And I express my appreciation to the boys and young men who opened themselves up to me and showed me what lethal youth violence looks like from the inside out. For legal and ethical reasons I cannot name them, but I thank them here in public, as I have in private.

Thanks to Dean Francille Firebaugh at Cornell for her support of the Making Sense of "Senseless" Youth Violence Project. And many thanks to my colleagues on the Project at the Family Life Development Center who played a role in the creation of this book, including Jane Powers, Joe Vorrasi, Matt Davidson, Sarah Weintraub, Denise Oliveira, Virginia Schuford, and Brian Bloom. I am grateful to Joe and Matt for helping me coordinate the details of the final manuscript, especially the references and the resouce list in the appendix; I could not have finished the manuscript without their help. Thanks also to my brother John, who works with troubled, delinquent youth, and to Robin Casarjian, who works with incarcerated men, for sharing their understanding with me, and to my colleagues at the Family Life Development Center who read an early draft of the manuscript. Thanks to Robin Hamlish, who provided wise counsel as I struggled with the emotional challenges of involving myself in the lives of young men on death row. And special thanks to Phillip Krist, whose perspective on youth violence has shaped my ideas.

Particular thanks go to my agent Victoria Sanders, with whom I clicked from the first moment and who guided this project to its natural home with the Free Press. At the Free Press the manuscript found a sympathetic, thoughtful, challenging, and generous friend in my editor, Philip Rappaport; I appreciate his skill and his tenacity. Finally, I thank my children—Josh and Joanna, and my stepson Eric—for being there.

February 5, 1999

THE EPIDEMIC OF YOUTH VIOLENCE

PROLOGUE: CHICAGO, JANUARY 1994

I lived and worked in Chicago for almost ten years, from the mid-1980s to the mid-1990s. My children grew up there. Throughout 1993, the *Chicago Tribune* published in-depth profiles of every kid who was killed in Chicago that year. As an expert on violence and trauma, I spent a lot of time talking with reporters in an attempt to help them make sense of what they had found during their investigation of each case. The reporters worked on the project all through 1993, and in a single issue at the beginning of 1994 the *Tribune* published the photo and name of every single child and teenager who had been murdered during the previous twelve months. It was a chilling and haunting sight to see the rows and rows of names and faces—sixty-one in all.

The same night the *Tribune* published the death toll from 1993, my seventeen-year-old son Josh was heading out for an evening on the town with his friends. "Be careful," I said. "It's dangerous out there, and I worry about you." He turned to me, with the *Tribune* in hand, and said, "Don't worry, Dad. Just how many white faces and names like mine do you see in the newspaper?" The reality was that in 1994 he could reassure me by this simple reference to the facts of the matter; you had to look long and hard at those rows of photos in the *Tribune* to find a white teenage face with a non-Hispanic surname. Even though we lived in the city, within walking distance of some of the most violent streets in America, Josh felt safe.

When my son's observation forced me to confront this reality, I recalled a meeting I had attended just weeks before. I was the lone white person on a panel of African American and Hispanic professionals for a community forum on violence. During the coffee break we panel members began chatting among ourselves, and it turned out that all of us had teenage sons. As we talked about being parents of teenagers in the city, it became clear to me that while I *worried* when my son went out at night, my African American and Hispanic colleagues felt *dread*, because they thought of their boys as part of an endangered species, even though the actual number of children killed that year was less than one hundred in a city of three million. But that number is a compelling feature of the violence problem; even a relatively small number of deaths can stimulate a profound sense of threat and insecurity in a community. Homicide *is* the leading cause of death for minority male youth, and each new death creates tremendous psychological reverberations. The feeling of extreme apprehension my colleagues experienced was neither paranoid nor far-fetched.

That was 1994. Fast-forward to 1998. By May of that year, I was living and working in Ithaca, a small university town located in the rolling hills of central New York State. Ithaca is a lovely place, mostly known for being the home of Cornell University. For many years and for most of its citizens, Ithaca has been a kind of idyllic paradise where the big news is likely to be the awarding of a prize to a member of Cornell's faculty or a local school board meeting (among vegetarians it is famous as the home of the Moosewood Restaurant, which inspired a popular cookbook).

On May 22, 1998, my fifteen-year-old daughter Joanna and my fourteen-year-old stepson Eric sat at the kitchen table reading the newspaper, which that morning was filled with accounts of the shooting of twenty-four students in Springfield, Oregon, by fifteen-year-old Kip Kinkel. Looking up from the front-page story, Joanna, shaking her head, said, "I wonder who it's going to be at our school."

NO ONE IS IMMUNE

The 1997–1998 school year will go down in American history as the turning point in our country's experience and understanding of lethal youth violence. *October 1, 1997, Pearl, Mississippi:* after killing his mother, sixteen-year-old Luke Woodham opens fire at his high school, killing three and wounding seven. *December 1, 1997, West Paducah, Kentucky:* fourteen-year-old Michael Carneal kills three students at a high school prayer meeting. *March 24, 1998, Jonesboro, Arkansas:* thirteen-year-old Mitchell Johnson and eleven-year-old Andrew Golden open fire on their schoolmates, killing four of them and a teacher. *April 24, 1998, Edinboro, Pennsylvania:* fourteen-year-old Andrew Wurst kills a teacher at a school dance. *May 21, 1998, Springfield, Oregon:* after killing his parents, fifteen-year-old Kip Kinkel walks into the school cafeteria and shoots twenty-four classmates, two fatally.

These cases made the national and international news. All the assailants were middle-class, white teenagers from small towns or the suburbs. But these headline-grabbing shooting sprees reminded some families and victims of youth violence of crimes that, although similar, did not seem to merit the attention of the national and international media. Standing just offscreen, beyond our gaze, were hundreds of other kids who had committed acts of lethal violence. Most of us never heard about the adolescents who shot and killed other kids in the inner-city neighborhoods of Houston, Chicago, New York, Los Angeles, and Detroit during that same school year. They remained mostly anonymous.

What about the fourteen-year-old African American kid who shot an eighteen-year-old convenience store clerk? The fifteen-year-old Hispanic kid who opened fire with an assault rifle on a street full of kids? The sixteen-year-old African American who gunned down three teens outside his apartment building? The fifteen-year-old Asian boy who executed a sixteen-year-old with a single shot to the head? Rarely do cases like these make the national news, and when they do, the perpetrators are usually described in dehumanized terms ("cold-blooded," "remorseless," "vicious") that lead us to speculate on whether or not these kids are even human. Rarely do we hear of inquiries into their emotional lives or of efforts to make sense of their acts. Why is that?

Is it because the high-visibility cases all involved white kids from the small towns and suburbs of the American heartland while the anonymous killers were poor kids, predominantly African American and Hispanic, living in inner-city neighborhoods? Is it easier for the media and the general public to forget or demonize the low-income minority kids who kill? Some informed observers of the role of race and class in our society have said publicly that they think the answer is yes.

3

Given our society's history of institutional and interpersonal racism, it would be naive to think that poor minority kids automatically get the same attention and concern as white and middle-class kids do. A number of respected African American psychiatrists, psychologists, lawyers, and community leaders addressed this point in interviews conducted by journalist Zachary Dowdy in 1998. Harvard psychiatrist Alvin Poussaint said, "When white middle-class kids kill, there is always a public outcry of why and a search for what went wrong, but when inner-city minority kids kill, the public is warned of demons and superpredators." Bill Talley, a public defender who has spent years representing inner-city kids in court, put it this way, "No one's calling these white youths 'maggots or animals.'" Judge Milton Wright noted that when Kip Kinkel committed his murders in Springfield, Oregon, *Newsweek* began its coverage this way: "With his shy smile and slight build, 15-year-old Kip Kinkel has an innocent look that is part Huck Finn and part Alfred E. Neuman—boyish and quintessentially American." Wright went on to say, "Quintessentially American? That always means white."

I have seen firsthand verification of this class and race bias. When I began working on issues of lethal violence and violent trauma in the lives of inner-city kids more than a decade ago, it was hard to get the attention of most Americans, beyond the professionals and parents who lived or worked in inner-city minority communities. The rest of America could afford to ignore the violence when it seemed to be "them," not "us." Perhaps the worst example of this came when a staff member from a congressional committee visited me in my office in Chicago to discuss the issue of lethal youth violence. He found out the problem was mainly confined to inner-city minority populations, and when he communicated this fact to the legislators he represented, they decided it wasn't worth holding hearings on the matter. Nasty, indeed, but brutally honest as an expression of politics as usual.

But the lack of interest among mainstream white America has its origins in more than racism and class bias. Until recently, most American parents *could* count on the fact that random youth violence was not their problem but a problem for others. After all, 84 percent of the counties in the entire country recorded no youth homicides at all in 1995, and parents and children in most places must have felt a kind of immunity—if they thought about it at all—because they, like my son in 1994, didn't see themselves in the pictures of the killers and the killed. But that was before Jonesboro and Paducah and Springfield, before the cast of characters expanded, and young middle-class Americans, like my daughter, came to see that this could happen to them and their schoolmates.

Now new voices of concern are heard, new faces appear in the newspaper, and new people show up for my lectures and my workshops on violence, trauma, and kids who kill. The killings in the small towns and suburbs during the 1997–1998 school year have served as a kind of wakeup call for America. But this is also an opportunity for Americans to wake up to the fact that the terrible phenomenon of youth violence has been commonplace for the past twenty years and to learn from the experiences of those who have lived with this problem for the last two decades.

In June of 1998, I was speaking at a meeting of mothers who had buried murdered sons. There were more than a dozen mothers in the audience, mostly African American and Hispanic women, bearing the black-draped photos of their dead sons and wearing the commemorative ribbons as testimony to an epidemic of lethal youth violence that is all too familiar to them. But they are no longer alone. The old faces and voices have not disappeared or grown silent but, rather, have been added to as every parent in the country now wonders, *Where next? Is my child safe? Could it happen here? What can we do?*

WHAT CAN WE LEARN FROM THE PAST?

What do the large number of anonymous killings have to do with the highly publicized killings in Jonesboro and Paducah and Springfield? What do they have in common? In this book we will find answers by moving beyond the surface differences between the two groups of violent boys—principally class and race—to see the profound emotional and psychological similarities that link them together. By getting to know the circumstances under which the epidemic of youth violence first took hold, among low-income minority youth in inner-city areas, we can begin to gain some insight into the lives of the boys in places like Jonesboro, Paducah, and Springfield.

My goal is to understand why kids kill and to help other parents and professionals understand so that they can do something to prevent it in the future. Certainly, there are individuals and cases that defy explanation; some youth violence is committed by kids who have totally lost touch with reality. But these truly are the exceptions. I believe we can make some sense of youth violence from the inside out, that is, by looking deeply into the lives of kids who kill and by listening closely to their own stories. In doing so we can see how problems accumulate and recognize the sequence of events in the life of a child that leads from childhood play to lethal violence, whether these events occur in urban war zones or in the small towns and suburbs of the heartland.

For the past twenty-five years I have studied children and youth in many different settings. My research fills books. Hardly a week goes by that I don't talk with a journalist or get on an airplane to go lecture to professionals or concerned citizens about murder, child abuse, war, and other violent trauma. How do I know what to say to people? Where do I find clues to understand how an innocent infant grows up to be a killer? In my work I always try to combine two sources of information: First, I listen to children who have killed to hear their individual stories. Second, I examine systematic research on the causes of violence in the lives of children and youth. In the pages and chapters that follow, I blend these two sources, drawing upon one to illuminate and make sense of the other, always with the intent to show how what we have learned about the epidemic of killing among inner-city boys can shed light on the boys of the American heartland who are the new casualties of that epidemic.

HOW MUCH KILLING IS THERE?

The FBI reports that there are about twenty-three thousand homicides each year in the United States. In about 10 percent of these cases, the perpetrator is under eighteen years of age. If we extend the age cutoff to include youth up to the age of twenty-one, the figure is about 25 percent. But while the homicide data, which are used widely for comparative purposes, may be reliable, their meanings are not transparent or unambiguous. There are many complexities and subtleties to be considered in making sense of the numbers.

For one thing, improved medical trauma technology has meant that an injury that would have been fatal just twenty years ago is today much less likely to result in death. Children survive gunshot wounds and stabbings that once were fatal, just as a 90 percent cure rate saves them from certain childhood cancers that forty years ago promised a nearly certain early death. An example of the change with respect to homicide is seen in Chicago, where from the mid-1970s to the mid-1990s the number of serious assaults (attacks that could lead to the death of the victim) increased 400 percent while the homicide rate remained about the same. This factor is particularly important when we try to look at long-term historical trends, such as when we compare the homicide rate of the nineteenth century with that of the twentieth century or when we compare data from the first half of this century with data from the last ten or twenty years.

Furthermore, any consideration of the overall homicide rate should be tempered by an appreciation of the role of age and gender in this crime. For instance, it is well known that young men are about ten times as likely as young women to commit murder. Thus, historical comparisons may be skewed by changes in the population's age and gender profile. For example, if a society with an average age of fifteen has the same total homicide rate as a society with an average age of thirty, it probably means that the first society has much less lethal *youth* violence than the second one.

American homicide data are subject to distorted analysis if one fails to consider two important facts: First, the average age of perpetrators of homicide decreased in the United States from thirty-three years of age in 1965 to twenty-seven years of age in 1993. Second, while the overall homicide rate has been relatively constant over the last thirty years, the youth homicide rate has risen. The period of greatest growth was from the mid-1980s to the mid-1990s, when the youth homicide rate increased by 168 percent. In other words, the problem of youth homicide is obscured when one looks at the total national picture, because the increased numbers of older Americans dilute the effect of rising youth homicide rates on the overall rate for the country as a whole.

Much has been made in the press and in city halls around the country of the welcome news that the total national homicide rate took a dip from 1991 to 1997. Similarly, after more than a decade of steady increase, homicides by juveniles dropped 17 percent between 1994 and 1995 (which still leaves the rate more than 50 percent higher than it was in 1980). Does this mean the problem is under control? Not necessarily, according to criminologist James Fox of Northeastern University's College of Criminal Justice. For one thing, homicide rates in general and our juvenile homicide in particular remain much higher in the United States than they are in other industrialized societies, such as the countries of Europe. Closer to home, Canada is reporting a youth homicide rate about one tenth as high as the United States.

What is more, criminologists expect fluctuations because of the many influences on the number of murders there are each year. For example, higher rates of incarceration for lesser offenses take some likely killers out of circulation. The lethal violence associated with the highly competitive nature of illegal drug dealing has been associated with the extraordinary levels of youth homicide reported for some inner-city neighborhoods. But since the mid-1990s, the drug business in some cities has settled down and become better organized, resulting in a decrease in the youth homicide rate. And several communities have been undertaking major campaigns to curtail violence in their inner-city areas. In the mid-1990s Boston was able to cut its youth homicide rate to zero for a period of two years. As we shall see in Chapter Seven, these city programs have a great deal to teach suburban and rural communities.

To reach a true understanding of why children kill, we need to look beyond short-term trends. Certainly, the long-term trends are very disturbing. According to the FBI, juvenile arrests for possession of weapons, aggravated assault, robbery, and murder rose more than 50 percent from 1987 to 1996. Looking back still further, we can see a sevenfold increase in serious assault by juveniles in the United States since World War II. But perhaps the most disturbing trend is that while the overall youth homicide rate dropped in 1997, the rate among small town and rural youth increased by 38 percent. And that last statistic highlights my conviction that no longer can any of us believe that we and our children are immune to lethal youth violence, because today almost every teenager in American goes to school with a kid who is troubled enough to become the next killer—and chances are that kid has access to the weapons necessary to do so.

KIDS WHO KILL THEMSELVES

Throughout this book we will be looking closely at children who lash out at other children or adults. But we shouldn't lose sight of the young people who turn their violence inward, the kids who kill themselves. Suicide among juveniles is a serious problem. According to recent statistics, each murder committed by an adolescent is matched by a suicide—about twenty-three hundred each year. And just as youth homicide rates have risen dramatically in recent decades, so too have youth suicide rates skyrocketed—400 percent since 1950.

According to the Centers for Disease Control and Prevention (CDC) survey of youth, 15 percent of high school boys seriously considered suicide in 1997. About 12 percent of boys made a suicide plan, and 5 percent actually attempted suicide. Two percent of the boys attempted suicide in ways that required medical attention. The CDC study also shows that while girls are more likely to contemplate, plan, and attempt suicide, more boys than girls complete the act, reflecting the more lethal methods chosen by boys. Boys use guns while girls tend to use pills.

Harvard University psychiatrist James Gilligan points out in his in-depth look at the world of incarcerated violent men that acts of self-destruction and the destruction of others often have a similar source in the psychology of men involved in lethal violence, namely, the sense that life is intolerable. Thus, the links between suicide and homicide for boys are an important part of the problem facing anyone who cares about kids. Sometimes only at the last minute does a boy choose between killing himself and killing others; sometimes he does both.

In some cases, the act of killing others is itself intended as a suicide attempt. The phrase "suicide by cop" has been used by journalists and police to denote the act of provoking a confrontation with the intent to be killed by police. The first words spoken by fifteen-year-old Kip Kinkel when he was wrestled to the ground by fellow students after his shooting spree in Springfield, Oregon, were reportedly, "Kill me! Kill me!" Understanding the frequent self-destructive impulses in kids who kill is a necessary element of the overall task before us.

WHERE DID THE EPIDEMIC OF YOUTH VIOLENCE START?

As I noted earlier, the federal government's Office of Juvenile Justice and Delinquency Prevention reports that 84 percent of all counties in the United States had no juvenile homicides in 1995 and 10 percent reported only one; in fact, 25 percent of all known juvenile homicides that year were committed in five cities: Chicago, New York, Los Angeles, Detroit, and Houston. Together these cities contain about 10 percent of the nation's population. Why was there such a concentration of youth violence in these cities?

Think about the characteristics that increase a teenager's risk of joining the ranks of boys who kill. As a result of their research, Chicago-based psychologists Robert Zagar and his colleagues published a paper in 1991 that offers a picture of this risk. These researchers found that a boy's chances of committing murder are *twice as high* if he has the following risk factors:

- He comes from a family with a history of criminal violence.
- He has a history of being abused.
- He belongs to a gang.
- He abuses alcohol or drugs.

The *odds triple* when in addition to the aforementioned risk factors the following also apply:

- He uses a weapon.
- He has been arrested.
- He has a neurological problem that impairs thinking and feeling.
- He has difficulties at school and has a poor attendance record.

The odds increase as the number of risk factors increases. This is a general principle in understanding human development. Rarely, if ever, does one single risk factor tell the whole story or determine a person's future. Rather, it is the buildup of negative influences and experiences that accounts for differences in how youth turn out. This is one of the most important things to remember in understanding boys who kill. If we try to find *the* cause of youth violence, we will be frustrated and confused; we may even decide it is completely unpredictable and incomprehensible. It is important to recognize the central importance of risk accumulation.

Understanding comes from seeing the whole picture of a boy's life, whether he is a troubled middle-class boy in a town like Springfield, Oregon, or a troubled poor child in inner-city Los Angeles.

Chicago, New York, Los Angeles, Detroit, and Houston have in common large and numerous inner-city "war zone" neighborhoods where many children experience a buildup of the risks identified by Zagar's group. These neighborhoods have the highest rates of adult criminality, child maltreatment, gang activity, illicit drug sales, possession of illegal hand guns by kids, health problems in newborns, and school failure. In addition, most of the children in such neighborhoods have experienced the ravages of racism. Sociologists have long recognized that the experience of racial discrimination provokes feelings of rage and shame, which play a potent role in stimulating violence.

Interestingly, the U.S. populations most affected by the epidemic of youth violence are the ones that have been disproportionately influenced by the particular historical and cultural patterns found in the South. Social analyst and journalist Fox Butterfield, who explored this Southern effect, reported that the highest homicide rates in the United States are found among those who have roots in the Old South. For example, in 1996 all of the states that constituted the Confederacy during the Civil War were on the list of the twenty states with the highest homicide rates. The ten states with the lowest rates were located in New England and the northern Midwest. Thus, for example, in 1996 Louisiana's homicide rate was twelve times that of South Dakota. This pattern was as true in the nineteenth century as it is today.

In his book *Murder in America*, historian Roger Lane of Haverford College points out that until the 1960s America's big cities had murder rates lower than the national average because Southern states had the highest rates and were predominantly rural. What is the reason for this connection between Southern culture and violence? Historian Samuel Hyde at Southeastern Louisiana University has explored this phenomenon and has concluded that it reflects the special cultural and political history of the South, notably the system of slavery and the violence associated with the prosecution and aftermath of the Civil War.

Institutionalized violence plays a role in breeding a cycle of violence across generations. But religious tradition is important as well. Sociologist Christopher Ellison at Duke University found that the public religious culture of the South plays an important role in legitimizing violence by making revenge a moral requirement. Those who transgress against one's honor or kin must be punished.

Psychologist Richard Nisbett and his colleagues at the University of Michigan have also studied this phenomenon and confirm that it is the code of honor that is passed on from generation to generation through childrearing that accounts for this cultural susceptibility to homicide. Nisbett's research has found that when a young man from the South encounters an insult (e.g., being bumped and called a jerk by a fellow student in a school hallway), his pattern of response differs from that of a young man from the Northeast. Southerners tend to react with anger, and their bodies show an increase in stress-related hormones. Northeastern young men are more likely to respond with laughter and without any detectable rise in hormone levels. Whereas Fox Butterfield has detailed these issues in his work, it is beyond the scope of this book to further explore the cultural and social forces in Southern history. Yet these forces do play a role in lethal youth violence. How?

One place to look for answers is in the fact that the African Americans who constitute the bulk of the population in inner-city neighborhoods have their origins in the Old South. This is not simply a matter of long-ago generations making the trip from the South to the cities of New York, Chicago, Los Angeles, and Detroit; it is common for younger generations to spend time in their family's ancestral homes in the Old South. When I interview boys in prison, I often hear them speak about summer trips to Alabama or Mississippi or being sent back to Louisiana or South Carolina when they get in trouble "up North."

It is not race per se but, rather, the *role of race* in the situation created by all the other influences that makes the difference in homicide rates. In 1994 the African American youth homicide rate was eight times the rate for white youth. Butterfield's analysis makes clear that this disparity has much more to do with the Southern origins of black youth than with their African heritage. Speaking to this point, psychiatrist James Gilligan reports that the homicide rates of blacks living in Africa are generally no higher than the homicide rates in other countries. And in the United States, the rate for African Americans outside inner-city neighborhoods is no higher than that of the rest of the population. The combination of racism and cultural values that promote violence as a response to perceived insult exerts a devastating influence on children wherever it is geographically concentrated and coupled with economic deprivation, such as is the case with blacks in South Africa, who have been shaped by apartheid, and the aboriginal peoples of Australia, who suffered through generations of cultural genocide. In fact, these two groups have homicide rates that are among the highest in the world.

What I have attempted to show is that the origins of lethal youth violence lie in a complex set of influences. The Southern culture in the United States as a single influence does not explain everything, of course. A code of honor by itself, no matter its origins, does not explain everything. Indeed, no single factor—neither racism nor economic deprivation nor child abuse—can provide the answer to the question of why kids kill. But this does not mean we are powerless to make sense of what is happening. Quite the contrary. We have at our disposal concepts that can take us far in our efforts to understand why our sons turn violent and how we can save them. Most important, these ideas shed light on the influences at work that are spreading the epidemic of youth violence.

The risk factors that Robert Zagar and his colleagues identified in 1991 as correlated with a boy's chances of committing murder continue to increase:

• *Child abuse:* According to the best study we have on the rate of child maltreatment, from 1986 to 1993 child abuse and neglect rose from 14 per 100,000 to 23 per 100,000. These statistics refer to children who have already experienced harm. If the standard used in defining maltreatment includes children who are at risk for imminent harm—what the study calls "endangerment"—the increase is even larger, with the rate nearly doubling, from 22 per 100,000 in 1986 to 42 per 100,000 in 1993.

• *Gangs:* According to research compiled by the federal government, more and more communities are facing the problem of youth gangs. Surveys find that more and more children and youth report that there are gangs active in their schools and community—up 50 percent from 1989 to 1995.

• *Substance abuse:* Hard drugs have spread throughout the United States; virtually every community in the country has a drug subculture. For 1997 the Centers for Disease Control and Prevention reported, in the annual "Youth Risk Behavior Surveillance," that 9 percent of all high-school-age males had used cocaine. Moreover, 50 percent of adolescent boys reported having used marijuana, and 30 percent had used it in the previous month. After a decline in overall drug use among teenagers, which started in 1976 (when 45 percent admitted to some drug use) and continued to 1994, the reported overall rate is on the increase again and now stands at 36 percent. What is more, heavy alcohol use among teenage boys is common: 37 percent of the boys reported that they drank five or more drinks on one occasion at least once in the previous month.

• *Weapons:* Surveys attest to an extraordinary increase in the likelihood that kids will carry weapons. They do so primarily because they feel threatened and can't count on adults to protect them. The most recent data, from the 1997 CDC survey, reveal that 28 percent of adolescent boys carried a weapon—a gun, a knife, or a club—in the previous month, with 13 percent carrying a weapon to school in the previous month. Fascination with guns often begins at a very young age. Eleven-year-old Andrew Golden of Jonesboro, Arkansas, and Kip Kinkel of Springfield, Oregon, were among them; both spent much of their time immersed in the gun culture.

• *Arrests:* Arrests of youth under age eighteen have increased dramatically since 1980—up 50 percent from 1980 to 1994 for serious offenses. In addition, law enforcement agencies in many communities have taken a much more active approach to arresting juveniles in response to community pressures, political directives, and court rulings that limit their discretion and their authority to use informal means of redirecting delinquent juveniles (e.g., taking kids home and confronting parents or ordering kids to make restitution without arresting them and involving court sanctions).

• *Neurological problems:* Surveys point to a significant increase among children with conditions such as Attention Deficit Disorder (ADD), which may reflect neurological problems and which certainly result in behavioral difficulties. Improved medical care for highly vulnerable babies means that more and more premature infants who might have died in previous decades are surviving today. For example, in 1960 only 10 percent of newborns weighing less than two pounds survived; by the early 1990s that figure had risen to 50 percent. This appears to mean that more and more kids are living with neurological difficulties, as a result of their prematurity, that can impair the processes of thinking and feeling. The rate of learning difficulties in children who were born prematurely is about 25 percent higher than the rate for those not born prematurely. The use of drugs and alcohol by pregnant women compounds this problem.

• *Difficulties at school:* Data show that for any thirty-day period, about one in three high school kids reports having skipped school at least one day. The likelihood of skipping is greatest among kids who live in a family constellation other than a two-parent household (the rates are 30 percent for two-parent households, 24 percent for mother-only households, and 37 percent for all others). The declining proportion of kids living in a two-parent household corresponds to an increase in truancy. What is more, research reveals increasing rates of behavioral, emotional, and intellectual problems that affect the ability to succeed in school. Since 1969 the percentage of high school students who have cheated on a test increased from 34 percent to 68 percent. According to the 1997 CDC survey, 20 percent of all high-school-age boys reported that they were in a physical fight on school property in the past year, and 26 percent of the boys said their property had been stolen or deliberately damaged on school property. Four percent of high school boys said that on at least one day in the previous month they felt too unsafe to go to school.

More children and youth across the country are experiencing the specific negative influences that increase the risk of youth violence. Where and when these negative influences show themselves in actual acts of aggression may differ from group to group. For example, the kids who committed the infamous school shootings in the 1997–1998 school year killed and injured multiple victims in a single incident and did not have some secondary criminal motive such as robbery or drug dealing. This is different from most of the lethal violence committed by inner-city kids. Also, while for most middle-class teenagers school is a very important social setting and what goes on there of vital emotional significance, for many inner-city kids, in contrast, school has lost its significance by the time they reach adolescence, and they have already dropped out. But once the shooting stops, the net result is the same for parents, friends, teachers, and civic leaders who must cope with the aftermath.

Epidemics tend to start among the most vulnerable segments of the population and then work their way outward, like ripples in a pond. These vulnerable populations don't cause the epidemic. Rather, *their dis-*

advantaged position makes them a good host for the infection. That the exact nature of the problem may change a bit as it spreads is not surprising. It is not uncommon for infections to mutate as they spread, with one strain being particularly successful in invading a particular host. The Black Death of the Middle Ages started in the poorest and most deprived homes and neighborhoods, where sanitation conditions and nutrition were most primitive, but it eventually reached into the palaces of the nobility. Unmarried teenage pregnancy over the past thirty years has shown the same pattern: the high rates observed among low-income, inner-city minority girls in the 1960s are to be found throughout America today, among small town, suburban, and rural girls. The same is true of the phenomenon of "latchkey children." Finding young children at home without adult supervision was once common among low-income families but almost unknown among the middle class. Now it is common everywhere.

The same epidemic model describes what is happening with boys who kill. The first wave of lethal youth violence in schools peaked in the 1992–1993 school year, when fifty people died, mostly in urban schools and involving low-income minority youth. In response to what we now call Stage One of the epidemic, inner-city high schools scrambled to devise and implement measures to teach teenagers nonviolent conflict resolution techniques, to disarm students before they could enter the school building, and to remove them if they did enter the school with weapons. American high schools have become the major market for worldwide sales of metal detectors. We are now in Stage Two, the spread of youth violence throughout American society. How did we get here?

HOW DO EPIDEMICS OF VIOLENCE SPREAD?

My use of the word *epidemic* to describe what's been happening with youth violence is deliberate. The study of epidemics (epidemiology) provides some useful tools for analyzing and understanding the situation of violent boys. For one thing, it helps explain how conditions can change so dramatically and quickly. One of these tools is the concept of the "tipping point," the moment in the development of an epidemic at which only a small change in the presence of the germ produces a big change in the rate of infection. Although the tipping point is characteristic of epidemics of physical illness, it is true of social epidemics as well.

Jonathan Crane, a geographer in Illinois, has identified the tipping point in the social decline of neighborhoods. He found that when the proportion of "affluent leadership class" families in a neighborhood drops below 6 percent, there is a rapid increase in such social pathologies among teens as delinquency, out-of-wedlock pregnancy, and dropping out of high school. Once this tipping point is reached, the neighborhood is ripe for becoming an "inner-city war zone." This is clearly what happened in many neighborhoods in cities like Chicago in the 1950s and 1960s, setting the stage for the dramatic upsurge of youth violence that occurred during the 1980s.

Harvard University sociologist William Julius Wilson documented this phenomenon in Chicago and other cities by demonstrating how an end to strict racial segregation allowed affluent and middle-class African American families to leave the ghettoes to which they had been confined by segregationist laws and policies and find homes in middle-class and integrated communities, thus leaving behind an ever-poorer and more isolated population to deal with the decline of the industrial sector jobs that had sustained them in earlier times. Neighborhoods that were once complete and resilient communities became homogeneously poor and socially troubled environments, the perfect "host" for an epidemic of violence.

Public policies have played a direct part in the latter process, for example, by clustering public housing in large projects, rather than dispersing it as scattered site housing, and then forcing middle-class families out of public housing by setting income limits. I know this from firsthand experience. As a three-year-old child, I lived in a large public housing project in New York City, a racially integrated project that included families of many varieties. Five years later my family was forced to move out because my father's income exceeded the ceiling set by shortsighted policymakers and administrators. As a result, what had been a very livable community in the 1950s joined the ranks of the urban war zones by the 1960s. Unfortunately, that story has been repeated over and over again in city after city around our country.

War zone neighborhoods are places where almost every fourteen-year-old has been to the funeral of a playmate who was killed, where two-thirds of the kids have witnessed a shooting, and where young children play a game they call "funeral" with the toy blocks in their preschool classroom. Since the 1960s, such war zones in the biggest, most crime-ridden cities have been the primary sites for kids who kill, but in the last two decades additional cities have spawned war-zone-like neighborhoods.

The change came first with the addition of a second tier of medium-to-large-sized cities like Denver and Minneapolis–St. Paul, which had long been held up as paragons of civic virtue and social well-being. These cities increasingly spawned microenvironments exhibiting the plague of gunfire in the climate of fear and pervasive insecurity that came to symbolize inner-city life. In some cities it may be only a few square blocks, but it is there nonetheless. Even Salt Lake City, Utah, the home of the Mormon Church, isn't immune, as I learned when I was invited there to address a gang violence task force in 1994. As the years have gone by, smaller cities have joined the ranks. Now, even places like Battle Creek, Michigan, the home of Kellogg Cornflakes, have had drive-by shootings. And in my own small town of Ithaca, New York, there is a small section of town from which there are regular reports of shootings, stabbings, gang activity, drug dealing, and all the other accoutrements of the urban war zone.

This development has a special significance for small cities, towns, and rural areas. In big cities the large population base has allowed for multiple large public high schools and for the maintenance of private high schools by affluent families and by others who wish to escape from the threat of inner-city youth violence. This means that "trouble spots" can by and large be avoided by most affluent families. But outside the largest cities, avoidance is not possible. For example, in Ithaca every teenager goes to the one public high school. This brings the problems of the micro-war-zone home to my daughter, who now goes to high school in Ithaca, in a way that was not experienced by my son, who went to high school in Chicago a few years ago. Ironically, she feels more threatened going to school in small-town Ithaca than he did going to school in big, bad Chicago.

But this account of the rise of micro-war-zones in small cities and towns is not the whole story. Another implication of the tipping point theory is that conditions in families and neighborhoods throughout society may deteriorate for years before suddenly achieving a critical mass for lethal youth violence. I have witnessed this in my professional lifetime.

As a young graduate student, I accompanied my mentor, psychologist Urie Bronfenbrenner, on a trip to the American heartland in 1970. We attended a community meeting in Racine, Wisconsin, a small city nestled in the American Midwest. Bronfenbrenner was there to talk to a group of civic leaders and parents about the trends he was detecting in American society that he thought boded ill for coming generations of children and youth, trends he had recently described in his book *Two Worlds of Childhood*. The assembled group listened politely to what he had to say, but their questions and comments following his presentation revealed that their overall reaction to his analysis had been, "This is all very interesting, but what does it have to do with us here in Racine?"

A quarter of a century later, I was invited to speak to a similar group of community leaders and parents in Racine. The meeting was held in the same room where Bronfenbrenner had spoken twenty-five years earlier. I was there to talk about my 1995 book *Raising Children in a Socially Toxic Environment*, in which I had taken Bronfenbrenner's analysis into the 1990s. The audience listened avidly as I described the unfortunate changes that were occurring in American life, changes that I said were "poisoning" more and more kids. At the end of my speech outlining the problem and what it would take to turn things around, there was sustained, loud applause. I then asked the group, "How many of you think what I have said today is relevant for the situation you face in Racine?" Every hand went up. One man exclaimed, "Yes. This is exactly what we are dealing with here. We have to act now!"

When I reported back to Bronfenbrenner, now retired but still active, his response was not a smug "I told you so" but, rather, one of sadness. He said, "Twenty-five years ago, when this was just starting, how much easier it would have been to turn things around. Now . . ." He sighed. Now we have come to the tipping point—and gone beyond it in many places in our country. In almost every community in America, growing numbers of kids live in a socially toxic environment.

Though they may weight the odds in one direction or the other, social conditions alone do not cause boys to kill. Those conditions must be incorporated into the way kids think and feel about the world, about *their* world, and about themselves. Ultimately, it is on the inner lives of boys that environmental influences take their toll, setting in motion the chain of events that results in the horror of Jonesboro, Springfield, or Paducah.

The surface conditions that we find associated with the inner damage to kids in, say, Washington, DC, and Detroit may not be entirely the same as those that play a critical role when the epidemic comes to the suburbs and small towns. As I mentioned earlier, school may be the site for some kids while the street plays that role for others. Exploring the links between external social conditions and the psychological conditions inside boys is the focus of later chapters, where I outline the role played by depression, shame, rage, alienation, and bloated self-centeredness in the origins of youth violence. I am concerned first and foremost with understanding *why* kids kill; I know that many individuals are desperate for answers, but do we as a society really want to know?

MAKING SENSE, NOT EXCUSES

Sometimes as I listen to people talk about violent youth, I doubt that they really want to understand the dangers that our boys face and to make sense of how their violent acts flow from their experiences in our society. Sometimes it seems that few people really care about hurt little boys who have grown up to be violent teenagers, except as potential threats to the community. It is as if we want to forget how they got to be kids who kill in the first place. We are willing to incarcerate them but not to understand them. Perhaps we feel that understanding them is unnecessary because punishment is the only issue, or perhaps we feel that an attempt to understand them is dangerous because it might excuse their actions.

In the days after the Jonesboro, Arkansas, shootings in March 1998, an opinion poll revealed that about half the adults in America believed that the two boys who shot their classmates should receive the death penalty. Throughout the months of their incarceration prior to the trial in August, the jail where they were being held received numerous letters containing death threats aimed at the boys. In the days leading up to and following the trial and the verdict, reporters recounted firsthand accounts of adults in the community explicitly stating that they would kill the boys if they were released. These threats continued when the verdict was made public (the boys were sentenced as juveniles, to be held in custody until their juvenile status ended).

In our anger and fear, many of us seem ready to impose the ultimate penalty against children. When fifteen-year-old Kip Kinkel in Oregon went on his killing rampage, it seemed that every newspaper account mentioned—often, it seemed, regretfully—that although he could be tried as an adult under Oregon law, the boy was too young to receive the death penalty. After the Jonesboro shootings, a Texas legislator gained national attention by bemoaning the fact that an eleven-year-old couldn't be executed in his state and announcing his intention to remedy the problem by lowering the age for imposing the death penalty to eleven.

A couple of weeks after the Jonesboro shootings, I was on a radio talk show to respond to some questions about the development of boys who commit such violence. One of the hosts said that at first she had thought the death penalty was justified for such an act but that now, as she learned about the boys' backgrounds (including the report that at least one of them had been sexually abused), she was changing her mind. She was learning about the life experience of boys who kill. This kind of learning is essential if we as a society are to choose the path of understanding, which leads to humane treatment and rehabilitation, rather than savage punishment to feed our hunger for revenge. This latter path produces an unending chain reaction of pain and suffering for our entire society. We build more prisons to punish these boys, and in those prisons their rage and despair hardens, so that they emerge even more dangerous than when they entered. Such a course of action only serves to validate the ancient proverb "If you start out on a journey of revenge, begin by digging two graves, one for your enemy and one for yourself."

On one side stands a simple moralism that says if kids can kill, kids should die (or at least serve long prison terms), as if they were adults. On the other side stands an impulse to understand and, if understanding is possible, to rescue the troubled and hurt child from inside the killer. I stand with the latter, which is why I do what I do to help people understand. But it's no easy task.

WHO CARES ABOUT THE CHILD INSIDE THE KILLER?

In 1995, I was called to testify as an expert witness in the trial of a Denver teenager charged with murder. The defense wanted my testimony to explain how this boy's history of abuse and exposure to violence in the community was relevant to an understanding of his motives and actions. By then I had become accustomed to hearing about the violent acts boys commit, so I was prepared to deal with the details of this boy's crime. What surprised me most about my experience in the courtroom was the prosecutor's response to my testimony. He had access to the same records I did and had heard the boy's account of life in his family and on the street. Nonetheless, the prosecutor denied the relevance of the boy's childhood experience, declaring indignantly, "Who cares what happened to him when he was a child?" As the prosecutor saw it, the only thing that mattered now was the crime the boy had committed. Nothing more. The only relevant question for him was, "Did he do the crime?" It's not enough.

Each of the violent teenage boys I meet moves and intrigues me as I come to know him as a human being rather than as just a "host" to an epidemic of violence. Many have committed monstrous acts. Their victims are testimony to that. And yet when I meet one of these boys, I can see beyond the facts of his crime. He is a sad woman's son, a young girl's brother, a baby boy's cousin. While never forgetting about the victims of his violence, I always seek to see him as more than a perpetrator, as more than his crimes. He is a boy, a dangerous boy to be sure, but still a boy. Sometimes I discover that the boy loves basketball or baseball, as I did as a teenager, or that he excels in a school subject that was particularly dear to my heart when I was in school. One boy I spoke with shares my love of mystery novels. Another shares my birthday.

Some of these boys appear so tough on the outside. But when I get a glimpse of their inner life, I am deeply touched by their vulnerability and their pain, and I come to see their toughness as a survival strategy, as something that helps them get through another day. In many ways their cold exterior is a defense against overwhelming emotions inside. They puzzle me, seeming in some ways so much like my own teenage son yet in other ways so alien. These boys are incarcerated as criminals, and they sometimes have long records that include multiple lethal assaults and armed robberies. Yet, young or old, they often seem naive and childlike as they talk about their life. More than one of the boys I have interviewed even sucked his thumb as he recalled the events of his life for me.

It was these experiences that led me to refer to them as "lost boys." Some boys get lost because they are systematically led into a moral wilderness by their experiences at home and on the streets, where they are left to fend for themselves. These are the boys upon whose behalf I testify in court, trying to help judge and jury see the injustice of their experiences and how they have been robbed of their childhood by abusive and neglectful parents, by malevolent drug dealers, and by the sheer viciousness of their daily life. And I argue that to simply punish them with death or decades of incarceration only compounds the injustice imposed upon them by the world in which they grew up.

Other troubled boys are better understood as having gotten lost through unfortunate accidents of human development. In their cases, no one set out to abuse or neglect them, but they ended up feeling rejected and humiliated nonetheless. Adults in their lives made ordinary efforts to teach them how to live in society, but these ordinary efforts were not enough. Sometimes the unfortunate circumstance is the absence or withdrawal of positive adults from a boy's life, a void that occurs not through some plan but as a result of the parents' fumbling efforts to deal with problems in their own lives—for example, a divorce—and their own disappointments. It is always something outside that becomes deadly when filtered through the lens of a boy's tormented inner life.

These boys fall victim to an unfortunate synchronicity between the demons inhabiting their own internal world and the corrupting influences of modern American culture. They lose their way in the pervasive experience of vicarious violence, crude sexuality, shallow materialism, mean-spirited competitiveness, and spiritual emptiness. These factors affect us all to some degree, but they poison these especially vulnerable kids. The unforgiving nature of modern life puts so much pressure on kids to grow up perfectly—perfectly powerful, perfectly sexy, perfectly rich, perfectly resistant to day-to-day pressures. However, whether they are deliberately misled or just unintentionally lost, some boys find their way to lethal violence. Every boy has his limit; some reach it earlier than others. With at least one gun in nearly half the households in the country, with two-thirds of our teenagers reporting they could get a gun in an hour, with virtually every kid exposed to vivid movie and television scenarios legitimizing violence, we live in dangerous times.

In my desire to understand these boys better, I needed to know how a parent, guardian, teacher, or coach might have diverted them from their downward spiral. And I needed to know how these boys could stop the violence in their lives once it started and how they could change the path they were on so that they would not spend their teenage years in prison or end up in the morgue when they should have been in school. I learned that I could only answer my questions by digging deeply into the lives of violent teenagers. I decided that rather than surveying large numbers of kids, where I might only have the results of a paper-and-pencil survey, or conducting an hour-long interview to get inside the head or heart of a number of boys, the best way for me to proceed was to focus on a small group of lost boys, taking time with each one to build a trusting relationship and to hear his story in depth.

SUCCESS STORIES

I know that some boys who enter into the world of lethal violence do find their way back into the mainstream of American life. I came to know one such success story quite well. His name was Julio, and he was a student in a course I teach at Cornell University. Julio had gone to a maximum security youth prison at age thirteen for the shotgun shooting of another kid who was competing with him as a drug dealer for a bit of turf. Julio had all the risk factors identified in Zagar's study: he came from a family steeped in criminality, he had been neglected and abused by his parents, his mother was a drug addict and his father a drug dealer, he was recruited early into a gang, and he lived in an urban war zone in New York City. As luck would have it, the boy he shot survived; Julio was therefore charged only with attempted murder, and he faced the prospect of release from prison within a few years' time.

Like many kids with the deck stacked against him, Julio developed a pattern of aggression that was well in place by the time he was ten years old. At thirteen, he was standing at the edge of the abyss, with one foot over the edge. But unlike so many other boys, Julio used the opportunity of being exposed to the prison program to turn his life around, to learn to read, and eventually to parlay his high intelligence, strong will, and sense of divine intervention into a college scholarship that put him on the road to a career in social work. What Julio found in the youth prison to which he was sentenced was not just more of the same but, rather, an opportunity for reflection and personal development in a safe setting. He became a monk in prison—reading, reflecting, and praying—and started the process of rebuilding himself from the ground up. Julio's path exemplifies the monastic model I will introduce in Chapter Eight as a strategy for reclaiming boys after they are lost. When I talk with kids who kill, I always hope and expect to find others like Julio so that I can deepen my understanding of why some kids turn their lives around and how we can use their experiences as a guide.

PSYCHOLOGICAL AND LEGAL REALITIES

One thing I have learned from talking to violent boys is that homicide is just part of the violence in their lives. Legally, there is a world of difference between violent assaults that end in death and violent assaults that fail to produce a dead body. I see this in the cases of boys I know. Michael shot two police officers; one died after being hit by one bullet while the other survived four bullets to the chest. He now faces the death penalty. Larry shot a police officer seven times, and the man spent only two nights in the hospital; Larry is serving two years. Conneel fired an assault rifle into a crowded playground and killed no one; he served three months on a weapons charge. Thomas fired a single "warning shot" from his .22-caliber pistol and felled a sixteen-year-old boy with that one small bullet; he was sentenced to twenty-five years in prison.

The legal system feasts on these distinctions, but I find them to be of very limited psychological significance in most cases. Thus, my concern is with potentially lethal violence as much as it is with homicide. We must look at kids who engage in assaults that *can* kill, even if they don't actually end a human life. It is very hard to predict with precision which boy will end up taking a life. Much more practical is to identify the boys who are at greatest risk for engaging in potentially lethal violence.

As I noted earlier, according to the surveys conducted by the Centers for Disease Control and Prevention, in any thirty-day period, nearly 30 percent of our boys attending high school carry a potentially lethal weapon around with them as they go about their business in the community, and 12.5 percent of our boys have carried a weapon to school. Recent research suggests that less than 10 percent of all juvenile killers are psychotic, that is, have symptoms of severe mental illness such as delusions and hallucinations. The rest commit acts of lethal violence in connection with, in roughly equal proportions, conflicts (such as disputes or arguments that get out of hand) or crimes (such as robbery or rape). This means there is always great potential for lethal violence in the day-to-day world of boys who attend American high schools. I talk mostly with the boys who have fulfilled that awful potential. Where do I find these boys who can help us understand youth violence? Sometimes they find me— or, rather, their lawyers find me and I am called upon to testify as an expert witness at their trials. But mostly I find them in a project I run with my partner, Claire Bedard, at youth prisons maintained by the New York State Office of Children and Family Services.

REAL-LIFE BOYS

The Austin MacCormick Center is located in a wooded section of central New York State, about fifteen miles from Ithaca. MacCormick is generally regarded as a model facility, and kids routinely report that it feels safer than any of the other secure facilities in which they have spent time. Still, it can be dangerous to work with these boys. In one two-month period in 1997, three staff members were sent to the hospital as a result of struggles with boys on the units: In one incident, a staff member had his nose broken as he tried to restrain a boy. In another incident, two staff members required stitches from a melee that ensued from their attempts to confiscate a razor blade found in the sock of a boy who had just arrived from another facility.

When I first see the boys I will come to know at MacCormick, they are usually part of a group walking down the hall. At first glance they are rather anonymous, with their generally guarded expressions and their MacCormick uniforms of red shirts, khaki pants, and white running shoes (the colors of the laces differentiate the boy's degree of progress within the facility's system).

Some are tall and very muscular, some are short and compact. Some have acne and the disproportionately developed bodies common to teenagers everywhere, and others are strikingly handsome. Some affect the "gangsta shuffle" they learned from rap music celebrities; other just walk. Most display a guarded expression, but some flash a menacing scowl and a few even smile. As I get closer, I see that many of them carry scars on their hands, arms, and face from beatings and fights, recent and long ago. With their shirt and pants on I can't know how many of them also carry physical reminders of wounds on their chest, back, and legs.

Like most teenagers in a group confronting adults, they don't want to let on that they are anything other than just like everybody else. I have to spend time with each boy alone, without the weight of peer scrutiny and the baggage of the "us versus them" attitude if I want to see and hear more. That's when I really meet a boy, when it is just the two of us alone in a small room and safely distanced from the outside world. At times there is instant rapport. Malcolm, sentenced to a term of four to ten years for second-degree murder, was such a boy.

Malcolm

The night before I met Malcolm, his mother called to tell him that his girlfriend, six months pregnant with his child, had been shot and killed while walking on the streets of his old neighborhood. Malcolm's loss is by no means unusual for violent boys. If anything, such loss is a common thread (not long after Malcolm's girlfriend was shot, the girlfriend of another boy was killed).

Malcolm's mother told him that the baby-to-be had died too. He recounted this as I sat with him in one of the facility's two isolation rooms, used both to punish boys who were in trouble and to keep a watch on boys who were sick or were thought to be suicidal (a reminder that more violent individuals die at their own hand than are put to death by a society committed to the death penalty).

Troubled as he was, Malcolm still was ready to talk. I learned later that talking was one of his strategies for coping with the traumas of his life. As the months went by, Malcolm opened up to me more and more, and I saw many sides to him. I discovered that he had started reading books while at MacCormick. Sometimes we talked about the books he was reading; the *Autobiography of Malcolm X* was a favorite of his (and of many of the other boys as well). His interest prompted me to buy a copy of a book he wanted to read but could not find in the prison library— *Street Soldiers* by Joe Marshall. When I gave it to him as we sat together, he looked at it, his head down, for a few moments. Then he looked up at me as a tear rolled down his cheek. "This is for me, really? Thanks, man. Nobody ever gave me a book before." A single tear is a precious commodity in the emotional economy of boys like Malcolm.

When the boys first speak of their experiences with violence, they are often cool and matter-of-fact about it. However, eventually, weeks or months later, some of them talk to me about the residue of trauma that results from living in a world where violence is so intense and pervasive. Inside almost every violent teenager I've spoken to is an untreated traumatized child. How do they cope? Each has his own strategy. Malcolm told me that he tried not to be alone, and he talked all the time. He once said, "When I'm alone, I see the faces of the people I killed in front of me, in a line. They be like ghosts. It's most bad at night, because then there's nobody to talk to, nothing to do except listen to those ghosts. It's bad, man." Then this tough, violent boy let a tear escape. Another single tear.

From Malcolm to Kip and Luke and Andrew and Mitchell and . . .

Malcolm and most of the others at MacCormick are among the most visible of those infected by the American epidemic of youth violence. But as we shall see in the chapters that follow, many of the elements of the stories I hear are also present in the lives of most young people who display lethal violence, wherever they come from.

These elements are often hidden and muted when a boy is from Springfield, Paducah, or Jonesboro rather than the inner city, but white boys from the American heartland reveal many of the same patterns in their most intimate and important relationships and in their inner lives as do their brothers at the Austin MacCormick Center. They may come from what appears on the surface to be a "good family" from the right side of the tracks, rather than one that is obviously dysfunctional. They may appear to be doing well in school, rather than dropping out for life on the streets. But the accumulation of risk factors is there to be found if we look carefully, deeply, and without prejudice. They are all our sons.

The risk factors are there to be found in the more subtle forms of psychological maltreatment, in alienation from positive role models, in a spiritual emptiness that spawns despair, in adolescent melodrama, in humiliation and shame, in the video culture of violent fantasy that seduces many of the emotionally vulnerable, and in the gun culture that arms our society's troubled boys.

There is an epidemic of youth violence, and no community is immune. This is the story I must tell in the chapters that constitute Part One of this book, as I trace how the inner life of a boy develops to the point where he is a candidate to become lethally violent. But we are not powerless. We can do more than simply watch this happen. What we can do will be the focus of Part Two.

Part One

HOW BOYS GET LOST

We are forlorn like children, and experienced like old men,
we are crude and sorrowful and superficial—
I believe we are lost.

—Erich Maria Remarque, *All Quiet on the Western Front*

$$\underline{2}$$

REJECTED AND NEGLECTED,
ASHAMED AND DEPRESSED

THE SACRED SELF

In a letter to a colleague after meeting the eight-year-old Hellen Keller, when her fame as a blind and mute child who nonetheless learned to communicate with eloquence was only beginning, Alexander Graham Bell wrote, "I feel that in this child I have seen more of the Divine than has been manifest in anyone I ever met before." Every infant contains a divine spark. I believe this as a psychologist; I know it as a person and a parent. Recognizing the reality of the sacred self is the foundation for understanding human development as something more than a matter of engineering, plumbing, chemistry, and electronics. Far too few social scientists take this into account in their professional work, but many recognize it in their personal lives. I start from this spiritual basis in understanding violent boys.

You can see this spiritual reality in the eyes of a child. This is one reason why I shamelessly "flirt" with babies everywhere I see them—in airports, in shopping malls, in the waiting rooms of prisons. I seek out their eyes to make contact with their souls, hoping to elicit a smile and to experience once again the delight that comes from contact with the divine spark within them.

Through the eyes you can tell a great deal about the well-being of the soul. We recognize this in the ancient proverb "The eyes are the window to the soul." When we see darkness, we are alarmed. I've seen both light and darkness in the eyes of children in my travels around the world, and in the eyes of children in the prisons, schools, and neighborhoods of our country. I see light sometimes in violent boys. When we see light in a child's eyes, we are joyful and reassured. Sometimes we are made intensely aware of a child's soul by virtue of the special circumstances or character of the child.

What kindles the spark of divinity in a child? And what consigns the human spirit to darkness? We begin our journey to understand lost boys by studying the quality of their early relationships, the psychological condition of their inner life, the development of their spirit. At the heart of the matter is whether a young child is connected rather than abandoned, accepted rather than rejected, and nurtured rather than neglected and abused. Naturally, all of this takes place at a particular intersection of biology and society. The individual temperament of the child does much to dictate the terms of engagement between him and the world, just as what the child's environment has to offer in the way of opportunities and threats does much to dictate the consequences of individual temperament and experience. In some situations this intersection produces unhappiness and violence; in others it brings joy and peace.

CAN A SOUL BE MURDERED?

Psychiatrist Leonard Shengold called his book on the effects of severe child abuse *Soul Murder*. He chose this title to reflect his belief that the catastrophically abused child, subject to so much internal devastation, is driven beyond the limits of humanness. I'm not in a position to debate the theological issue of whether or not souls can die or be killed, but I do believe that Shengold's view contains an important insight: at the very least, souls can be wounded. At the extremes of human deprivation and degradation, it may well be true that the human psyche can be so terribly mutilated that the soul departs, leaving behind something else to fill the void—or perhaps just leaving an unfilled void.

From what I have seen, the more likely course of development is that when forced to live in hell, the soul withdraws, perhaps shutting itself off from the world outside in a desperate attempt at preservation. Once hidden away, it covers itself with layers of insulation. As the years pass, this protective shell may harden to the point where eventually the soul seems dormant, so out of touch with the day-to-day self has it become even to the tormented person himself.

There are such individuals in our midst, although most of them seem to end up in prisons or mental institutions. Some are violent boys. In such boys, the soul is buried deep under layers of violence and distorted thoughts and emotions. But is such a soul dead or dormant beyond revival? I don't think so. I find inspiration in the life of psychotherapist Robin Casarjian, whose work with adult prisoners focuses on efforts to help them reconnect with their buried souls. In her book *Houses of Healing*, she provides a road map for people seeking a pathway from the darkness into the light.

I side with Sister Prejean, the author of a moving testimony to her work with men on death row, *Dead Man Walking*. Sister Prejean has found her vocation in ministering to the spiritual needs of these prisoners, men whose souls have often spent decades in a state of suspended animation. Faced with physical death but in the company of her spiritual love, these souls often reawaken, if only to be present at the time of the execution. For all its terror, waste, and defeat, death row can be a soulful place.

In August 1998, I was called upon to interview a young man on death row so that I might participate as an expert witness in his appeal. This was my third visit to death row. Byron is there because he shot and killed a police officer in 1994. His social history is perhaps the most appalling litany of child abuse and neglect I have ever encountered. Indeed, a social worker who evaluated him said that in her twenty years as a protective service worker she had investigated more than two thousand cases of child maltreatment and had never seen or heard of a more horrible story. Yet the reports speak of this young man's tender love for his children, his patience working with disabled adults in a halfway house, and his efforts to befriend and mentor a fourteen-year-old boy in his neighborhood.

What did I find when I entered the small interview room at the prison where Byron was being held? After a moment of initial awkwardness as we dealt with the circumstance of being strangers—one visiting, the other shackled—I found a beautiful soul. His eyes were alight with life as we talked for the next two hours. When we were done, I understood something of the contradiction of his life: the rage he lived with and sometimes expressed (as a response to the torture he had suffered at the hands of his abusive father) coupled with the impetus for goodness that was in him.

Byron admits that the four years he has spent in prison awaiting the results of his trial and appeals have provided him a first opportunity to reflect and ponder his life—indeed, the very meaning of life. Like most of us, he was previously caught up in the day-to-day search for diversion. Most of us allow everyday life to divert us from the essential business of our souls. But most of us don't have to face what Byron faces. Obviously, he has put this time to good use. More and more, he has become a monk serving time in a monastery of someone else's making. Now, as he awaits the results of his appeal, he is at peace, saying that his only goal is to live to see his son grow up. I was not the first visitor to comment on his soulfulness: he told me with a smile that a visiting poet from Chicago spoke with him and told him that his eyes shone with light and life.

THE SOUL IN HIDING

How does a soul survive in a world of torment? What keeps a soul from dying? The conventional psychological answer has several parts. The first is temperament, the fact that children differ in constitution and in the emotional predispositions they bring with them into the world. Some are very sensitive to upset or threat; others seem naturally hardy. Some children seem to have a positive orientation to life, to be sunny and light; others are burdened with negativism, gloomy from the start, predisposed to depression. Temperament plays an important role in determining which souls survive and which depart.

A second part of the equation is resilience, the ability to bounce back from or overcome adversity. Much has been made of the role played by differences in resiliency in accounting for the fact that most children who have had a bad time in early life *don't* become delinquents or murderers. In Chapter Six I will explore the origins, meaning, and limits of resilience as a concept.

There is a third force at work. This is the role of love, of being unconditionally loved. In an abusive family it may be the one small voice of kindness that comes from a relative too weak to change the situation but nonetheless able to feed the child's soul enough tidbits of love to sustain it during its hibernation, its long winter of discontent. In a cold, impersonal orphanage it may be one friend who kindly shares her own meager resources. I would be bluffing if I said I can always specify what in this world can sustain a child living in the midst of an earthly hell.

Beyond these findings from social science, there is a fourth force, yet another answer to the question of why some souls stay active and others hibernate. Removing my psychologist's hat for a moment, I would have to call it divine intervention, a single thread of light that feeds the spirit. Sometimes it seems like an amazing grace that finds the spark in a child's soul before it dies out entirely and that keeps it alive, ready to shine brightly if the child's social conditions ever permit that to occur. At other times the fourth force is a special talent or ability in the child, or an image he possesses of some better world.

I see this in Byron. What or who sustained his soul while he was being held hostage in the torture chamber of his father's house? Listening to him and reading the documents in his social history, I recognized his small connections to love and to the divine amidst the horror. For one thing, despite her many failings his mother loved him. She could not protect him from his father, who terrorized them both. And she herself sometimes whipped him in a mistaken effort to guide him. But she did love him, and we must never underestimate the value of love as the most important nutrient for the soul.

Noticing the cross around his neck, I ask Byron about his religious beliefs. "I believe in God, and I believe that God has a purpose for me," he replies. "Where does that come from?" I ask. "My grandmother. She believes, and she taught me to believe, too." Simple faith. Even if Byron's life is spared by the courts, the best he can hope for is life in prison. But he does hope for that. When he fired on the police officer he killed, the officer's partner returned the fire, and Byron was himself shot seven times. He looks back on that now and sees a divine plan. "God spared me that day for something," he says. "I believe it was so that I can look out for my son as he grows up."

Psychologists Patrick Tolan and Nancy Guerra at the University of Illinois in Chicago document that the most effective treatments for delinquent and criminally violent youth emphasize changes in thinking (cognitive restructuring) coupled with opportunities to practice nonviolent behavior (behavioral rehearsal). Faith is the most profound cognitive restructuring that I know of. I will return to these lessons in Chapter Eight, where we explore issues of rehabilitation for boys imprisoned for murder.

CONNECTION

The process of kindling the divine flame begins with connection. Child development is fundamentally social: a human infant can neither survive physically nor develop normally on its own. This is why there is no such thing as "a baby"; there is only "a baby in relation to a someone else." An infant cannot survive psychologically and spiritually on its own. To begin the process of human development, a child needs not so much stimulation as responsiveness; children need to make connection through entering into a relationship. Working in Israel, psychologist Jack Gewirtz demonstrated this in his classic study of smiling, one of the building blocks of human social life. Smiling is one of those mutually satisfying behaviors that link infant and adult; it keeps each motivated to invest more in the relationship. Human babies are primed to smile. That is their part of the initial social contract. The adult's part is to respond to those smiles. Gewirtz's research shows that if normal infants receive positive responses to their first smiling gestures, they accelerate the rate of their smiling; they enter into a relationship. But if their smiling is ignored, they eventually stop smiling. Missing the opportunity for connection, the divine spark is not kindled.

Gewirtz's results attest to the validity of Russian psychologist Lev Vygotsky's conception of child development as inherently and fundamentally social. While most psychologists usually see this process in concrete and mechanistic terms, it is more than that. This social process is meant to fan the divine spark that I discussed earlier in this chapter. Most kids who kill have damaged souls, unable to connect with love to the world around them. Or perhaps some combination of temperament and early experience has sent them looking for love in all the wrong places.

Developmental science and theory point to this fundamental fact: human development proceeds from attachment in the first year of life. Starting at about three months of age, babies come to know and love the people who care for them. By the age of nine months, most babies have formed a specific attachment to one or more caregivers. This attachment is a mixture of *knowing* them in their particularity and *feeling* for them, as special individuals, a special sense of positive connection. This is why, by nine months of age, most babies the world over will shy away from strangers and cling to a familiar person, who is the focal point of the baby's social world and of his or her emotional development.

In the presence of this "object" of their attachment, infants are free to explore and develop their skills in mastering the world. In the absence of the beloved object, they become wary and withdrawn, defensive rather than exploratory, captured by their anxiety. This relationship becomes one of the important mediators between a child's temperament and the challenges of entering and mastering the world outside the family. Good attachment does not inoculate a child against later misfortune, but it does get the child off on the right foot.

After the concept of attachment was accepted as a central theme in the study of child development, psychologists began to ask more varied and complex questions beyond simply whether or not a child developed an attachment. Exploring varieties of attachment, they came to focus on four forms: secure, insecure-avoidant, insecure-ambivalent, and disorganized-disoriented. In contrast to secure attachment, insecure-avoidant indicates a generalized wariness and distancing on the child's part whereas insecure-ambivalent indicates a high level of distress and inconsolability. The disorganized-disoriented pattern indicates a mix of behaviors from the other three classifications. *In general,* parents who are responsive and gentle in their interaction with their baby end up with a baby who is securely attached. Some babies are more temperamentally difficult than others, of course, and this makes the task for parents more difficult. But even most difficult babies can become securely attached. In a project conducted by psychologist Dymphna Van den Boom, visits to the mothers of irritable babies in the first year of life by a counselor who helped each mother become more effectively responsive to her child resulted in 68 percent of these difficult babies being securely attached at twelve months of age, in comparison with only 28 percent of the babies whose mothers were not given this extra help. This is an important investment, because follow-up studies show that securely attached infants are more likely to become competent and well-adjusted children. As one of the leading researchers in this field, psychologist Alan Sroufe at the University of Minnesota, puts it: "Not all anxiously attached children later show acting-out behavior problems, but a young child manifesting such problems in an extreme form is likely to have a history of avoidant or resistant attachment relationships." That describes the lost boys to a T.

DOES PARENTAL BEHAVIOR MATTER?

In her book *The Nurture Assumption,* Judith Rich Harris marshals theory and evidence to challenge the idea that parental behavior is the principal influence on child development. She offers voluminous evidence highlighting the role of what the child brings to the family (in the form of genetics) and what the family brings the child to (in the form of neighborhood and school influences that have their effects through peer groups). Harris cites studies that show that parental behavior has little *direct* effect on the various themes in a child's life—academic achievement, personality, talents, and moral behavior—once genetic similarity, peer groups, siblings, and other experiences outside the parent–child relationship are taken into consideration. Thus, she reasons, the effect of parents is very much *indirect.* There is much truth to this perspective.

Parents do matter, however (as Harris acknowledges). Parents choose or otherwise influence where children live and how often they move—and thus who their peers are and how stable their relationships with those peers are. Parents decide how many siblings a child will have—and thus the extent to which they have a peer group in the family. It is the actions of parents that determine the social class of children and which school they will attend—and thus the opportunities and expectations that will surround them as they make their way in the world outside the home. Thus, much of the effect of the parents is not to be found in the subtle ways they directly shape the personality of a child but in the bigger picture of how parental behavior organizes that child's life.

But there is more to it than that. Parental behavior plays a critical role in at least two other very specific ways. First, at the extremes, parental behavior determines whether a child will live or die. In the United States each year, about two thousand children are murdered by their parents through fatal child abuse or neglect. Second, it is impossible to dispute the undeniable developmental effects of severe psychological deprivation and rejection, particularly in early childhood.

Psychiatrist René Spitz carried out the best-known study of such extreme psychological deprivation. He looked at what happens when early attachment is either disrupted or prevented from forming in the first place. Spitz carried out this research in Mexico in the 1930s and 1940s in institutions for unmarried mothers. Some of these institutions maintained a policy that required a mother to leave her baby six months after the baby's birth, in order to free the child for adoption. Other institutions forced mothers to leave within days after the birth of their child. In both cases, the babies without mothers were fed, washed, clothed, and given medical attention, as needed, but they were not loved. No one cooed to them, no one played with them, no one sat with them and "flirted." In short, no one took over the role of their mothers.

The first group of babies had a chance to form an attachment to their mothers, but were then psychologically abandoned. Many of these babies died, despite receiving good medical care and nutritious feeding. These babies lacked someone to fill the emotional void created by the departure of the beloved person; they starved to death emotionally, and their souls departed. The second group of babies never had psychological mothers, and they never connected with anyone. They, too, languished developmentally, although they did not die.

René Spitz showed that a child removed from the attachment figure grieves the loss deeply. If someone else steps in to take over the role of primary caregiver, children are generally able to transfer their capacity for forming attachments, a capacity developed with their first caregiver, and to establish such a relationship with a new person. But without a new beloved, children move beyond grief to deep depression. Human beings need connection. Disconnection is a threat—particularly if there is some temperamental vulnerability to developing depression. René Spitz's most important message is that human babies can die from depression. It can kill adolescents, too, and depression is a particular problem for violent boys.

THE SPECIAL CHARACTER OF MALE DEPRESSION

Research by psychologist Ronald Kessler at Harvard Medical School reveals that the rate of serious depression among American youth has increased from 2 percent in the 1960s to almost 25 percent in the 1990s. Particularly important is the finding, reported by Columbia University psychologist Suniya Luthar, that these high rates of depression are being found equally among affluent and poor youth. Our research shows that violent boys often have problems with depression as a prelude to their lethal crimes. Michael Carneal, the fourteen-year-old shooter in West Paducah, Kentucky, and Kip Kinkel in Springfield, Oregon, are two infamous examples of this. Both were diagnosed with depression prior to their attacks on their schoolmates, attacks in which a total of five people died.

But simply diagnosing depression is not the whole story. We need to go deeper into the special character of depression as it develops and affects boys; in particular, we need to understand its links to anger. This is stunningly clear in the case of Malcolm; his father never made an effort even to meet him after being present for his birth, and now this incarcerated teenager carries a ton of anger about this abandonment. Although he keeps his rage about his abandonment bottled up most of the time, sometimes it slips out. The last time his father tried to talk to him on the phone, Malcolm would have nothing to do with him. "I took the phone and gave it to my mother. I just don't care no more." Knowing him as I do, I find it hard to believe that he doesn't care. Deep down, he cares too much. I suspect that his apparent lack of emotion about being abandoned exemplifies a common male strategy for dealing with very powerful negative emotions. In his book *I Don't Want To Talk About It*, psychologist Terrence Real explores this characteristic emotional disconnectedness among boys and men. The subtitle of his book, *Overcoming the Secret Legacy of Male Depression*, refers to his observation that while troubled women are likely to express depression through overt suffering, men are more likely to experience hidden depression, what he calls covert depression.

When afflicted with covert depression, males hide the darkness within them both from those around them and from their own conscious awareness. For boys and men, the experience of depression is typically a mixture of two things: loss of the capacity to feel at all and externalization of their pain so that they attribute it to the actions of others, feel victimized, and deal with their distress through action, particularly violent action. Some boys are temperamentally primed to experience this depression; the neurochemical processes that keep people basically happy and on an even keel malfunction in them. This creates a special vulnerability. This potential for depression is actualized when a boy's experiences of abandonment combine with the cultural messages he receives about masculinity, messages that devalue the direct expression of feelings and emphasize the necessity of burying feelings, particularly feelings of emotional connection, vulnerability, and softness. As boys experience increasingly more disrupted relationships at home and in the community, these factors combine to put them on the road to trouble.

My intimate time with troubled boys often permits me to glimpse the intensity of their sadness—and thus their rage—at being abandoned. The extent of their disconnection from their deepest, darkest feelings is often extreme. It is so extreme that sometimes they evidence a lack of memory when it comes to emotion-laden experiences. Terrence Real calls these experiences "the building blocks of depression, a condition which, conceived in the boy, erupts later in the man." Many boys I have spoken with exhibit this kind of emotional amnesia, but none more than Rasheen.

When I first met fifteen-year-old Rasheen, whom I found to be a nervous boy, he was serving a ten-year sentence for his involvement in an armed robbery that turned into a shoot-out with the shopkeeper and the police. In our first interview I tried to learn about the structure and composition of his family—who was around when he was born, whom he lived with over the years before he was incarcerated, what the family's financial situation was.

The early years of his childhood were a complete mystery to Rasheen. He didn't remember much of anything. "Where were you born?" I asked him.

"I don't know."

"Was your father around then?"

"I don't know."

"Did you live with your mother after you were born?"

"I don't know."

It turns out that he lived with his great-grandmother for as long as he could remember, she raised him and his mother's aunt's children (his "cousins" he called them, although they were technically his first cousins once removed).

"Did you ever ask about your mother?" I inquired.

Rasheen lowered his eyes and twisted his fingers. "Yes. I would ask my grandmother, but she wouldn't tell me anything."

"Did you see your mother?"

"Sometimes, but my grandmother didn't want her around . . . I didn't either."

Rasheen was clearly humiliated by the fact that he was abandoned by his mother in favor of her addiction to drugs or alcohol (he wasn't sure which).

What shame a boy feels when he is abandoned by his mother! What lengths he will go to in order to defend himself against these feelings. Inside, he "forgets" so that he doesn't have to feel. Outside, he punishes the world so that he feels avenged. Shame at abandonment begets covert depression, which begets rage, which begets violence. That is one of the powerful equations of life for lost boys.

PARENTAL ABANDONMENT

Some parents disappear from their child's life, psychologically and/or physically. Some mothers experience what psychologists call postpartum depression during the early months of their baby's life and for a time are psychologically unavailable to their newborn, unable to form a secure attachment. Violence within the home, illness, extended hospitalization—all are factors known to impair the development of the attachment bond. Some women have strongly ambivalent feelings about being a mother, perhaps feeling they were pushed into motherhood by social or family expectations when what they really wanted was to focus on their careers outside the home.

Whatever the particular circumstances or barrier, social issues and psychological problems can prevent otherwise competent, caring individuals from succeeding in basic parenting tasks. And when this earliest parent–child relationship doesn't take hold and thrive, a boy is left emotionally high and dry and his soul retreats deeper and deeper.

It is commonplace for the general public and politicians to attribute youth crime and violence to a breakdown of the family. In truth, the problem is not the breakdown *of* the family but the breakdown *in* the family. Disruption in the basic relationships of the family figure prominently in the lives of violent boys. These boys often have a strong sense of family, and they often speak about their families. In this sense, they are very big on family values. For example, Malcolm's rhetoric on family resembles that of my own Italian father in his description of where loyalty fits into his value scheme. He says, "Nothing is more important than family, nothing. I would kill anyone to protect my family. I would die for my family, man."

But existing side by side with this feeling of family that many violent boys have is a record of the disrupted connections and abandonments they have faced, often early in life. Sometimes in talking with them I get glimpses of how boys feel about these abandonments. When I ask Malcolm whom he trusts, he replies, "No one." I ask, "What about your family?" "My family," he replies, "only to a limited degree. I mean, you can't trust nobody all the way in this world."

To anyone who knows family life in America, it should come as no surprise that fathers play a crucial role in the development of boys. Two particular patterns of father influence are most important in understanding the development of violent boys: (1) the *presence* of an abusive father and (2) the *absence* of a caring and resourceful father. The presence of an abusive father teaches sons some very dangerous lessons about being a man, often lessons that are only unconsciously learned.

Fifteen-year-old Terrel is in jail for killing a convenience store clerk. As he talks about his history, he returns over and over again to his need to dominate people. "People are afraid of me," he says. "I like that." Terrel recounts how he assembled a group of boys who would do anything he told them to do. "I enjoyed having that power, making people do what I want. And if they disobey me, they get hurt. That's the way things are." He is currently serving a life sentence because the convenience store clerk dared to oppose him when Terrel demanded all the money in the cash register. "He said he couldn't do it," Terrel says. "So I says, 'Don't talk to me like that. Don't you ever talk to me like that.' And then I shot him."

Where did Terrel learn to be the boy he is? Having heard the story of his father's brutal treatment of Terrel and his eighteen-year-old brother, who is serving a life sentence in an adult prison, one doesn't have to look far. What Terrel describes happening between him and the convenience store clerk echoes his description of his relationship with his father: Do what I say or get hurt; submit or feel pain. When asked about this parallel, Terrel seems surprised, even stunned. "Hmm," he says after thinking it over a minute. "I never thought of it that way, but I guess you're right." Sometimes a boy is better off with no father at all than one who teaches him these lessons about manhood and violence.

But boys also suffer from the absence of a caring father. Research shows that having an absent father is associated with a greater likelihood of chronic juvenile bad behavior. The link comes through at least three effects of living without a father:

First, being fatherless increases the odds that a boy will grow up in a neighborhood where resources of all kinds are in short supply, thus, the normal opportunities for success in the world will be limited. In America today, being fatherless is one of the most powerful predictors that a child will be poor, will be moved from home to home and neighborhood to neighborhood, and will therefore have more difficulty establishing stable and positive relationships with peers. Thirteen-year-old Mitchell Johnson of Jonesboro, Arkansas, is but one example of a young boy who suffered through such instability in the years leading up to his infamous shooting spree.

Second, growing up fatherless increases the chances that a boy will lack a male guide, protector, and mentor. This is itself a risk factor for later delinquency, because boys in an environment with many negative possibilities require every possible counterforce to keep from succumbing to them. Having a father is no guarantee of protection (particularly if he is abusive), but it does increase the odds of success. We know that in Pearl, Mississippi, Luke Woodham fell under the influence of a particularly pernicious peer group, one that capitalized on his emotional vulnerability and drew him ever deeper into violence. Tragically, Luke's mother was unable to move him away from that group.

Finally, growing up without a father always leaves the question of why. "Why don't I have a father?" often goes unanswered. And there is always the possibility that a child will answer that question by concluding there is something wrong with him that he doesn't have a father. The repercussions from this negative conclusion pose a bigger danger for some children, particularly those with a temperamental predisposition to depression and aggression, than for others. Imagine the powerful chemical reaction when many boys who have grown up in similar circumstances, similarly hurt, get together.

An absent father is one thing—and the consequences for boys of this absence are not surprising to anyone familiar with the correlation between father absence and delinquency—but what is surprising is the prevalence of absent *mothers*. Many of the boys involved in lethal violence lose their mothers for significant periods in their early years; some lose them permanently. Some have a mother in jail or in a drug treatment program. Sometimes mothers move away and leave their boys with relatives; some mothers die. The pain and rage associated with maternal abandonment is often buried deeply, but it is there nonetheless.

Matt speaks to me about his postrelease plans and says that he hopes he might be able to relocate so that he can be closer to his mother, who is herself serving a life sentence for murder at the state prison. This is the same mother who gave up caring for him when he was four and turned him over to *her* mother. Why? She wanted to protect him from his father—her pimp—who was beating and tormenting him mercilessly, and she also wanted to be rid of him because he interfered with her "lifestyle." This double abandonment may cut more deeply than the hurt other boys experience, but Matt is far from unique.

THE COSTS OF ABANDONMENT

British psychiatrist Michael Rutter has studied the chain reactions that are likely after a child experiences abandonment and other disruptions of early relationships. In his research it is clear that for a boy to be separated from his mother in infancy and early childhood is a very significant risk factor for future development. Rarely does one risk factor by itself tell the whole story about development, but most child psychologists recognize that early detachment is a very powerful negative influence all by itself.

In Jonesboro, neighbors report that Andrew Golden, the eleven-year-old who partnered with thirteen-year-old Mitchell Johnson to shoot down kids at their school, was raised mainly by his grandparents while his parents worked long hours. In the weeks before the shooting, his dog was lost for a time, and when it returned it was suffering from a bullet wound. For a boy whose principal activity with his father seems to have been shooting and involvement in the gun culture and who was already angry, this kind of hurt could easily have been too much to bear.

In Moses Lake, Washington, fourteen-year-old Barry Loukaitis brought an assault rifle to school a few weeks after his mother announced that she was divorcing his father and that she was suicidally depressed about this planned breakup.

Of course, none of these abandonment experiences necessarily lead to violence. Thousands of boys live with the same losses each year, yet very few take extreme measures to cope with their pain. Many become depressed and mask that depression by self-destructive behavior such as alcohol or drug addiction. And many others express it though nonlethal violence (but violence just the same). But when an abandonment experience is put in the broader context of a troubled boy's life, particularly a boy with uncontrolled access to guns, such an experience can be the spark that ignites a powder keg.

WHO IS THERE FOR ABANDONED CHILDREN?

Why is parental abandonment so dangerous? For one thing, it leaves children dependent upon people other than those with the greatest biological investment in them. Working at McMaster University, psychologists Martin Daly and Margo Wilson documented this risk. While not denying that most of the adults who hurt children are biological fathers and mothers, Daly and Wilson present data that show that the *odds* that children will come to harm increase the further away they are from the care of their biological parents. Their data indicate that there is a special danger faced by children in the care of nonrelatives. For example, while the overall odds that a child will die at the hands of an adult with whom she or he lives is small (totaling about two thousand cases per year in the United States and Canada), the likelihood that a child will be killed is eight times greater if that child lives with one or more substitute parents than if he or she lives with both biological parents.

At particular risk is a child who is exposed to a man who is sexually involved with the child's mother but is not biologically related to the child nor legally or socially committed to serve as a surrogate father. This is the "mother's boyfriend" who appears so disproportionately in reports of child abuse of all kinds. Of course, many children are truly blessed with a loving foster or adoptive parent or a loving stepfather who cares for them. But too many others get dealt men who are negative influences. In Jonesboro, Arkansas, the mother of thirteen-year-old Mitchell Johnson married a man who had served time in prison on federal drug and weapons charges. Mitchell mourned the loss of his father (due to divorce), and to help heal this hurt he needed a stepfather who was especially kind and caring. It would appear he lost out on this score. While we know little about this stepfather's relationship with Mitchell, we can hazard a guess that the relationship did little or nothing to help an already troubled young boy and may even have undermined his development.

I visited seventeen-year-old Tyrone to find out how his background influenced his entry into the drug dealing that eventually brought him to the point of killing a neighborhood rival. Tyrone's father did come around sometimes, he reported. "He would give me money and things." "Can you remember something fun you did with your father?" I asked. Tyrone thought for a moment. "No. I don't think so," he replied. Being abandoned is a tough challenge for any child. Ironically, it may be better to lose a parent to an early death (even though many young children interpret this as a kind of abandonment) than to have a neglectful parent. At least then a child can accept the separation as inevitable and not of the parent's choosing.

REJECTION IS A PSYCHOLOGICAL CANCER

Deliberate abandonment evokes in boys a deep shame. When I sit with him, I cannot help but be aware of the pain Tyrone feels. It's physically hard for him to sit there awash in his shame. The shame of abandonment appears over and over again in the lives of kids who kill. Boys feel the shame of rejection.

Shareef Cousin, a boy who exemplifies the potential of parental rejection for pushing a boy already at risk over the edge, is on death row in Louisiana. He spent his first decade of life believing he knew who his father was—a man who was involved with his mother but who did not live in the house. One day Shareef approached this man, Robert Epps, for validation of their relationship. Here's the way *Time* magazine reports their meeting:

"Do you know me?" Shareef asked. Epps said that he did. "You're my father, right?" Shareef asked. "No, I'm not," Epps replied. "I don't know why your momma would tell you that." Shareef was crushed. And in front of his friends. "I started crying," Cousins said in an interview in prison. "That was like him telling me, I'm sorry I made you. Like I wasn't worth anything." Family members said that day was the start of Cousin's descent. His grades fell. He developed a bad attitude. His mother began to suspect he was using drugs.

Being explicitly rejected by his father was the last straw for an already vulnerable boy. In just a few years Shareef committed the murder that landed him on death row. In Shareef's case, rejection was twice fatal—once for his victim and now for himself.

Anthropologist Ronald Rohner has studied rejection in more than a hundred cultures around the world. His findings are clear: although cultures differ in how they express rejection, rejected children everywhere are at heightened risk for a host of psychological problems ranging from low self-esteem, to truncated moral development, to difficulty handling aggression and sexuality. This effect is so strong that Rohner calls rejection "a psychological malignancy" that spreads throughout a child's emotional system wreaking havoc.

John, one of the boys in prison, told my partner Claire that he knew from his earliest years that he was unwanted. His parents only had him in the hope of having a daughter to complement his older brother. Their disappointment in having a second son became the primary theme of John's young life, and the happiness surrounding the birth of a sister a few years later only magnified his perception of his parents' rejection of him. Psychologists report that Kip Kinkel struggled with a similar feeling of rejection, always feeling second best to his "perfect" older sister. It appears that Michael Carneal in Paducah, Kentucky, felt the same way about his successful sister. Many of the lost boys have this kind of comparative rejection at their core, even when parents try to overcome it.

How does a boy talk about rejection? It's not easy. I sit with 18-year-old Stephen, a boy from New York who is serving a life sentence for shooting a police officer, struggling to find a way to help him communicate his thoughts and feelings about rejection. I know that his mother rejected him in favor of his older brother, a palpable hurt that seems to lurk in everything he says about her. For example, he tells me that one day when he was twelve years old, he borrowed a pair of his brother's pants and wore them to the park. While he was there playing with his friends, his mother drove by. She recognized the pants as belonging to his brother and immediately stopped the car. After calling Stephen over to her, she made him take off his brother's pants right there in the park and hand them over to her, whereupon she drove off, leaving him standing there in his underwear. His shame at the time was profound and the words are still difficult to retrieve, so I am searching for some other way for him to tell me about it.

On the desk between us are two beverage cans (I had bought Stephen a soft drink on this hot day as a small gesture of solidarity). See-ing the cans gives me an idea. "Let's think of this whole desktop as your mother's love," I say to him. He nods his understanding. "Now, this can is you," I say, holding up one of the cans. "And this one is your brother," I continued, gesturing toward the other can. "How full of your mother's love is your can? And how full is your brother's can?" Stephen clearly un-derstands that I am giving him a chance to tell me what could not be said before. He bows his head in thought for a moment, then he shows me that he received about 20 percent of his mother's love, and his brother got 80 percent. Stephen's feeling that he received even 20 percent of his mother's love may be the starting point for his redemption. Even this lit-tle tidbit of love was enough to nurture the light in his soul. If it had been the whole story, it might even have been enough.

I then say, "Now let's use the desk to show being accepted or re-jected." I point to one end of the desk. "This end means complete accep-tance, the other end is total rejection. Choose places for the two cans to show how much your mother accepted you and how much she accepted your brother." Again Stephen bows his head in thought. When he raises it, he puts "his" can almost all the way to the end of the desk that means rejection and puts the can representing his brother all the way to the edge at the other end of the desk, the end indicating complete accep-tance. "Ninety percent rejection for you and a hundred percent accep-tance for your brother?" I ask. "Yes," he says softly. That's a hurt that lasts.

Listening to Stephen and thinking about the violent crimes he has committed, I reflect upon how things might have been different were he a girl. While boys are encouraged to act out their feelings through aggression, girls are taught to talk about how they feel. And, boys learn to punish other people, while girls are taught to keep that hurt inside, even if it eats her up. A boy is likely to spill that hurt into the world through his violent behavior.

Children who are rejected by one or both parents are likely to attribute the rejection to something lacking in themselves. "What's wrong with me that my parents don't want me?" is their inevitable, often silent, question. Adults who were adopted as young children often cannot even ask this question without the aid of counseling. It is no wonder that it is too big a question to be asked directly by many kids. Who among us could bear to confirm that a father or a mother *chose* not to be in our life? When I sit with Tyrone or Michael, the question hangs in the air between us. I can feel the weight of it in their lowered eyes.

WHO PAYS THE PRICE FOR ABANDONED AND REJECTED CHILDREN?

British psychiatrist John Bowlby was a pioneer in understanding attachment. I recall him telling the story of a little boy who had missed out on developing attachment. How did this happen? It resulted through a combination of the child's temperament and his parents' psychological unavailability. While seeing this young patient in the study of his home, Bowlby was called out of the room to answer the telephone. While out of the room, Bowlby remembered that he had left the cat in the room with the little boy and rushed back—only to find that the boy had very calmly thrown the cat into the fire.

Attachment is one of the crucial building blocks in the process of emotional development. As Bowlby's shocking story shows, children who don't develop attachment have trouble making appropriate emotional connections. They have trouble with their own feelings and with the feelings of others. They often lack the emotional fundamentals for becoming a well-functioning member of society and are prone to become infected with whatever social poisons are around them. In short, they have trouble learning the basics of empathy, sympathy, and caring. The relevance for violent boys everywhere is clear.

The big family issues for lost boys are not abstract formulations or political pronouncements about family values. They are very concrete and specific: rejection, abandonment, disrupted family relationships. The latter can take many forms and have multiple consequences, but one of the most important is that disruptions affect the child's ability to form and sustain secure, positive social relationships. These relationships serve as a psychological anchor, helping to hold a boy in good society rather than allowing him to drift into the dark side. As always, it is a matter of temperament and experience; a boy's fate is neither totally predetermined by genetic programming nor totally the result of social influences.

The problems violent boys show in truly understanding normal social relations in the community is sometimes startling, even to someone, like me, who is sympathetic to them. While few of them have the kind of cold-blooded character evident in the little boy who threw Bowlby's cat in the fire, some of them do seem clueless when it comes to conventional standards regarding humane behavior in our society.

Later, in Chapter Five, I will explore in depth what this alienation means for moral development, but here I want to just mention some of its implications. Sitting with Michael one afternoon as he awaited trial for killing a police officer, I asked him, "What was the worst thing you ever did? What was the worst thing that ever happened to you?" He thought for awhile and then told me he couldn't think of anything really bad that he had ever done. After a brief pause, he added, "Of course, the worst thing that ever happened to *me* is the present situation." A minute later, he added that there were illegal things he had done that some people might consider bad from *their* point of view.

Michael had erected such strong defenses against his own deep feelings of hurt that he had great difficulty recognizing the feelings of others. Accurately seeing and hearing what others are feeling is one feature of what psychologist Dan Goleman calls "emotional intelligence." And it is in this sense that many violent boys suffer from a kind of "emotional retardation." Like most forms of retardation, it can arise from a mixture of biological predispositions (less than usual neurological capacity for empathy) and experiences of deprivation (being treated with emotional brutality rather than empathy).

Emotional retardation is one of the socially expensive side effects of surviving rejection in childhood, particularly in boys whose temperament puts them in jeopardy for emotional compartmentalization in the first place. When thirteen-year-old Mitchell Johnson and eleven-year-old Andrew Golden opened fire on their classmates in Jonesboro, Arkansas, the two boys seemed surprised at the results—at both the carnage and the adults' reactions. In the hours and minutes leading up to their crimes of carnage, some violent boys seem genuinely unaware of the human significance of what they are about to do. After the fact, they have trouble connecting with the emotional pain they have caused others. Shortly after Michael Carneal was apprehended following his shooting spree in Paducah, he told police, "It was like I was in a dream."

With their emotional retardation and great difficulty recognizing the feelings of others, it's no wonder that animal abuse is common among kids with difficult attachment histories. If our society were uniformly caring and nurturant toward animals, this might not be such a big problem, but our society kills and feasts on animals of all sorts and regularly exposes children to images of violent treatment of animals in movies and television. For example, how is it that we find the throwing of a cat in the fire hideous and yet are quite content with tossing live lobsters into pots of boiling water? From the perspective of a troubled boy, our society has rather ambiguous moral standards about the treatment of animals. This helps create a moral space for cruelty by boys who seem to lack the regular emotional feedback systems that cause most children to stop the hurting once they receive the victim's signals of distress and pain.

Sixteen-year-old Malique recalls his experiences abusing animals when he was twelve. "Any animal—a cat, a dog, a bird, or anything that we saw that was moving—it could be shot. That's where I learned to shoot my first gun. One time we had a long knife that we used to cut open this stray dog. It was disgusting, 'cause his insides fell right out." It should come as no surprise that Kip Kinkel, the fifteen-year-old who killed his parents and schoolmates in Springfield, Oregon, has a history of animal abuse, as do some of the other middle-class boys who opened fire on classmates at schools in recent years. In Pearl, Mississippi, Luke Woodham and a friend were observed beating Woodham's dog with a club, wrapping it in a plastic bag, setting it afire, and tossing it in a pond.

Early in our relationship Malcolm spoke about using his pit bulls in dogfights in a way that I found particularly disturbing. It was not until we had spent months together and I felt a close relationship evolving that I heard him change his tune about the dogs. What began as a relationship with me matured into a larger capacity for relationships in general, and eventually Malcolm told me he didn't think he could participate in the dogfighting anymore. Perhaps our relationship was somehow starting to fill the void in his heart and soul. In a small way I was becoming the positive parental figure that Malcolm lacked.

But even when there is such a parent figure in a boy's social map, there are often other problems that arise from rejection and abandonment. Thomas had grandparents who filled the void left by his drug-dependent mother. But it was not enough, because Thomas still wonders why she wasn't there for him. Andrew Golden in Jonesboro spent most of his time with his grandparents while his parents worked. Malcolm's was separated from him for four years, serving in the army. She returned for him, but it may have been a case of too little too late. In fact, her presence provoked a crisis that grew out of the hole left in this family by the "missing" father and Malcolm's efforts to fill that hole.

THE COSTS OF BEING THE "LITTLE MAN OF THE HOUSE"

When boys grow up without fathers, there is always a possibility that they will be drawn into the role of the "man of the house." Without stable partners in their lives, some mothers turn to their sons for intimacy or protection. This is not necessarily a problem in and of itself. Indeed, learning commitment to another human being brings many developmental rewards. But premature responsibility and responsibility that is too big for a child to shoulder gracefully can cause big problems in the long run.

While Malcolm had no real contact with his biological father, he did have contact with his mother's boyfriends. Much of that contact was very negative and exposed Malcolm to domestic violence. His mom would fight with a boyfriend, and he would beat her up. She would then throw him out, and he would return. It became a routine, and Malcolm watched it all. One incident, however, stood out in his mind:

One night, as eight-year-old Malcolm and his ten-year-old brother tried to sleep, the shouting and fighting got so bad that they thought the current boyfriend was going to kill their mother. Little Malcolm and his brother peeked out into the living room and saw the man beating their mother bloody with his fists and his belt. The two little boys grabbed baseball bats from their room and rushed to their mother's defense, knocking the boyfriend unconscious. Malcolm's mother hugged and kissed him until she stopped crying, and then she called the police. What Malcolm said next, after he described this incident to me, is crucial to understanding his story. He told me, "Ever since then, I've been over-protective of my mother." This admission is crucial, because it shows that Malcolm was cast in an inappropriate role in his family—that of "man of the house."

This kind of role reversal—where the child is the protector and the parent is needy—is common in the lives of violent boys. Alfred sold drugs to feed his younger brothers and sisters, because his mother was incapacitated by her own drug addiction and there was no father present to take charge. Corneel used proceeds from his drug dealing to pay the rent for his mother. Tyrone said it "felt good" to be able to take care of his mother.

For boys already in jeopardy because of their temperament and the social situation of their family, this role reversal can be a big problem in adolescence, the time when boys are in greatest need of a strong authority figure to steer them away from the negative influence of peers. It is then that the consequences of role reversal in childhood are most keenly felt, these being greatest for the boys facing the most negative social environments, that is, those that promote delinquency and the buying and selling of illicit drugs. In the worst of these situations, almost no parent can have much influence, but weak mothers who are trying to do the job of parenting alone are at a special disadvantage. They may seek to discipline and exert control, but it is usually futile, because once he has been his mother's protector, a boy is not about to see her as an authority figure.

Some violent boys actively despise their mothers. For example, Luke Woodham in Pearl, Mississippi, told friends he hated his mother because she was powerless and inept; he stabbed her before beginning his assault on his schoolmates. Many violent boys express strong affection for their mothers. However, rarely do they express genuine respect. Sixteen-year-old Robert explained, "My mom was trying to keep me out of trouble, but I wouldn't listen to her. She tried everything she could. She even told me that she should have called the cops and gotten me straight, but I didn't want to listen. There was no force, and I think if my dad was around, things would be different because he would have been able to use force. We wasn't scared of our mother in that way, so we didn't listen."

Many violent boys love their mothers but do not feel that these women can protect them. Indeed, they often have direct physical evidence to the contrary. And usually there is no one else in their lives who can demonstrate to them the protection that a powerful parent figure can provide. This void makes them ripe for the negative influences of the street and the dark side of adolescent culture.

PSYCHOLOGICALLY ALONE, SOCIALLY VULNERABLE

Disrupted relationships in childhood predispose boys to trouble in adolescence. Whether it is outright abandonment or psychological rejection, violent boys often leave infancy and early childhood with one of the biggest strikes against them that a child can have—disrupted attachment relationships. Some boys are predisposed to this emotional isolation. To prevent this predisposition from manifesting itself requires special efforts on the part of their caregivers. Some boys may even be virtually "unattachable" in the normal course of things.

These disruptions in his early relationships challenge a boy's every effort to find a place for himself in the world. The emotional pain and isolation these boys feel can push their souls into hibernation. When what they need is a robust sense of connection to the deepest resources of the spirit, they experience only emptiness. When what they most need is to feel they belong to someone positive and strong, they feel only disdain and see only weakness.

Research on resilience documents the crucial protective role of a secure, strong attachment and the importance of being loved unconditionally by a parent or uncle, aunt, older sister, father, *someone*. Violent boys demonstrate the emotional vulnerability created by weak or broken early attachment. It may take years to do its damage, but unsatisfactory childhood attachment sets in motion the chain of events that results in lethal violence when these boys reach adolescence. How can responsible adults in the community begin to repair this damage? First, they can provide emotional support for parents who are dealing with boys demonstrating attachment problems. It is emotionally grueling to be the parent of such a boy. By all accounts, Kip Kinkel's parents worked hard at trying to find a way to connect with him and bring him under control. As his behavior worsened, they became more desperate. And so did he. It was a race against time, and they lost.

Second, adults outside the family can engage the child and caregiver in therapeutic relationships that examine the nature of the child's attachment problems. For a child predisposed to isolation, only a skilled therapist may be able to figure out effective ways to relate to the child. Third, adults outside the family can go out of their way to provide opportunities for stability and continuity in the child's relationship with them. For example, although conventional programming in elementary schools has children changing teachers every year, vulnerable boys would do better if they had the same teacher over a period of years. This continuity can provide an opportunity for some remedial attachment experiences.

Fourth, when parental abandonment occurs, whether voluntary or enforced by the court, the focus of public policy must be to counteract the emergence and expansion of relationship problems in the child. This means offering therapy to children separated from their parents as well as making systematic efforts to ensure that children find stable homes. It means implementing what social services workers call "permanency planning," that is, carrying out a permanent plan in which children establish and maintain solid relationships while they are in foster care (and even after adoption). The goal is to stop early relationship problems from blossoming into long-term issues of shame, rage, and aggression.

TOXIC SHAME

In his book *Homecoming*, therapist John Bradshaw coined the term "toxic shame." This isn't the healthy sense that you have done wrong and are temporarily ashamed of your actions, and it is very different from feeling guilty over a specific transgression. People who live with toxic shame feel fundamentally disgraced, intrinsically worthless, and profoundly humiliated in their own skin, just for being themselves. Bradshaw links toxic shame to having a "wounded inner child," a concept he popularized in the 1980s. I would associate it with being a hurt soul. But whatever we call it, toxic shame arises when an individual's inner core is tormented through rejection. I have seen it firsthand.

I attend my first Family Day at the Austin MacCormick Center on a fine, sunny Saturday in May 1997. I have come as Malcolm's guest so that I can meet his mother, his aunt, his sister, his brother, and his daughter. Ordinarily, family members may visit once a week, in groups of up to four at a time (no girlfriends are allowed), but from my perusal of the visitor sign-in log at the receiving desk and from talking with the boys, it seems to me that few families make the trip. There is no public transportation to the prison; the closest bus depot is in Ithaca, twenty miles away. Some families have cars (or at least access to cars), but it is a long trip for most of them. Some of the boys come from New York City, five hours away; others from Buffalo or Albany, a three-hour drive; still others from Rochester, two hours distant; and a few lucky ones from Syracuse, only an hour's commute. But physical distance alone doesn't account for the relatively few family members who make the trek. Most boys don't have fathers in the picture, and not every stepfather or mother's boyfriend has the time or the interest to make the trip (and some would not be welcome if they did). Some mothers are just not available. They have other children to take care of, or they may not have the money to pay the fares for buses and taxis. Furthermore, it's not uncommon for moms themselves to be in jail or in a drug treatment program—or dead.

While the typical week's log of visitors to MacCormick reveals little evidence of family visitors, the annual Family Day is different. The Mac-Cormick administration arranges for buses from major cities in New York State to transport family members. And many do come. For this special occasion, the prison grounds are set up for a barbecue. There's music, too. I arrive as the bus from New York City pulls into the parking lot. The door opens, and families pour down the steps. There are mothers in their thirties and grandmothers (in hats); there are even young women who turn out to be not the mothers but the grandmothers of the boys. There are the incarcerated boys' little sisters and daughters (all done up in frilly dresses, their Sunday best) and brothers and sons. Some of the big brothers have been here before, on the inside. Many of the little brothers will probably find their way inside in the years to come, judging by the stories the boys tell me about them. There are grown men, too: fathers, stepfathers, boyfriends, uncles, and grandfathers. And there are even some teenage girls, who are officially supposed to be sisters but who are in reality the boys' girlfriends.

There's an air of excitement and anxiety about the crowd that anyone who has ever been to sleepaway camp or boarding school would recognize. But before this reunion can start, MacCormick, unlike a summer camp or a boarding school, requires that each family member sign in, go through the metal detector, be searched, and leave all contraband (unauthorized reading material, food, CDs, audio tapes, and virtually everything else) in the makeshift reception center set up in the training building outside the main gate. Everyone must pass through the checkpoint and receive a visitor's badge. It is a chaotic and seemingly endless process, but eventually it does end and, in groups of eight to ten, the visitors are led through the security gates to be with their boys.

Sometimes the greetings between the boys and their families are guarded. Sometimes there is pure, simple warmth, and many eyes are filled with tears. Claire has asked me to deliver a birthday card to Gino, one of her favorites. I find him sitting at the head of a picnic table, surrounded by eight female relatives—mother, aunt, sisters, and cousins. This is a boy who has impressed Claire with his seriousness, particularly about family matters, and with his anxiety about his upcoming release back into "the world." He once told her that his biggest dream was to live to be twenty-five, and that returning to the city makes him fear for his survival. The card I am delivering says HAPPY 17TH BIRTHDAY. When I present the card to Gino, his mother shows great pride in seeing that someone has acknowledged her son's birthday. I don't really know Gino, so I quickly move on to my primary mission—finding Malcolm and meeting his family.

When I do find Malcolm, he is sitting alone. I see him before he sees me, and I am privy to the tense, worried look on his face. Obviously, his family is not yet here. When he sees me, his face lights up with his trademark smile, and I sit down with him to wait. Before long, Malcolm begins to ruminate about why his family is late. He envisions his mother or aunt oversleeping, or maybe his girlfriend (who has recovered from being shot eight months earlier) was late bringing his daughter over for the trip. Or maybe his aunt had trouble getting the car from her brother. There are lots of reasons why they might be late—all the *normal* reasons why family members get delayed. Knowing Malcolm as I do, I expect that he fears the real reasons have something to do with his lifelong experience of re-jection and abandonment.

A half hour passes. Visibly agitated, Malcolm asks if I would call his mother to find out what is happening. Doing so means having to go back through the security gate to my car phone, which I agree to do, given the circumstances. Malcolm writes out a phone number for me on a piece of paper. When I dial the number, there is only endless, unanswered ring-ing. After twenty rings, I go through the laborious process of re-entering the prison grounds, back through the security check. Malcolm figures the unanswered phone must mean that family members are on their way, so he brightens up considerably. He is such delightful company when he's happy.

An hour passes. It's getting late for lunch, and Malcolm asks if I will try calling again, this time adding his aunt's number to the piece of paper. Once again I make the trip back through the security gates to my car, and once again there is no answer. When I return with the bad news, Mal-colm is stoical at first. "No problem," he says. But his hands are working nervously. Time passes. "Do you want to eat something?" I ask. "No," he answers. "Do you want to sit with some of the other boys and their fami-lies?" Again, "No thanks." We opt to sit and wait.

Malcolm is not the only boy whose family has not arrived. By them-selves and sometimes in groups of two or three, the unvisited stroll around the compound or drift back inside to their rooms. A few join up with other families, but Malcolm still sits and waits. As unvisited boys walk past us, Malcolm introduces a few to me and then later tells me what they are in for—mostly for murder or assault. One is the seventeen-year-old boy with a life sentence who is the only boy at the facility to have achieved honors in MacCormick's system for ranking boys by the level of their compliance with the rules and the extent of their participa-tion in the program.

Now it is clear that Malcolm's family is not going to make it in time for the official ceremonies, including the presentation of academic, so-cial, and athletic achievement awards. Still we sit—a very disappointed black teenager and a very sad white man. Malcolm's family never does ar-rive. I joke awkwardly that he will have to settle for me as family. The time eventually comes when I must go home. "No problem," he says again, but when I next see him, he is bitter about being let down—again.

There is some story about his aunt not getting the promised car to make the trip, but it is clear that this is not the first time Malcolm has felt rejected and abandoned. Chances are it won't be the last. Each such experience forges another link in the chain of events that leads to lethal violence in boys.

HOW EARLY VULNERABILITY
BECOMES BAD BEHAVIOR

HURT LITTLE BOYS BECOME AGGRESSIVE BIG BOYS

What comes next in the chain of events that leads from disconnection and hurt in the early years to the act of committing lethal aggression in adolescence? Chapter Two explored the roots of vulnerability in young boys, emphasizing the process of connecting and the consequences of psychological abandonment and rejection. What stands between this early psychological vulnerability and later youth violence? That is the question I am seeking to answer when I talk with Dennis.

Dennis was sixteen when I first met him, the youngest of two children. Tall with short hair and very intense dark eyes, he grew up in a small city in the care of his mother and father. Both parents worked—he at the post office, she in a hospital. While his parents worked, he was cared for by his grandmother a few days a week and at a day-care center the rest of the time. When he was six years old Dennis started first grade at the school three blocks from his home.

It is my first interview with Dennis. I have been going through the chronology of events in his life—where he lived and with whom, where he went to school and how he liked it, and so on. He lists four different elementary schools he attended as a child. "Why did you change schools so often when you were a child?" I ask. "I was bad," is his simple answer. "How bad?" I ask. "I'd get in trouble and get suspended," he replies with a smile. "After getting suspended a few times, I'd get expelled and then move on to another school. That's the way it went until I got to high school, and then I stopped going most of the time." He says his parents told him he was always more difficult than his older sister. "I did have one good year, though," he reports. "At the Alternative School." There, he tells me, he didn't get into much trouble. The classes were small, and there were only a hundred kids in the whole school. "The teachers made an effort to understand my problems," he says. Whatever good they did for Dennis, it was either too late or simply not enough to set him on the right track.

The following year, when he was transferred back to the regular high school program, all Dennis's old problems resurfaced, and by May of that year he had stopped going to school altogether. A year later he was arrested on a charge of being part of a drug-dealing network in his neighborhood. Convicted of this crime, he served four months in a juvenile detention center. After he was released, he didn't even bother to go back to school. He simply picked up where he had left off. Six months later Dennis was arrested again, this time in connection with the shooting of two boys in the park across the street from the school he no longer attended.

Fourteen-year-old Thomas tells much the same story. I talk with him while he awaits trial for murdering a seventeen-year-old in a street confrontation two blocks from his home in a small town in rural upstate New York. "I was a terror," he says, recounting a litany of troubles. Like Dennis's, Thomas's problems started in early childhood, beginning with an escalating pattern of disobedience and graduating to fights at school. He lived with his grandmother and her husband, the only child in a household with two middle-aged adults.

When Thomas talks about his childhood, he is quick to point out that he wanted to do better than he did—in school, with his grandparents, and with the neighbors. His grandmother says, shaking her head, "Thomas is a nice boy, but he was always a handful. My husband and I tried our best with him, but . . ." Her voice trails off. I've seen the records in Thomas's case, and they document an ongoing saga of misdeeds: stealing money from his grandmother's purse, calling in a false fire alarm to his elementary school, skipping school with some older boys when he was nine years old, smoking in the bathroom in sixth grade, not coming home when he was supposed to after school, and getting into fights on the playground.

Malcolm, too, was a difficult child whose problems started early. Recall from Chapter Two that his mother was absent for the first four years of his life. She was in the army, and Malcolm lived those years with his grandmother. Once his mother did return, she tried to impose her will on a little boy who knew her only from pictures, cards, and phone calls, and he rebelled. Malcolm was a troublesome child in kindergarten, always into mischief. If there was a wad of gum in the goldfish bowl, Malcolm was the most likely suspect. If there was a tussle in the back of the line on the way to the gym, Malcolm was probably involved. In second grade he was suspended for a day for punching another boy so hard he knocked the wind out of him. By the time he was in third grade he had started fighting for real, not just the tussles common to many a boy's childhood but full-fledged fighting. At ten years of age he was suspended from school for a fight that landed another boy in the hospital with a seriously injured eye and a broken nose.

Such stories are not unusual in the accounts of childhood told by violent youths, who by and large started misbehaving early in life. These boys say that the adults who took care of them often remind them of their early misbehavior, even today. Such stories are in the social worker's notes in Michael's case file; Michael's mother had told the caseworker, "The boy has always been a problem—willful and disobedient. No matter how hard I punished him, he wouldn't behave." Michael has the scars on his back to validate her claim about using harsh punishment. But he also has taken her words to heart and has folded them into his own self-portrait. Now nineteen years old, Michael says that he was "a rogue" but that his brother Robert was "submissive." The pattern was set by the time the brothers reached elementary school: Michael fought with other children, disobeyed teachers, and destroyed property, whereas Robert submitted to adult authority in every situation in every way. Today's violent high school boys are, for the most part, the bad boys in elementary school from five or six years ago.

I saw such bad boys during my own brief stint as an elementary school teacher in the 1960s. I recall one such child as if it were yesterday. As I watched him on the playground, six-year-old Damon dropped a banana peel on the ground and ran off. The principal saw him commit this minor act of delinquency and tracked him down. "Pick it up," he said to the boy. Damon did, and then promptly dropped it again. "Pick it up and put it in the trash," the principal commanded. Damon did so, paused, and then pulled the banana peel out of the trash and dropped it on the ground again. "Pick it up, put it in the trash, and leave it there!" the exasperated principal yelled. These are the children who leave their teachers weary every day.

Coupled with aggression, this sort of chronic misbehavior lays down the foundation for bigger problems in later life unless teachers and parents intervene early to get these boys back on track. The good news is that this redirection is possible. According to the results of a study conducted by Johns Hopkins University psychologist Sheppard Kellam and his colleagues, violence prevention programs and effective classroom management techniques in first grade can have a dramatic effect on the likelihood that an aggressive six-year-old will become a violent thirteen-year-old. Kellam's group found that highly aggressive six-year-old boys placed within well-managed first grade classrooms run by effective teachers were three times less likely to be highly aggressive by the time they reached eighth grade than similarly aggressive boys who were placed in a chaotic classroom with ineffective teachers. This is a critical issue to which I will return in Chapter Seven.

WHEN BAD BEHAVIOR STARTS EARLY

Research by psychologist Leonard Eron and colleagues documents that by age eight boys' patterns of aggressive behavior and attitude are already crystallizing, so much so that without intervention such patterns tend to continue into adulthood. When they began their studies in the 1960s, Eron and his colleagues asked eight-year-olds to identify the aggressive children in their classrooms. "Who are the children in your class who hit people, who start fights, who kick people?" they asked. When they followed up on these children three decades later, they found that, by and large, the children who had been identified as aggressive at age eight became adults who at age thirty-eight hit family members, get into fights in the community, and drive their cars aggressively. (By the way, this gives a developmental spin to the problem of road rage: it may start as "tricycle rage.")

There is a formal name for the pattern of behavior that Dennis calls being "bad" and Thomas calls being "a terror." Psychologists and psychiatrists call it Conduct Disorder. For children to be labeled as having conduct disorder, they must meet a set of criteria developed by the American Psychiatric Association and published in its official *Diagnostic and Statistical Manual of Mental Disorders* (DSM). The current edition, DSM-IV, defines Conduct Disorder as "a repetitive and persistent pattern of behavior in which the basic rights of others or major age-appropriate societal norms or rules are violated." The manual's criteria include aggression to people and animals, destruction of property, deceitfulness or theft, and serious violations of rules. This is a familiar pattern to me; I see it often with incarcerated boys. That is not surprising, for at least 80 percent of boys in juvenile prisons and rehabilitation programs, boys like Dennis, Malcolm, Thomas, and Kip, carry with them this rather cold diagnostic label.

Particularly important for understanding lethal youth violence is the question of when a boy's pattern of chronic bad behavior starts, that is, whether it begins early (childhood onset) or later (adolescence onset). British criminologists Farrington and Hawkins report that when conduct disorder begins in childhood rather than adolescence, it is more likely to continue into adulthood. Other investigators, such as psychologist Alan Kazdin, agree that youths with childhood-onset Conduct Disorder are more likely than those with adolescence-onset Conduct Disorder to engage in aggressive and criminal behavior and are more likely to remain chronically dysfunctional into and throughout adulthood.

Why is childhood-onset Conduct Disorder more severe? There are no simple answers, but there are some compelling ideas from child development research. First, if bad behavior starts in childhood rather than adolescence, it has a longer period to build up and interfere with normal development. When it begins in adolescence, a boy is more likely to have positive experiences and relationships from the past to fall back on, and the troubling behavior is more likely to be a temporary phase reflecting difficulty in meeting the special challenges of being a teenager, such as dealing with complicated issues of peer relations. Indeed, surveys show that *most* boys and many girls exhibit some delinquent behavior during their teenage years, with more than 60 percent engaging in some combination of aggressive acts, drug abuse, arson, and vandalism. I know I did, as did most of the teenagers I have known.

The second reason childhood onset is a bad omen is that when young children exhibit a pattern of bad behavior, it more than likely is linked to some underlying problem in them rather than to simple negative peer influence. According to Kazdin's research, underlying problems include a difficult temperament, neurological deficits and difficulties (often associated with pregnancy- and birth-related complications), separation from parents, violence in the family, and harsh parenting practices.

Of the boys I've interviewed, nearly all would qualify as childhood-onset cases. Dennis reports that he regularly beat up other kids in school. Devon took money his mother gave him to buy sneakers and used it to purchase drugs instead. Adam stole a purse. All these things happened before any of these boys turned ten. Their own self-reports fit within the American Psychiatric Association's set of criteria for Conduct Disorder.

I sit listening to fifteen-year-old Aaron remember the places he lived in and the schools he attended over the years. He's a cherubic-looking kid with an engaging smile and a very dignified way of talking. (I can picture him with a herringbone tweed jacket, an ascot, and a pipe.) I am taking it all in, perhaps lulled by his apparently sweet disposition. After he has finished, I turn to the task of verifying the sequence of events he has just reported. "Why did you move from the house on Ferry Street?" I ask pleasantly.

His answer takes me aback. "I burned down the house playing in the kitchen," he replies, smiling sheepishly.

I pride myself on being unflappable with the boys, so I pause a moment and then say, "Tell me about that."

And he does: "I burned the house down 'cause I was playing with spaghetti sticks. I was putting them in straws, and the melting plastic was dripping on the floor. I think I was like seven."

I ask, "So when the fire started in the house, were you by yourself?"

"No, my mother, she was braiding my sister's hair in the living room. And I was running back and forth playing in the kitchen. My mother was telling me like, 'Don't be back there playing with nothing.' But I didn't listen, and I climbed up on the wood thing, I got some spaghetti strings and the straws, I took some straws out the drawer, and I stuck them in there. And I lit the stove and stuck it in the fire. And the straws was burning, the plastic was dripping. And when that happened, when the plastic on the floor started burning up, I went in the living room and sat down next to my mother. And she was like, she knew I did something 'cause usually I just was running around the house, but I came and sat next to my mother. I was sitting there watching her braid my sister's hair. She was like, she looked at me like, 'What did you do?' I was like, 'Nothing.' So she went in the kitchen and saw it, and that's when it was already burning up. So we had to leave, and we moved down the street by my grandmother."

I ask him, "Were you scared when the fire started?"

"Yeah," he says. "But my mother, she wasn't surprised I did it, 'cause I was always hyper."

UNDERSTANDING, NOT LABELING

Although violent boys obviously don't use the term Conduct Disorder to describe themselves, their self-descriptions certainly match the criteria for this disorder. But the term is only a label. It simply describes a pattern of chronic bad behavior: a boy steals, hits people, hurts animals, destroys property, disobeys parents and teachers, fights with other boys, and victimizes girls. When this behavior occurs over and over again, it is called a chronic pattern of behavior, or Conduct Disorder.

But using this label for a boy can easily become the end of the story rather than the beginning. To go beyond diagnosis, we need to know *why* a boy is behaving badly and what we—parents and professionals—can do to improve his behavior. We want to understand why a boy would engage in a pattern of chronic bad behavior, but it seems that the process of diagnosis often simply leaves us with the fact that he does habitually engage in such behavior, without shedding light on its origins. For example, during Thomas's trial, the prosecution's psychologist diagnosed him with "Conduct Disorder, childhood onset" and left it at that, as though simply pronouncing the diagnosis explained anything and everything the court needed to know. In fact, it explained nothing other than the fact that Thomas's act of homicide as a teenager was the culminating point of many years of aggressive behavior.

It took hours listening to Thomas's life story for me to understand how and why he reached the point of killing someone. It took hearing about his being emotionally abandoned by his mother and father, about his early problems controlling his temper and his grandparents' ineffective responses, about his frustrated attempts to find friends, about his being sent to visit his drug-addicted mother in the war zone of the city. In short, understanding him required hearing his life story, not just learning which diagnostic label he had been assigned.

What is more, labeling a child pushes us away from remembering the human being behind the diagnostic label or category, a consequence of most clinical diagnoses. No one likes to be reduced to a diagnosis. I don't like being known only as a "white adult male college professor" any more than Malcolm likes being seen only as a "black teenage felon with a history of Conduct Disorder." So while I rely on research that uses the term, I avoid the term Conduct Disorder as much as possible, and instead will simply focus on the questions of how and why boys get to be who and what they are.

Avoiding dehumanizing labels is particularly important when dealing with adolescents and issues involving adolescents. Many adults have a prejudice against teenagers. We make jokes about it as parents. I SUR-VIVED BEING THE PARENT OF A TEENAGER, says one bumper sticker. We tend to shy away from teenagers in groups, for example, at the mall or on the street. Thirty years ago, when I told people I had volunteered to teach junior high school, and thus to spend my day with classes full of kids just entering adolescence, many thought this was clear evidence of insanity on my part. One reason for this bias is that while most adults find children familiar and comprehensible, they find teenagers alien and inscrutable. Part of this is the myth that adolescence is a time of unpredictable changes and that it represents a disconnection from childhood. Child analyst Anna Freud promoted this view. In fact, as she saw it, there is something unhealthy about a child who *doesn't* go crazy and become rebellious, defiant, and troublesome as a teenager. Our culture has a tendency to see adolescence as a time of dramatic changes that come out of nowhere, unpredictably. In her book *Children Without Childhood*, social critic Marie Winn refers to the "myth of the teenage werewolf": the idea that well-behaved and nice children become monsters when the hormonal surges of adolescence take over.

But research conducted by psychologist Daniel Offer in the United States and psychiatrist Michael Rutter in the United Kingdom generally tells a different story. Only about 20 percent of kids demonstrate a tumultuous adolescence, one full of crisis and turmoil. Most kids do *not* evidence the dramatic changes for the worse that the myth of the teenage werewolf would lead us to expect. Rather, they show a pattern of continuity from childhood into adolescence, particularly if the circumstances of their lives remain relatively constant and supportive. Psychologist Aaron Ebata finds that children with depressive tendencies generally become depressed teenagers. A report compiled for the American Psychological Association documents that aggressive children generally become aggressive teenagers.

Yes, adolescence brings about changes and intensification, but generally these are along the lines laid out in childhood. Kids who experience a tumultuous adolescence generally had a difficult childhood. Violent boys are not so different from other boys in this regard. It is a question of their intensifying the negative while other boys are accentuating the positive. The process is the same, but the negative outcomes can be as disastrous as the positive outcomes can be wonderful. And in some boys it is a time when problems that were swept under the rug in childhood come bursting out into the world, as the suddenly powerful teenager replaces the previously powerless young child. For example, University of Pennsylvania sociologist Richard Gelles reports that most teenagers who assault their parents were once children assaulted *by* their parents. This is the domain of the lost boys, the boys who go beyond the bounds of normal male aggression to become violent teenagers. The recognition of adolescence as the culmination of what begins in childhood directs us toward an understanding of the core question, Why would a boy be so bad at an early age in the first place?

ARE BOYS BORN BAD?

Some people are tempted to say that some kids really are just born bad. That is where the popular expression *bad seed* comes from. Some of the troubled boys' parents and grandparents seem to accept this explanation, as do some professionals who work with them. Yes, some boys are born with difficult temperaments; they are irritable, hyperactive, and resistant. And, yes, being born difficult increases the challenges faced by parents and other caregivers and thus increases the likelihood that such boys will be rejected, abandoned, abused, neglected, and mishandled. But this is not synonymous with being "hardwired" in the womb to behave badly and become a violent teenager.

The question of whether bad behavior is preprogrammed genetically is one of the central controversies in child development. An informed starting point is to remember that child development requires the interplay of biology *and* society, the characteristics children bring with them into the world *and* the way the world treats them, nature *and* nurture. Sociobiology emphasizes a genetic origin for social behavior: some characteristics promote survival, and thus reproduction, more than other characteristics. In contrast, what researcher Benjamin Pasamanick calls social biology concentrates on the social origins of biological phenomena (e.g., the impact of poverty on infant health). Sociobiologists look for the origins of biological phenomena (i.e., genetically transmitted characteristics in a population) in its social history (i.e., the differential life success of individuals and groups in reproducing and thus passing on those characteristics). The key is that there are *social* implications of *genetically based* individual behaviors; the social impact of biologically rooted traits can affect the survival of individual people and groups of related people, and thus the likelihood that a particular genetic pattern will be passed along to surviving offspring.

From a social biological perspective, one can say that children face different opportunities and risks for development because of their mental and physical makeup *and* because of the social environment they inhabit *and* because of how well their inborn traits match up with what their social environment offers, demands, rewards, and punishes. Social environment also affects the very physical makeup of the child. These effects may be negative (e.g., the impact of poverty on birth weight or the influence of industrial carcinogens in one's neighborhood in producing birth defects) or positive (e.g., intrauterine surgery or nutritional therapy for a fetus with a genetic disorder). A social biological perspective on the question of lethal youth violence accepts the premise that biologically based predispositions to violence only translate into behavior when they occur in social situations that permit or encourage their expression.

So when all is said and done, I think the best theory of child development comes down on the side of a focus on the social context, what psychologist Urie Bronfenbrenner has called an "ecological" perspective on the question of nature and nurture. How genetic influences, such as temperament, and environmental influences, such as early trauma, will affect a child's development depends upon the context in which those influences are played out. One of the challenges we face in understanding human development is the central importance of these contexts. Few processes work universally and independently of specific situations. Rarely does any specific X cause a specific Y in every time and place and with every human being. Indeed, in matters of human development, when the question is "Does X cause Y?" the best answer is almost always "It depends." *It depends*.

The critical importance of social context is as true of the consequences of child temperament as it is of any other characteristic relevant to understanding youth violence. Does it matter if a child is born with a minor physical anomaly, such as low-seated ears and a slightly misshapen head, which are indicative of minor neurological problems arising from disorders of pregnancy, particularly in the first trimester? Does being born with these anomalies predict that a child will end up as an aggressive adolescent? *It depends* upon the family the child is born into and in which the child grows up.

Sarnoff Mednick and Elizabeth Kandel studied the impact of being born with such a minor physical anomaly on the development of violent behavior, speculating that the neurological damage signaled by the physical anomaly might be biologically linked to such behavior. They found that such children who grow up in well-functioning, stable families have no greater risk of being arrested for violent crimes by age twenty-one than do physically normal children (the arrest rate was about 15 percent for both groups). However, when such damaged children grow up in unstable, troubled families, they are three and a half times more likely to end up being arrested for violent crimes by age twenty-one than are physically normal children in similar families (70 percent vs. 20 percent).

A study conducted by German psychologists Friedrich Losel, Doris Bender, and Thomas Bliesener tells a similar story about the role of social context. These psychologists looked at the role of child temperament in high-school-age bullies and victims. They started from the general finding that a low resting heart rate in children is associated with antisocial behavior. Why? The hypothesis is that such children have a low resting heart rate because the emotional reaction system in their body is set low.

This means, among other things, that they don't show as much fear in response to the threat of punishment and are more impulsive. Apparently, they are less likely to be frightened off by scary situations and are more willing to take the risks associated with antisocial behavior. By the same token, timid children typically have high resting heart rates, suggesting that their emotional response systems are highly reactive and that they thus are easily frightened.

Losel and his colleagues went beyond this simple dichotomy to look at the role of temperament (as measured by heart rate) in two situations: low-risk families (i.e., those with low levels of stressful events and trauma and a high level of effective family functioning) and high-risk families (high levels of stressful events and trauma coupled with a low level of effective family functioning). The heart rates of bullies and victims were quite different in the two groups of family situations. In low-risk families there were significant differences between the heart rate of bullies and that of victims: in contrast to other children (who had rates of 70 beats per minute), bullies had low heart rates (62 beats per minute) and victims had high heart rates (75 beats per minute). But in high-risk families there was no difference in the heart rates of bullies, victims, and other youth (at about 70 beats per minute). Context matters in the impact and expression of temperamental characteristics. We must never forget that.

THE STORY OF ONE DIFFICULT CHILD

Being born difficult does not mean that a child will end up displaying a chronic pattern of aggression and bad behavior in adolescence. I know this from firsthand experience. I myself was a difficult infant and toddler—cranky, troublesome, willful, and aggressive. At two I was found standing on the wall of the balcony outside our sixth-floor apartment and talking to the cats in the courtyard. When my mother ordered me in, I refused. That same year, I ran away from home one night and was found wandering the streets in my pajamas. When I was three, the neighbors routinely came to my mother to complain that I was beating up their six- and seven-year-old children. When I was six I would stand at the top of the monkey bars on the playground, let go with my hands and challenge other children to try to shake me off.

But by the time I reached adolescence, my aggressive days were over and I became something of a model citizen. I was vice president of the student council and editor of the yearbook in my high school; I was even sent to Washington in 1964 as an exemplary youth by the Lions Club in my town. Few who saw the difficult child I was at three would have predicted the model citizen I became at sixteen.

Why did I turn out as I did while other difficult children do not? My success had a lot to do with the social context in which I grew up—my family, my neighborhood, my community, my school. I was the first child in my family and for more than four years the only child, so I had my parents all to myself. My mother devoted her every minute to me, literally "taming" me as one would a wolf pup. My father was there for me, a positive force in my life. When I started elementary school, I was assigned to strong and effective teachers in the early grades who took charge of me and the rest of their students and made sure we behaved in a civilized manner. Although I lived some of my early years in a public housing project in New York City, it was when "the projects" were still a safe and sane place, before they began the descent that transformed them into a war zone twenty years later. I was taken to church every Sunday morning, and the president of our country was a trusted and reassuring father figure. When I turned on the television or went to the movies, the violence I saw was very tame by today's standards and the sexiest thing on either screen was a slow kiss. When I reached adolescence, I went to a small high school where I felt safe and was taught by teachers who cared for me. There were no gangs, guns, or drugs in my neighborhood.

Each of these elements of my life supported, protected, guided, and nurtured me. A boy like Malcolm experiences a negative mirror image of my early life: for each protective factor I experienced he is dealt a risk factor. Context matters, and one of the most important features of context is the balance between protective influences and threatening risk factors.

RISK ACCUMULATES

Threats accumulate; support ameliorates. The presence of only one or two risk factors does not disable a child. Rather, it is the accumulation of threats that does the damage. And trouble really sets in when these threats accumulate without a parallel accumulation of compensatory "opportunity" factors. Once overwhelmed, defenses are weakened the next time the child faces threat. Children and adolescents become highly sensitive to any negative social influences around them. I look at it this way: Give me one tennis ball, and I can toss it up and down with ease. Give me two, and I can still manage easily. Add a third, and it takes special skill to juggle them. Make it four, and I will drop them all. So it is with threats to development.

This accumulation approach to developmental threats offers hope to those responsible for policy and programming on behalf of youth. It tells us that life need not be risk free for development to proceed successfully. And one way to succeed with kids is to inject compensatory opportunity factors into the equation of their life. Then we can expect to see positive results—as long as we can prevent the coping capacity of youth from being overwhelmed. If there are one to two threats to our children's development beyond our immediate control, they need not be destructive. At the same time, they should be an urgent warning, telling us to protect the children in our care from any further risks and to marshal our resources to build opportunities to enhance their development.

As threats accumulate, children's intellectual development suffers and they cannot bring to bear cognitive strength in mastering the challenges they face. In a study by University of Michigan psychologist Arnold Sameroff and his colleagues, eleven-year-olds with less than three risk factors had above-average IQ scores; those with four such risk factors had below-average IQ scores.

The threat to intellectual competence compounds the effects of negative social influences in the environment by undermining a child's resilience and coping processes. With the accumulation of threats—an absent father, a low resting heart rate, ineffectual teachers, whatever—children not only achieve less but, as a result, value themselves less. Thus begins a downward spiral: those who enter adolescence lacking the reservoir of skills and attitudes they need to deal with negative peer influences in their communities are drawn into or seek out aggressive peer groups, including gangs.

We always need to look at the whole picture, not just one element of the situation. Psychologist Alan Kazdin speaks of "packages" of risk factors that interact to produce chronic patterns of bad behavior in boys. Psychologists Carl Dunst and Carol Trivette speak of the "accumulation of opportunity factors" in improving the prospects of children with disabilities. When I look back on my own childhood, I see a healthy social environment rather than a toxic one; when I listen to Malcolm's story, I hear the opposite. I will return to this exploration of just how toxic or healthy our social environment is in Chapter Four and again in Chapters Six and Seven, for that is what we must try to change in our effort to save violent boys.

THE SEEDS OF BAD BEHAVIOR

In her book *The Nurture Assumption,* Judith Harris pinpoints a series of temperamental traits that put a child at risk for becoming troubled and aggressive. These include high activity level, insensitivity to the feelings of others, lack of physical fear, being easily bored with routine, tendency to seek excitement, and less than average intelligence. Put these characteristics together in one child, and you have a parent who faces a very difficult challenge.

But why do some difficult children become well-socialized youth while others end up troubled or in trouble? One important reason lies in early experience. As I pointed out earlier, chronic bad behavior and aggression are more than a simple matter of male biology or hardwiring in the brain. They result from experience, experience that may start with an infant's nonresponsiveness in the early months of life, which is mostly an adaptation to early mistreatment, rejection, and inept parenting. In a study by child psychologists Stuart Erickson, Byron Egeland, and Robert Pianta at the University of Minnesota, children who were maltreated at an early age were noticeably less cooperative than children who had not suffered harsh punishment at the hands of their parents or guardians. Indeed, the early badness of violent boys—that is, being noncooperative and resistant to parental directions and commands—often starts as a reaction to maltreatment. Many incarcerated boys echo sixteen-year-old Scottie when he recalls, "I wouldn't listen. I just was not going to be told what to do by anybody." This makes the task of anyone who would reform these boys very challenging indeed. By the time these boys reach prison, they often have a decade and a half of noncompliance under their belts. It's a tough habit to change, and much easier to prevent in the first place.

Some parents believe that the way to encourage cooperativeness and obedience in a child is to be harsh and punishing from the very start. But in her classic study of the relation between maternal responsiveness in the first three months of life and the child's compliance at twelve months, psychologist Eleanor Maccoby and her colleagues found just the opposite. Rather than producing "spoiled brats," responsive mothers were rewarded with obedient children. In fact, Maccoby found that the more responsive mothers were in the first three months of life—for example, going immediately to pick up the baby when he or she cried—the more obedient the child was at one year. Maccoby measured obedience by how long the child would stay away from a desirable toy if the mother said, "No. Don't touch." Babies who had more responsive mothers were more obedient than babies who had less responsive mothers. Of course, Maccoby's study did not directly measure how easy or difficult the children were, temperamentally, from the start. But psychiatrist Stanley Greenspan has taken this part of the equation into consideration, and he finds that although it takes a special kind of responsiveness from the mother (including a lot of physical soothing), even temperamentally difficult children can learn to behave well.

It is ironic. Mothers who seek to prevent the disobedience they believe comes from spoiling a baby can end up producing exactly the opposite of what they desire. University of Oregon researcher Gerald Patterson and his colleagues found that chronic bad behavior is most likely to arise in the early years of life when parents use harsh, inconsistent punishment practices instead of clear, firm, but warm responses when the child exhibits unacceptable behavior. The former approach reflects inept parenting, the latter competent parenting. As it turns out, parents who use harsh punishment and mainly pay attention to their child's negative behaviors and ignore the positive ones are unintentionally encouraging aggression.

This is a good starting point for understanding the seeds of a troubled boy's behavior. Mothers and fathers who parent according to the rules I have just described, or whose own psychological condition or history makes them emotionally unavailable to the child, are setting the stage for their child's disobedience and defiant behavior. Not surprisingly, early disobedience and defiance are building blocks for trouble later on, particularly if the child's peers are themselves disobedient and defiant.

One of Patterson's contributions to our understanding is to highlight the fact that parental behavior affects child behavior and vice versa. Alternative behavior patterns are possible for the same parents and children. Behavior is not fixed as a matter of personality. How a child eventually turns out is not decided solely by what goes on inside the family, between parent and child, of course. The world outside the family, particularly the school environment and peer group, plays a powerful role in translating the child's personality traits and predispositions into behavior.

Children may start off on a negative path in part because parents mistakenly withdraw from them in the first months of life (perhaps because they have been taught that leaving a young infant to cry in the crib is the best medicine or because they find the baby too much to handle). The truth is, in the early months of life the big danger is not too much attention but, rather, *in*attention. It is only later that effective parents begin to shape their child's behavior by responding to desirable and undesirable behavior in different ways. Infants require unconditional attention, regardless of how undesirable their behavior may be. "Discipline" only comes later.

It is hard to know what goes on inside the head and heart of an infant, but I believe babies are angry and confused when no one comes to them when they cry and that they are pleased and reassured when someone does come. Is this the beginning of a pattern of estrangement and isolation that builds up through childhood? It certainly seems so when I listen to violent teenagers talk about the way they see the world, that is, with distrust, suspicion, and rage. Malcolm says, "I don't trust nobody. You can't count on anyone except yourself. That's a fact." Scottie tells me, "I just say, forget them. They don't want me, I don't want nothing to do with them," and Bobby has arrived at this conclusion: "I've learned one lesson about life: it sucks." Where did they learn these bitter lessons about life? I believe they learned them first as infants and found reinforcement for those beliefs as they passed through childhood into adolescence.

Psychologist Byron Egeland and his colleagues report that children whose mothers are psychologically unavailable have more behavioral problems than other children. These problems include most forms of emotional and intellectual dysfunction and disability, as well as aggression. Why do some mothers ignore their children? There are many reasons, of course, some having to do with temperament and others with circumstances. Some mothers may be self-centered or self-absorbed or may be the product of an abusive childhood themselves; others may suffer from drug or alcohol abuse, depression, or domestic violence. Whatever its origins, a parent's psychological unavailability is a form of child maltreatment, and maltreatment plays a central role in the development of bad behavior and aggression in children.

Recall that in Chapter Two I mentioned that problems with early attachment are one of the sources of vulnerability among children. Byron Egeland, Alan Stroufe, and their colleagues at the University of Minnesota explored the relationship between attachment problems and aggression by studying preschool-age children in social situations. They identified two groups of children for the study: those who often took the role of victimizer and those who were frequently the victimized. They found that the "victimizer" children had displayed avoidant attachment as infants. (Recall that avoidant attachment describes children who fear their caregivers. It is often a sign of some significant disruption of the parent–child interaction early in life, perhaps including maltreatment.) Egeland's research suggests that early maltreatment plays a role in diverting the development of young children toward aggression.

THE PSYCHOLOGICAL COST OF ADAPTING TO CHILD ABUSE: NEGATIVE SOCIAL MAPS

Nothing tells us more about the link between child maltreatment and aggressive bad behavior than the research of psychologist Kenneth Dodge and his colleagues at Vanderbilt University. Child maltreatment teaches children to adapt their behavior and thinking to the harsh fact that those who are in charge of caring for them are the same people who hurt, terrify, ignore, and attack them. This very adaptation ultimately becomes the source of their problems in later years. According to the studies by Dodge and his colleagues, *children who are maltreated are much more likely than non-maltreated children to develop a chronic pattern of bad behavior and aggression*. The key lies in the fact that the child comes to understand how the world works through the lens of his own abuse. Put another way, a child's worldview is a matter of how he draws his social map.

Of course, all children develop social maps and codes of behavior, which are initially the products of their experiences as filtered by their temperament. For most children, the social map portrays the world in positive terms: *I can trust people. If I behave well, I will be treated well. I am lovable. I have allies in the world.* And as a result, these children naturally develop benign codes of behavior: *Listen to adults. Cooperation pays off. Be patient. Share. I will keep my hands to myself.* Such social maps and codes of behavior give direction to life.

Abused children develop their social maps by adapting to an abusive environment. The more they learn these lessons, the more likely it is that they will learn a code that is compatible with a pattern of bad behavior and aggression by the time they are eight years old. There are four specific elements of this code that are especially important for subsequent behavior and development.

1. *Children become hypersensitive to negative social cues.* Thomas sits with me watching staff and other kids pass by the window of the interview room. As each one goes by, he has something to say that marks them as dangerous. "This one looked at me funny yesterday," he says. "That one is bothering me," he tells me. "See that guy there? I think he's got a blade hidden." No one escapes his watchful eye. He continues: "Just the other day one of the teachers insulted me. She made me feel stupid for asking a question in a class."

2. *Children become oblivious to positive social cues.* Michael cannot think of one nice thing that anyone has done for him in the past year of his incarceration, yet I know of at least three staff members who have gone out of their way to offer him a kind word or some special bit of help. And I know that the teacher who Thomas says insulted him makes a point of praising him whenever she can.

3. *Children develop a repertory of aggressive behaviors that are readily accessible and can be easily invoked.* Malcolm tells me, "I know how to fight. Someone touches me, I'm going to finish it. Somebody hits me, I hit him back twice as hard. I hit him until he bleeds 'cause that way he's not going to hit me again. You know what I mean." I do.

4. *Children draw the conclusion that aggression is a successful way of getting what they want.* Dennis says, "I learned early in life that there's winners and there's losers. The winners end up on top. The losers bleed. I can take care of myself if I need to. I know the rules." He learned that lesson

first at home, at the hands of his parents, and it was later reinforced on the playground and on the street.

The code of violent boys and the social maps it reflects partially explain the nature of their bad behavior. They are not dumb. They observe and they experience, and they draw conclusions based on what they see and feel. Specific experiences become general patterns that together become the lenses through which they see the world. In early childhood they begin to draw negative psychological conclusions about the world and about their place in that world. With these negative social maps in place, they act accordingly.

According to psychologist Alan Kazdin, about 4 to 7 percent of kids exhibit chronic patterns of bad behavior and aggression that are serious enough to constitute a diagnosable mental health problem, such as Conduct Disorder. Boys are anywhere from three to four times as likely to display this pattern as are girls. How specifically are the social maps that abused kids develop linked to their later bad behavior and aggression? Dodge and colleagues found that if a child is maltreated and develops none of the four critical code elements associated with a negative social map (described earlier), the odds that he will exhibit chronic bad behavior and aggression are 5 percent, about what's normal for the population as a whole. But if the child manifests at least three of the four code elements, we can expect a sevenfold increase in the risk that the child will exhibit the pattern of chronic bad behavior and aggression that defines Conduct Disorder.

WHY DON'T MOST ABUSED KIDS DEVELOP BAD BEHAVIOR AND AGGRESSION?

While most kids don't become violent criminals, of course, it is true that the majority of boys incarcerated for violent crimes were subject to abuse or neglect as children. But what about the abused kids who don't develop the negative social maps and don't develop chronic bad behavior and aggression? What about them?

Only 35 percent of abused kids with negative and aggressive social maps become violent, according to Dodge. Why is it that 65 percent of the kids who have been abused and have negative social maps do not develop a pattern of bad behavior and aggression? Why do some boys who are abused develop some or all of the self-defeating behaviors and activities that characterize bad boys while others do not? Some children probably respond by developing other kinds of problems, perhaps confining their response to the internalizing problems of depression, low self-esteem, self-destructive behavior, and bodily troubles like headaches and stom-achaches.

Some children do seem resilient. Why? With some boys, the answer seems clearly linked to a compensatory relationship—that is, a relation-ship with a devoted grandmother, a father who balances out an abusing mother, a loving mother who compensates for an abusive father, perhaps someone outside the family who is positively crazy about the child and who does not let the child's emotional life wither on the vine but lov-ingly helps redraw the child's social maps. The resilience of some chil-dren is due to the fact that the abuse they experience is limited to physical assault and they are able to feel a measure of love and accep-tance from their parents at the times when they are not abused.

Some at-risk children are saved by an intervention program, perhaps a highly effective early childhood education program or the work of a child guidance clinic. Therapists can help children improve their atti-tudes and their behaviors. Some of the same psychologists who study the origins of bad behavior and aggression in children also remedy those problems. For example, the same Gerald Patterson who studies the emer-gence of aggressive and oppositional behavior among children develops and implements therapeutic programs to help parents and children es-cape from being entrapped in coercive relationships. All around the country there are professionals doing this good work with young chil-dren.

The mystery remains, however, as to why some children have the fortitude and strength to resist adapting to abuse and other experiences in ways that put them at risk for becoming violent. Some boys achieve a state of grace in which, though victimized, they find a positive path. This is resilience at its highest level, and I will return to it in Chapters Six and Seven.

There is, of course, another question implied by Dodge's research: Why do some *nonabused* children develop bad behavior and aggression? Perhaps the answer in this case comes from research on parents who withdraw from but do not actively abuse their kids. These are neglectful, passive parents, about whom much less is known. But some things are clear: neglect often results from parents who are incapacitated by drugs or depression, by what social worker Norman Polansky called the apathy-futility syndrome. Also, some parents find themselves unable to cope with temperamentally difficult children and gradually withdraw from them. Their goal each day is only to avoid the aversive experience of confronting the child and dealing with the resulting shouting, screaming, crying, hitting, punching, slamming of doors, stamping of feet, destruction of property, and general mayhem. These parents find an escape from their children, but the result is often emotional and physical neglect.

In fact, neglect is more common than abuse: more kids are emotionally abandoned than are directly attacked, physically or emotionally. According to the federal government's National Incidence Study of Child Abuse and Neglect, there are almost 900,000 cases of neglect and about 750,000 cases of abuse. Neglect leaves a social vacuum that may send a young child looking for connection somewhere else, or with someone or something else. That somewhere else may include television, where the child can learn countless negative lessons about violence and antisocial behavior.

Someone else may include peers who actually have been abused and who thus can model and teach neglected children the ins and outs of bad behavior and aggression. A significant proportion of the acts of violence committed by boys occurs in groups, and in groups there is often a psychological chemistry that makes the violence potential of the group greater than the potential for violence of the individual members. Acting under the influence of peers, any boy may be led to do things he might not do alone, and boys who have a desperate need to fit in may be particularly likely to join in hurtful, aggressive, and dangerous activities.

BEYOND SOCIAL MAPS: DISSOCIATION AND EMOTIONAL NUMBING

There is more to the link between child maltreatment and the development of violence and antisocial behavior than its effects on the child's social map, however. Actual brain damage may be involved, perhaps accounting for some of the unexplained differences between children who become violent youth and those who don't. Baylor University psychiatrist Bruce Perry and his colleagues documented damaging effects to children's brains as a result of the trauma of child abuse. Particularly vulnerable to such damage is the cortex of the brain, where higher thinking that controls moral reasoning takes place.

There is a third explanation for the link as well, lying in the emotional disconnection that psychologists and psychiatrists call *dissociation*. Much has been made of the famous fight-or-flight response to threat. But as Bruce Perry points out, rarely do children have the option of either fighting or fleeing a situation physically, particularly when, as often is the case, the situation is their membership in an abusive family. Perry notes that the fight-or-flight response is mainly observed mostly in male adults, who, when confronted with a stressful threat, can actually choose between fighting or fleeing. Trapped in their home, in a schoolyard, or in a neighborhood, how do children respond?

The most likely option for children is to flee psychologically, that is, to shut down emotionally and disconnect themselves from their feelings *so that they don't have to feel them anymore*. It's a survival strategy that seems to work—in the short run. By cutting off or disowning the feelings that threaten to overwhelm them, children can survive traumatic threats. But at what cost?

John was six years old when his mother was murdered. He knows that because he was there. The day of the killing his stepfather showed up at the door at three o'clock in the morning, hoping to sneak back into the house after having been thrown out the day before by John's mother. The little boy awoke when he heard the kitchen door open, and he got out of bed to see what was happening. He found his stepfather opening the refrigerator to get a can of beer. "Shush," the man said as John appeared in the doorway to the kitchen. "I don't want your mother to hear me." "Welcome back, Daddy Bill," little John said. "Are you supposed to be here?" "It's okay, boy," John's stepfather replied, patting the boy on the head and moving down the hallway to the master bedroom. John stood in the middle of the kitchen, sleepy but hoping for a glass of milk. In a minute Daddy Bill was back in the kitchen, but he looked very angry. At first, John drew back in fear, because he had experienced his stepfather's anger before.

But Daddy Bill was not angry with little John this time. "Don't be scared, boy," the man said. "You okay. Now just reach in that drawer there," he continued, "and get me that big knife your mother uses to cut meat." John did as he was told. He reached into the drawer next to him and pulled out the big knife, then handed it over to Daddy Bill, who took it in his hand and disappeared down the hallway toward the master bedroom again. The next thing John heard was shouting and screaming coming from the bedroom. He stood there, frozen to the spot, for five or ten minutes, until he felt the pee running down his leg onto his foot. Then he walked down the hallway to the bedroom and looked in. Years later, he says that what he remembers is the red walls. His stepfather killed John's mother, stabbing her fifteen times.

"How did you feel?" I ask him, now two decades later. "I don't remember," he says. "I suppose scared, but I would be lying to you if I said I really remember anything but giving Daddy Bill the knife, hearing the screaming and the shouting, and seeing the red walls." He remembers the events, but he has no memory of the feelings. Poor little boy. As I talk with him, he sits on death row, awaiting execution for stabbing to death a fifty-year-old woman in her bedroom. "How did you feel when you killed that woman?" I ask. "I don't remember," he replies.

Emotional dissociation becomes a hard habit to break. It becomes generalized, giving others the impression that a boy has *no* feelings. In fact the reverse is true: his feelings are so powerful that they must be put in a box and pushed aside to ensure his survival. When incarcerated boys talk about their lives—and sometimes their crimes—they often seem emotionless. But I know it's not that they don't have feelings; their feelings are locked up inside the young child they have banished for his own protection.

This is emotional territory that is familiar to most males. Boys are routinely taught to ignore or deny their feelings by parents and others who are training them to be men in a culture that demands male stoicism. It is no secret that boys and men in many societies, including our own, are encouraged to put their emotions in boxes, to keep them out of consciousness, and to regard the expression of powerful feelings of pain and sorrow as a highly dangerous activity. We call this *compartmentalization,* and it is dissociation's first cousin. One of the emotions specially targeted for compartmentalization and dissociation is fear.

Fear

For teenage boys, particularly those who have to be tough on the streets or in their families, fear is a dangerous commodity. Boys often talk about the testing that goes on among their peers, whether it be in school, on the streets, or in prison. They are virtually unanimous in their belief that to *show* fear is to invite victimization. But do they *feel* fear? While the boys I see generally won't admit to feeling fear when they talk to their peers or even to adults who have power over them, they sometimes do so in the privacy of our interviews.

Sharnell is a tough kid. He's battle scarred from his life on the streets and in the juvenile detention facilities where he has spent four years of his life since he turned twelve (he is now sixteen). We sit and talk about his life. Forty-eight armed robberies. He tells me how he and three of his friends would take the subway out to middle-class neighborhoods and rob other teenagers there at gun point. Drug dealing. He explains how the most dangerous point in a drug deal comes when the money is in sight. Once he had to punish a buyer who tried to cheat him; he hit the man on the head with a lead pipe. "Did he die?" I ask. "No," he replies. "My mistake, 'cause a week later the guy surprised me in the hallway of my building and stabbed me in the chest." He shows me the scar. When I ask him about fear, Sharnell tells me, "Nah. I ain't afraid of nothing. Nothing." At which point he rocks back and forth in his chair and sucks his thumb, an act of self-soothing carried over from early childhood. What is going on inside this boy?

As I watch Sharnell rock back and forth, I think of Bruce Perry's study of the children who survived living in the Branch Davidian complex in Waco, Texas, and who had lived through the confrontation that took the life of its leader, David Koresh, and most of his followers. After the shooting and fire, when the surviving children were safely evacuated, Perry interviewed them. Even though they seemed calm on the surface, their hearts were beating at 148 beats per minute (far above the normal 70 beats per minute for young children at rest).

Violent boys often erect this facade of fearlessness early in their lives. I suspect for some it reflects a biological predisposition, an element of temperament. Recall the study in Germany conducted by Friedrich Losel and his colleagues showing that in low-risk families, high school bullies had unusually low heart rates (62 beats per minute, compared to 70 beats per minute for other boys) and victimized children had high heart rates (75 beats per minute). This may reflect a temperamental predisposition to fearlessness.

Some boys are temperamentally primed to take on aggressive roles, while other, more timid, boys are likely to be targeted as victims—and thus develop the elevated heart rate indicative of traumatic response. This pathway is evident in families where environmental conditions permit temperament to shine through. But in high-risk families the trauma affects all the boys, and neither bullies nor victims differ from the normal heart rate patterns found among other children of the same age (70 beats per minute). Perhaps this means the bullies among them have had their heart rates accelerated from dealing with traumatic experiences while the timid victims have used dissociation to train themselves to deaden their emotions so they can get through their stressful days without exploding.

Some boys are too fearful from the start to react delinquently to parental mistreatment or to the threatening environment they find on the streets. They simply try to conform to parental dictates and seek out some small measure of safety in conforming to adult conventions. Michael's brother Robert was one such boy, and Michael referred to him as "submissive," a highly undesirable trait for most boys because it flies in the face of dominant images of masculinity, images that are reinforced nightly on television and in the movies. Thomas reflects the culture around him when he derisively labels as "sissies" the boys who cave in to parental pressure or who stay at home to avoid dealing with the challenges of the streets.

This is always an issue for boys in a situation of social conflict and danger. I sat in a home in the Gaza Strip in 1988 with a fifteen-year-old Palestinian boy named Hamad and his parents at the height of the uprising against Israeli occupation. Hamad's older brother was serving time in an Israeli prison for his acts of political violence. While I sat in his living room with Hamad, other boys his age were on the street in front of the house throwing stones at the Israeli soldiers, and getting teargassed in repayment. His parents had made a deal with the authorities. If they kept him inside and out of the conflict for another three months, the police would release his older brother from jail and the whole family would be allowed to emigrate to Canada. If the younger son joined the conflict, he too would be arrested and both brothers would spend years in jail. I watched Hamad as the battle raged outside. His shame at being safe at home was terrible for him. He was a sissy in Thomas's terms, a "kit kat" in the local youth slang of the Palestinians.

Some boys do cave in, but other boys fight back against the world when they experience trauma at home. Compare Michael, who is facing the death penalty for first-degree murder, with his brother, who is working in a record store. But some boys are given no choice. They live in environments in which failure to participate in violent peer group activity is not an option. Billy was such a boy.

When I interview him on death row, Billy recounts his struggle as a timid child to find a way to avoid joining in with the violence that was all around him. He is now a slight man with fine features and a soft voice. I can imagine him as a small, skinny child, a frightened child, easily bullied. He tells me how the more aggressive boys in his neighborhood were bound and determined to get him to join them. They threatened him. They beat him up day after day, on his way to and from school. Finally, they threatened to kill his mother if he didn't join them. At that point he succumbed and joined the program. It was all downhill from there as he went further and further down the path of aggression and bad behavior, learning to hide and bury his feelings as he went. He was nineteen when he killed on the orders of his gang.

Unlike violent boys such as Billy, who start out as victims and later make the switch to bully as a matter of survival (who are, in effect, drafted), other boys seem to volunteer to join the ranks of violent youth. These boys often remember a physical fearlessness from an early age. Robert speaks of eight-year-old playmates with whom he jumped from second-floor window ledges onto mattresses below. Rasheen recounts walking a plank between two buildings four stories off the ground. "Was I afraid?" he said, extending my question when I asked him how he felt four stories off the ground on a single plank. "Nah. No problem, man. It was cool." "How about when you heard shooting outside your building?" I asked. "Nope. I ain't afraid of nothing," he replied. Where is the fear? More important, where are the feelings at all?

Dissociation as a Way of Life

The dissociation of violent boys is more than simple temperamental fear-lessness. It goes beyond that, so far beyond that it makes me wonder about their overall emotional life. Where is the hurt? Where is the anger? I asked Michael what he did with the anger he felt toward his mother for the beatings she inflicted on him and for the favoritism she displayed toward his older brother Robert. He thought and thought with an intense look of concentration. Then he shook his head and said, "I guess I just held it inside." I asked him how he felt about his mother's preference for his brother. "It's just a fact of life," he replied. But it's an overwhelming *emotional* fact of his life. Most people would find the feelings intolerable. How did Michael deal with these feelings? One small clue appeared when he told me that the only thing he was ever afraid of was that he would lash out at his abusive mother and do to her what she had done to him, take an electric cord or a fist and even the score. Here was the fear that grew out of the hurt. And here was the anger. How are they related? Anger is repressed sadness, and sadness can mean depression.

In *I Don't Want to Talk About It*, Terrence Real provides a road map to the hidden emotional life of boys and men. He traces the links be-tween masculine culture and covert depression, and the detour sadness takes to become violence. By burying their feelings in silence and exter-nalizing them through aggression and addiction, sad and hurt men find a way to get through the day. Speaking of one of his patients, Real reports, "A life-time of inattention to his emotions and his relationships was perched precariously over a childhood of profound psychological ne-glect."

That's what the future holds for aggressive boys if they are not helped to reconnect with their emotions and see clearly the role these feelings play in producing their acts of violence and thus wrecking their lives. This redirection can happen for boys, but it takes a lot of work and a lot of skilled psychological and spiritual leadership. Cuts to mental health services in schools and juvenile detention facilities and the secular na-ture of most programs put this desperately needed leadership in short sup-ply. It is a major public policy issue for citizens and governments to address.

For a young child, this is not a grand issue of public policy or institutional practice. It is a matter of inner life or death. Without loving guidance, spiritual counsel, and psychological nurturance, children see little alternative but to cope as best they can, and that generally means dissociation—no matter its cost to a child's inner life and his external behavior. For a child, the intolerable can be made tolerable by being stripped of its emotional content and consigned to the world of simple fact, with the emotional content being locked away in a psychological vault. That's the point of dissociation as a survival strategy.

But while they are locked away in that psychological vault, the emotions that arise in response to rejection, abuse, and abandonment don't just sit there, inactive. They earn emotional interest. Rage compounds. And the negative emotional bank accounts of the lost boys are often bloated with rage and shame and fear and humiliation. For some boys the psychological vault cannot hold all the hurt and anger that is stored there. Events—sometimes what appear to be trivial events—trigger a break that results in violence. I will return to this issue in Chapter Five when I take a look at the moral development of violent boys, and how their concepts of justice and right and wrong reflect their troubled emotional lives.

These boys need someone to help convert their negative emotional stockpiles, to therapeutically take the anger and make it over into insight and eventually into something constructive for the soul. Terrence Real and Robin Casarjian find in their therapeutic work with the men these boys become that without this psychological and spiritual help violence sometimes becomes a chronic addiction for the men, something to divert attention from their pain and sadness and a way to punish the world and themselves.

HOPE

When I think of helping violent boys find their way, I often think of one particular troubled youth who grew up in Jamestown, New York, in the early years of this century. The boy had to deal with the emotional predicament of living in a household dominated by an alcoholic and abusive father. To escape his horrible family life, the boy wandered the hills and found solace in nature, particularly in birds. This fascination with birds sustained him, but by the time he reached high school he was a lonely, troubled boy. A teacher in his school formed a Junior Audubon Club so that the boy would have at least one positive setting at school in which his interest in birds could be nourished. This act of acceptance was decisive. It provided a positive link for the boy to peers and adults. As a result of this experience, the boy did not get lost. He went on to become an internationally acclaimed expert on birds and wrote a best-selling guide. His name was Roger Torrey Peterson. When I met him near the end of his long life, we talked about his personal history, and he told me this story as a testament to the potential power of a caring teacher, to the power of hope.

I believe that one of the most important elements in the developmental equation for violent boys is the larger social environment *outside* the family, for it is there that one of three things happens: (1) an early pattern of bad behavior and aggression is identified and treated; (2) an early pattern of bad behavior and aggression plays itself out in a socially benign setting (in which no matter how bad the boy's behavior gets, there is little danger); or (3) an early pattern of bad behavior and aggression falls on fertile ground and grows into chronic violence and delinquency as the child partakes of the dark side. All three courses are possible options.

Option one is the most likely outcome in families and communities that are rich in social and educational resources, where parents, teachers, and mental health professionals have the time and energy to focus on redirecting troubled little boys. I saw it in my own life when I was in elementary school. In my school and in our community, most boys were doing pretty well, but there was enough time and energy to go around for the boys who were in deep trouble.

Option two still exists in some places and certainly was more common in our society in decades past. When a troubled boy lives in a safe and peaceful social environment, there is a cushion for him. In the past, a boy living in a small town found a slow pace of life, without drugs and gangs and guns. In such an environment, a boy with bad behavior tests the limits, but his being bad is very unlikely to result in lethal violence. After all, other societies tell a different story from our own. For example, Canadian kids get in fights, too, but their youth homicide rate is less than a quarter of ours. Even American girls have a higher homicide rate than boys in many countries, such as Japan and Sweden.

Context is critical. Enter option three. It is because of the dangerous larger social environment many boys find themselves in today that we are so concerned that early "childish" bad behavior and aggression will turn into lethal behavior in adolescence and young adulthood. In the next chapter we see how learning the secrets of the dark side plays a role in the evolution of youth violence.

DISCOVERING THE DARK SIDE

PEOPLE ARE MORE SIMPLY HUMAN THAN OTHERWISE

Working in the 1950s to understand the blatantly crazy behavior of schizophrenics, psychologist Harry Stack Sullivan realized that *human behavior is more simply human than otherwise.* Nothing is more basic to understanding youth violence than remembering this point. We dehumanize adolescents—like Malcolm, Peter, Kip, Andrew, and Luke—who appear in the newspapers and in the courtrooms of our nation by calling them "super predators," "monsters," or "crazies" or by trying them as adults and sentencing them to life imprisonment or death. We do it by creating barbaric prison conditions meant to "teach them a lesson" rather than rehabilitate them. Our goal should be to find the human sense in senseless youth violence, to translate Sullivan's principle into practice.

It is not a matter of simply forgiving or excusing. Boys who commit violent acts need our help to change and recover. Simply letting them walk away is, of course, not the answer. Intervention must take place. We can see this in the cases of fifteen-year-old Kip Kinkel (who shot his parents and classmates in Springfield, Oregon) and Andrew Wurst (who shot a teacher in Edinboro, Pennsylvania). Each case illustrates the dangers of insufficient intervention. The day before he went on his killing spree, Kip was apprehended at school for purchasing a stolen gun. He was suspended from school, brought to the police station for booking, and then released home to his father. This boy needed to be placed immediately in a facility capable of assessing his state of mind—particularly since he had been heard by other students to threaten retaliation for the humiliation of being arrested and expelled. In Edinboro, fourteen-year-old Andrew had talked of being tortured by his social failures and of hating his parents and teachers and had proclaimed his attraction to murder and suicide. He showed friends a pistol in his house. Like Kip, Andrew declared his homicidal intentions, saying, "I am going to go to the dinner dance and kill some people." He needed intervention on at least two fronts: his suicidal thinking and his threat to kill other people. The kids who heard his statements didn't report them to adults who could take action, and as a result Andrew was able to make good on his threats. A troubled boy in need of serious attention, he ended up getting attention—except that it was too late. Intervention delayed too long can have irreversible consequences, and this, I believe, is a crucial lesson to be learned from the Andrews and Kips of America. Recognizing the humanity of troubled boys does not mean ignoring or rationalizing their lethal behavior. The kids and adults in their lives must take their threats seriously, and in the wake of what happened in Springfield and Edinboro, now they are.

Within months of these violent assaults, schools around America were scrambling to institute more effective methods for screening and responding to student threats. By September 1998, the Center for Effective Collaboration and Practice, in collaboration with the National Association of School Psychologists, had issued a handbook entitled "Early Warning, Timely Response." The handbook includes a wide variety of responses to the problem of youth violence, (some of which are detailed in Chapter Seven). One central message to kids and adults alike is this: Take these boys seriously. But merely increasing security and the severity of punishment is an inadequate response. Solving the problem requires that we also look at its origins in the exposure of boys to the dark side of human experience.

One day in 1986, I was invited to participate in a small seminar on ritualistic child abuse and serial killers. I sat in a room for two days with other professionals who were dealing with child abuse at its absolute worst. To begin, we heard from an FBI agent who was in charge of a task force on serial killers and fatal child abuse and neglect. He turned on the slide projector and showed us crime scene photos. It was horrible beyond what any mere words can describe. The pictures shocked and disgusted everyone in the room, even though all the participants in the seminar considered themselves emotionally tough from their years of training and experience. One person rushed to the bathroom to throw up; others wanted to.

There is a dark side to human life, a place where human beings are tortured, maimed, and killed; where blood spurts out on the walls; where children are starved and weigh twenty-five pounds when they die; where women are raped and locked in closets. This is a place where things are done that mock expressions like "human dignity." Horror lurks here.

As adults, we usually try to put away somewhere the knowledge that this dark side of human life exists. We try to lock it up in memory or at least limit access to it to those professionals among us who have no choice but to know. Police, physicians, nurses, child protection workers, judges, lawyers, and soldiers have a tacit understanding that they must see what the rest of the world would rather not see. Of course, they suffer for it. This is one reason why soldiers mostly won't or can't talk about their experiences in combat. And why cops who investigate grisly murder scenes often develop an exterior emotional hardness that is shocking to outsiders and painful for their loved ones. And this is why social workers, nurses, and physicians indulge in gallows humor, an attempt to bring some comic emotional relief to horrible situations faced on a daily basis. Children are more vulnerable than adults to the traumatizing and corrupting effects of exposure to evil, so we adults try to keep such evil a secret from them—or at least we did before all the rules about what could be shown to children broke down to create a free-for-all of horror on television and in the movies.

Through my research I have learned that understanding how and when children learn the secrets of the dark side is a tool to unlock the mystery of how an innocent baby becomes a lethally violent teenager. When we look beyond the stereotypes and simple characterizations of kids who kill, we see boys who have been exposed to the capacity for evil in human nature and society. Some troubled boys seek out images of this evil and become addicted to them as a way of responding to the emptiness they feel inside; they may then engage in violence as a way of experiencing acts that they have already committed in their imagination. Exposure to evil images prepares the child to pull the trigger.

PETER'S STORY

I meet Peter for the first time in his cell. He's a gawky kid, several inches taller than I. His face is pasty and pimpled after spending almost one year in lockup, awaiting trial for murder. Peter is only thirteen years old, and he is being tried for first-degree murder. He shot a seventeen-year-old boy who had threatened him. Now, at the beginning of the interview, he is nervously wringing his hands. His eyes have an intense, almost haunted look. It takes me a while to focus on Peter as an individual boy, however, because he reminds me so much of my own son. Seeing Peter in profile, I can see my Josh. Were my purpose for being here to render psychoanalytic treatment, I would have a major problem in *countertransference* (i.e., I would respond to Peter through the lens of my relationship with Josh). It requires a lot of concentration for me to see and hear Peter for himself, but after a while I manage to do so.

Peter was arrested at his home in a small town in the northwest corner of New York State. I've been to see his home and his neighborhood, and there is nothing remarkable or sinister about either. I've met his grandparents, with whom he lived until he was arrested. Nothing is apparent there that would lead anyone to predict that this boy would one day be facing a possible life sentence for murder. His grandparents are very pleasant people. Peter's grandfather is a retired military man, his grandmother a homemaker who in recent years has joined her husband in operating a small cafe.

When Peter shot and killed Charles on the street, near his home in a middle-class area of his small town, people asked, "How could it happen here?" Newspaper reporters quoted neighbors and friends as being "shocked" and "stunned" that Peter could do such a thing. Nonetheless, the prosecutor in the case successfully argued to have Peter tried as an adult, because he found the crime reflected a "callous disregard for human life." He called the shooting "cold-blooded," and said that Peter was a gangster who was a danger to the community. In his view the community could only be protected by putting Peter away for a very long time. And the prosecutor succeeded in his mission: Peter was sentenced to ten years in prison for his crime.

Where did Peter's violence come from? What do the facts of his case reveal about his interior life and compulsions? The story is there beneath the normal surface of his life in small-town America.

Peter started life as a difficult child, but he had experiences that capitalized on that vulnerability in devastating ways. He did the shooting with a sawed-off .22-caliber rifle he kept hidden in his bedroom closet, but the reason he had the gun and felt compelled to use it one day when threatened by an older boy is not obvious. During the summers of the years before he committed murder, Peter visited his mother and her boyfriend in New York City. With both of them frequently doped up (which was why he was being raised by his grandmother upstate in the first place), Peter was left to his own devices much of the time. One summer, within days of his arrival, he was recruited by the local gang as a lookout, and within a couple of weeks he was carrying a gun and helping his newfound friends defend their turf against local rivals. Peter was a psychologically vulnerable boy who struggled with issues of abandonment by his mother, the total absence of his father, and his emerging difficulties in school and at home with his well-intentioned but inept grandparents. Left to fend for himself in a very dangerous world, he learned some very damaging lessons. Peter himself tells two stories about these lessons:

One time, one of the guys I was hanging with told me I had to run over to a neighborhood half a mile away where our competition hung out. I said, "I don't want to go over there, man!" He said, "Go over there! Just go over there real quick. It's all right!" They were *cool*. They were my friends. They said, "Go over there and go up to apartment ten and drop this off to Big Al." So I took off over there. I was waiting for Big Al to come, and these guys came up. And they're like, "We're going to get that punk right there!" And then the next thing I knew, I got *socked* in the head and I was on the ground and I was getting beat up. And like, six of them came on me and started *pouncing* me. I finally got up, but they locked the gates. They locked me in. So I ran to the gate and started climbing. I started climbing the fence and I got out of there, but I ripped my shirt and I cut my arm. I cut my arm all up. I started running as fast as I could—I didn't get to drop the stuff off—and I was feeling really dizzy and my ear was all just huge right here—like, my whole temple area. One of them I think hit me with a crowbar. And I got away from this, and I ran to where my guys were at. I told them about it, and they got their guns and they said, "We're going to get those bastards, man! We're going to get those bastards!" I saw one of them had a .38 and one of them had a shotgun, and they just ran up in there. They were looking for them, but they couldn't find them. So we just left.

Another time, I had been getting these threatening phone calls, like, "We're gonna get you." Stuff like that. So when I walked to school, I carried my gun with me. I'd stash it in a bush, in between my house and the school, 'cause I didn't know what was going to happen. One day I was walking by the cement building right there, and this red car pulled up behind me and these guys were in it. All I saw was a barrel coming out of the roof of the car. And then—boom—I heard a gunshot and then I—this stuff hit me in the eye, pieces of the brick wall, they hit me in the eye. It hit me right there [*points to his eye*]. I was like [*groans*] and then boom, boom, boom, boom! Gunshots. And then there was more powder . . . and all of a sudden [*makes a sound like tires squealing*] the tires skidded off. And then I heard a police siren going . . . so I just sat down, and I fell to the ground. And that was the third time I had ever been shot at in my entire life. But that was the time that it was actually about from here [*points*] to about the other side of the door over there. The first time I had been shot at that closely. I think they were just shooting at the wall to scare me.

Peter was twelve years old at the time of these experiences. A year later he faced murder charges for killing one of the boys who he believed had threatened him.

SOCIAL POISONS

When I lived in Chicago in the early 1990s I tried to avoid watching the local news, because each night seemed to bring more violence and death. One night I did watch. The lead story dealt with a teenager who had been murdered by other kids from his school because he had insulted one of them at a basketball game. Listening to this story, I recalled an incident from my own youth, nearly thirty years earlier.

As a teenager growing up in the New York metropolitan area in the early 1960s, I wrote a column for my high school newspaper. One week I wrote a column in which I made fun of the fraternities in my high school. This angered some of my teenage peers, and they exacted their revenge when, two nights later, a car pulled up in front of my house and dumped garbage on the lawn of my house as an act of retribution. In today's terms, you might say that I was the victim of a "drive-by littering."

I think of this incident often when I reflect on the world in which today's youth live. Today in a neighborhood like the one in which I grew up, a boy who similarly angered his peers might well be the victim of a drive-by *shooting*. Malcolm certainly was, and Peter was similarly threatened by a carful of angry boys with guns in the days leading up to his own crime.

It's not that kids have changed since I was a teenager. It is the social environment in which they live that has changed. The risks of misjudging one's peers have increased. The costs of being in conflict have been magnified by adolescents' access to guns and their willingness to use them. Children are routinely exposed to vivid and explicit scenarios of death and destruction.

It pains me greatly to recognize that boys all over America witness terrifying scenes on television or the movie screen. Although some experts dismiss this as too simplistic an explanation, I am convinced that this is one reason for the spread of lethal youth violence to small towns and rural areas. What I saw in the FBI agents' photos of horrible crime scenes at that meeting in 1986 is now routine fare in the entertainment of many American children. This explicit and vivid imagery of scenes of horror is a kind of social poison, part and parcel of what I described as "social toxicity" in my 1995 book *Raising Children in a Socially Toxic Environment*.

Understanding the concept of social toxicity means in part recognizing how the quality of the social environment has changed over the decades, how social and cultural poisons are manufactured, and how they contaminate the social world of children, youth, and families. But it also entails recognizing that some individuals and groups are more vulnerable than others. For example, in a smog alert, public health officials and private citizens worry particularly about children with asthma and old people with emphysema, that is, individuals with some special vulnerability to the poisons in the air. The same applies to social poisons.

Psychologists like Urie Bronfenbrenner have been issuing increasingly serious "social smog alerts" for the past twenty-five years. Bronfenbrenner's 1970 book *Two Worlds of Childhood* sounded the alarm, and the social environment for children and parents has continued to deteriorate. (His most recent book, *The State of Americans*, updates that analysis.) His analysis explains some of the trends that professionals have witnessed over the last forty years in the changing face of the troubled population of children and youth. Bronfenbrenner's analysis focuses on the overall level and effects of social poisons on children and youth in general, but we can bring his analysis to bear particularly on the vulnerable boys introduced in the previous chapter, the boys who early on show themselves to be special cases because of some combination of difficult temperament and early disruption in their relationships with caregivers and because of the emergence in them of patterns of bad behavior and aggression.

Vulnerable Children and Social Poisons

A few years ago I was asked to visit a day treatment school for emotionally disturbed kids in Chicago. The school's director presented the situation to me as follows: "We need help. I started this program in 1970, and I've run the program since then continuously. I've always used the same program models. I've trained the staff the same way, used the same diagnostic criteria to admit children into the program, and take children from the same neighborhoods we always have. This program used to work, but now it doesn't." I had no way of knowing for sure whether the program ever worked. I did look at some of the program's data on its outcomes over the years, however, and they did seem to present a positive picture. But after spending some time at the school, I certainly agreed with the director's assessment that it simply wasn't meeting his charges' needs any longer.

I believe that the social environment across most of the country has become less welcoming to highly vulnerable children, that is, those who live under difficult social and emotional conditions and therefore soak up social poisons. The program I visited in Chicago literally broke down under the weight of the violence and the sheer nastiness that these emotionally disturbed children incorporate. This is a story that many human service professionals can tell, if they've been in the field long enough. Vulnerable children have to be understood as "psychological asthmatics." Their increasing distress is a measure both of the increasingly harsh and toxic social environment and of their own personal vulnerability.

Peter's temperament and his early experiences seemed to conspire to make a psychological asthmatic of him. By the time he left his grandparents' home for an extended stay with his mother and her drug-dealing boyfriend in New York, he was primed to succumb to the social poisons he encountered there. He soaked up those experiences, incorporated them into his day-to-day map of the social world, and brought them back to his small town. It is impossible to understand the murder he committed without linking the shooting to the social poisoning he experienced.

Social poisons affect us all in one way or another. Even if we are good parents, we cannot protect our children fully from them. As Judith Harris makes abundantly clear in her book *The Nurture Assumption*, there are many powerful influences on a child's behavior and development outside the family, and parents have only limited direct influence. Peter was especially vulnerable, and the social poisoning he experienced was especially intense. And ready access to firearms was the very last poison a boy like Peter needed in his life.

ARMED IS DANGEROUS

Few Americans would disagree that guns hold a prominent place in our culture. Surveys consistently report that nearly 40 percent of all households in our country contain at least one gun (with estimates at nearly 50 percent for households in the Southern states). As Americans—white, black, Hispanic, Asian, Native American—we all live in what I would call a gun culture. A few years ago I interviewed middle-class, white, suburban eight-year-olds in Illinois, a third of whom were quite convincing as they related how and where they could get their hands on a gun. Although I consider myself an expert on violence, I was shocked that one-third of this third-grade class claimed to know where and how to get a gun. It is fortunate for all of us that most of these children did not think they needed a gun . . . yet.

In 1993 I interviewed a nine-year-old California boy who lived in a dangerous neighborhood. After hearing him talk for a while about the ins and outs of what happened in his neighborhood, I asked him what it would take for him to feel safer where he lived. He thought for a moment and said, "A gun of my own."

My evidence is anecdotal, but research shows that the increased use of guns by American kids to deal with conflict is a vital factor responsible for the increase in youth homicide rates in our country since World War II. Understanding why kids use these guns is imperative if we are to make the lives of children and youth safer.

A study by psychologist Jeremy Shapiro and his colleagues in Cleveland reveals that a series of four motives plays a central role in whether or not a child or teenager will be drawn to guns. The first motive is called the aggressive response to shame, which refers to the code of honor that says, "If someone insults you, you have to fight"; kids who have incorporated this belief are more likely than other kids to be drawn to guns. The second motive is comfort with aggression, meaning that a kid is not worried or upset by being around other people with guns. The third is excitement; that is, guns evoke positive feelings in a kid. The final motive is power and safety; that is, kids associate power and a feeling of security with carrying a gun and being with other people who carry guns. Less than one percent of kids who have none of these motives possess a gun while fully one-third of those studied who did possess a gun appeared to have all of these motives.

BEING LEFT OUT IS POISONOUS

In Chapter Two, I presented the psychologically devastating consequences of parental or family rejection. But rejection is more than a family issue. It includes the social poisons at work that devalue and isolate many children and youth who don't fit the mold for success in America. Although racial and cultural diversity exists in America, racism and ethnic discrimination are also present. To be anything other than white and Anglo heightens the risk that a child will feel rejected for who he is or for the group to which he belongs or for the sound of his name.

Racism coupled with economic impoverishment is a huge generator of a sense of alienation, which can easily become shame when a boy finds in society's response to him echoes of the rejection he feels at home. Unless you have lived with it, it will be difficult for you to appreciate the psychological significance of the double dose of shame that results when a sense of community alienation is coupled with parental rejection. You can hear it in their voices when boys say things like "If you call 911 in my neighborhood, they don't come" or "Pizza Hut won't deliver in my neighborhood."

It's often easy to recognize this sense of alienation and disenfranchisement when it occurs among an identified minority. When it occurs among white youth who have fewer clearly recognizable grievances, the task of comprehending their shame and pain is made difficult. A particularly shocking example comes from the small city of Gloversville, New York. In the spring of 1998, two teenage boys—Ron Johnson, sixteen, and Bruce Insome, also sixteen—killed a seventy-seven-year-old man whom they had been harassing for months.

The killing was bad enough—and it was the second youth homicide in Gloversville in a year—but what most disturbed the adult community was that these boys drove the dead body around town for two days afterward, inviting friends for rides. As many as thirty adolescents knew of the killing, but not one contacted the authorities to report it. This indicates the profound estrangement felt by many kids in our society. Gloversville is not an inner-city war zone, but it is a small town that has been left behind economically and that is struggling with social decay. The sense of despair grows. One teenage girl said, "I think in the beginning they're all, like, shocked, but I think in a couple of months it's going to happen again. And I really think somebody has to do something about Gloversville."

Some of the small-town shooters of the 1997–1998 school year referred to this feeling of alienation and despair in what they said before or after their attacks. Luke Woodham told ABC News that he felt so isolated and rejected in his community that he was easily drawn into a group of boys who were self-proclaimed Satanists. Of the group's leader Luke said, "I tried so hard to get his acceptance because he was the only one who would accept me. He just put a lot of bad things into my head and it built up after time." He also admitted, "My whole life I felt outcasted, alone. Finally, I found some people who wanted to be my friends."

"People are more simply human than otherwise," said Harry Stack

Sullivan. A Christian might say, "There but for the grace of God go I." Here's what Malcolm says of the life he leads:

> People on the outside, they go on TV and they say, "Damn, look at them killing, just killing each other." But they don't know what this stuff is about. They think it's really stupid stuff, but to us it's big stuff 'cause we live in that environment and we've got to learn how to survive. You place any one of them people outside, you put them in that predicament, and they are going to do the same thing. They're not always going to try and call the cops. They're not going to. They're not going to. They're going to try to handle it themselves 'cause they're going to fear for their lives.

That's a message more and more kids are hearing from their peers and from the dark recesses of their own fears as the sense of being endangered grows among American children and youth. More kids know the dark side of not belonging in a way that is more intense than what the traditional adolescent "outsider" feels. In Paducah, Kentucky, fifteen-year-old Michael Carneal felt so desperately alone that he told a psychologist after the shooting, "I felt mad about the way kids treated me. Sometimes I'd hit the steel drum in my backyard to let out the anger." That didn't work for Michael, and, as we will see in Chapter Seven, this kind of expressive behavior doesn't reduce anger for anyone else either.

THE TRAUMATIC SECRET ABOUT THE PHYSICAL MEANING OF LIFE

Our bodies are fragile vessels for our spirits. This is a basic fact of human existence. Our souls may be eternal, but our bodies are vulnerable to damage when they are subjected to violence. Rather than being strong, powerful, and tough, the human body is really a fragile envelope filled with gooey lumps and breakable stuff. Learning this dark secret is traumatic for children. We can see this in Peter's remembrance of his traumatic encounter as an eleven-year-old:

> I was playing with this kid. His mom lived right down the street, and she invited me for lunch because we were playing in the yard. And then she brought out the family album, and she was sharing some stuff with us. And then she. . . . she told me a lot about how her husband was crazy,

how he had stalked her before. Then she showed me a picture of him in the photo album, and pictures of her daughters, and stuff like that. We were all just sitting around having a nice time, and she told me, "You know, he drives a blue truck, so if you ever see him around here, let me know. You know, if you ever see him creeping up the house." I go, "I will," 'cause I lived right down the street. "I'll let you know." After lunch I went outside to get some fresh air, and I was looking around, and I saw a blue truck! And I saw a guy look at me like that, looking at me. I was like, "Okay, we were just talking about this guy!" And I went inside and I go, "There's some guy out front! Yeah! . . . He drives a blue truck." And then she started like screaming, like, "Oh God, that's him! Oh God . . . !" I'm ready to walk out the door. I'm like, "Oh, I want to go home now. I'll see you guys later. I'll come back a little later, when everything's okay." And she goes, "No, no, no—don't go outside, don't go outside!" And she locked it. "Come on!" she yells. "We're going upstairs, we're going upstairs!" She just ran up the stairs, without us. And my friend was running up behind her, so I said, "I'm not going to stay down here!" But I grabbed the cordless phone! Nobody knew I had it. I grabbed the cordless phone, and I ran up the stairs behind them. Then she put us all in the closet . . . and I dialed 911. And I told them about it. I told them, and then I heard a big boom! And he knocked the door down in the front of the house. And then he started yelling about something, like, "I know you guys are in that closet!" And I was like—I had asthma, so I'm thinking now I didn't want to breathe too hard 'cause I didn't want him to find us. Then he goes, "You guys better not come out of there or I'll shoot you!" Then I heard the door shut and it was quiet. When we came out after a while, it turned out my friend's mom had a butcher knife with her there in the closet, and on the way down the stairs she fell and accidentally cut herself. After that I didn't have anything to do with the family. I was just a friend. But then I had *dreams* for the first two weeks. And then it stopped . . . and after, ever since after that, I've been edgy around people . . . like not really wanting to go into somebody's house . . . kind of like a *fear*, like an anxiety. Yeah. And I took things real seriously after that.

Trauma occurs when overwhelming ideas (negative cognitions) combine with overwhelming feelings (negative *arousal*). As Cambridge,

Massachusetts, psychiatrist Judith Herman wrote in her book *Trauma and Recovery*, "trauma is the coming face to face with both human vulnerability in the natural world and with the capacity for evil in human nature." Learning about the destruction of human bodies at the hands of nature or at the hands of fellow human beings is traumatic. How and when we learn it seems particularly important. To learn it vividly, visually, and experientially in childhood can be an event from which we never fully recover. In Chapter Three, I recounted John's experience of being his stepfather's unwitting accomplice in the bloody murder of his mother's lover. That trauma became the defining fact of John's life, and its influence on him continues to this day.

Vulnerable and defenseless children often learn the dark facts of life early, in their witnessing of shootings, stabbings, and beatings in their homes, schools, and neighborhoods. Like many other boys in prison, Malcolm learned these facts at home, at school, and in his neighborhood. I have a lot of experience with violence, but Malcolm's litany of violent incidents in his life still staggers me. He has participated in drug-related kidnappings, both as victim and as perpetrator. He has been the target of drive-by shootings and has retaliated with drive-by shootings of his own. He has committed numerous armed robberies. He has scars on his body from beatings administered by his mother, his uncle, his stepfather, drug bosses, and neighborhood rivals. He has been beaten up by the police (and has a three-inch scar on his head to show for it after one of the cops hit him in the head with a flashlight). As a thirteen-year-old he killed so that he might avoid being killed. His life story is awash in the traumatic details of violence.

But the fact of the matter is, psychological, physical, and sexual violence exists in homes and neighborhoods throughout the country, regardless of geography. Such violence occurs in small towns and suburbs, in cities and rural areas. And images of it are accessible to almost every child in America simply by turning on the television. When I visited Kuwait in 1991 at the conclusion of the Gulf War, I interviewed children who had been traumatized by firsthand exposure to Iraqi atrocities. A follow-up study conducted a year later by UCLA psychologists Kathi Nader and Robert Pynoos revealed that many children were traumatized *after* the war was over because they were made to witness Iraqi atrocities on videotape as part of a political education campaign conducted by the

Kuwaiti government. Many American kids watch hours and hours of atrocities, day after day, week after week. While some may label it entertainment, it is—from the point of view of a child's development—a documentary of atrocities with the potential to traumatize and corrupt.

Analyses of television content reveal that a typical American child can witness more images of death and destruction from the comfort of his living room than any cop or soldier witnesses in actuality in the line of duty in a lifetime. A recent analysis for the American Psychological Association highlights some important elements of this exposure: "good" characters or heroes commit 40 percent of the violent acts, more than a third of the bad characters aren't punished, and more than 70 percent of the aggressors show no remorse and experience no criticism or penalty for their violent actions.

Psychologist Leonard Eron and his colleagues have demonstrated the negative influences of violent images by following a group of kids from childhood into adulthood. Their results can be stated as follows: just as some people are more vulnerable to developing cancer from smoking than are others, so too are some children more affected by televised violence than are others. There is no simple one-to-one correspondence between watching television and committing violence, just as there is no simple one-to-one correspondence between smoking and developing cancer. But there *is* a *direct* connection in both cases.

The American Psychological Association's expert panel looked at all the research studies and concluded that the evidence linking televised violence to real-life violence is about as strong as the research evidence linking smoking to cancer. But smoking is not the only cause of lung cancer. Neither is television the only cause of youth violence. But it does play a significant role, accounting for about 10 to 15 percent of the variation in violent behavior. And the most psychologically vulnerable among our children are the ones most likely to show the effects.

YOU ARE ON YOUR OWN OUT THERE

One day in Chicago several years ago, a seven-year-old-boy named Dantrel Davis was killed on his way to school. Dantrel was walked to school by his mother every morning, because she worried for his safety. Yet one morning he didn't make it to school. One hundred feet from the front door of the school, his mother let go of his hand and he turned to walk up the steps. Because he lived in Cabrini Green, a notoriously dangerous neighborhood in Chicago, on the street corners near the school were cops and on the school steps were teachers. Despite the presence of his mother, the cops, and his teachers, as Dantrel started to walk the one hundred feet to the front steps of the school, he was shot in the back of the head and killed. This is another feature of the dark side of life that our children are learning at progressively earlier ages: *adults can't protect you*.

The breakdown of child protection and the realization that adults can't or won't protect them figures prominently in the life stories of violent youth. Thomas, now eighteen and serving a life sentence for killing another boy, talked about how he, as an eight-year-old, watched helplessly while his friend was being beaten bloody on the playground. His lasting memory and recurring nightmare is of his teacher walking away rather than intervening.

Over and over again, the boys speak of this betrayal by adults, their supposed protectors. We know from generations of research that the failure to protect children in war zones is crucial to understanding the psychological impact of war on them. Psychologist Victor Papanek wrote about kids and violent trauma as an observer in London in 1942, during the bombing of London: "Children measure the danger that threatens them chiefly by the reactions of those around them, especially their trusted parents and teachers."

Once children understand that adults cannot protect them, the next logical step is for them to find ways to protect themselves. Some resort to social withdrawal (such as staying home to avoid the streets). Others turn to "juvenile vigilantism," assuming responsibility for their own safety, including taking up weapons and joining gangs:

I was twelve. I spent the night with five other kids at the apartment of an older guy we knew who sells drugs. He has guns there, and he was selling drugs, and there was a lot of girls there who wanted to get it on. It was a good party, and by the end we was too drunk and too high to go home. The next morning we left. He had a party there again the next week. When I came to the party, he was in my face and he goes, "Where's my gun? Somebody took it last week the night you was here. You spent the night. I asked everybody else where my gun is at and nobody is saying nothing, so I figure you took it." Then he pulled out a .44-caliber. This big. And he was like, "I better have my gun. If I hear that you got my gun, I'm going to shoot you." And then he just pointed the gun down at me with this look in his eyes. That made me break down. I was crying. I couldn't believe I got threatened like that, because I never had the intention of stealing somebody's gun. And that shocked me. My friend Duane was there—he's the one that got shot. I was like, "Duane, why'd he do that? Why'd he threaten me like that? Why would I take his gun when I'm cool with him?" That made me disconnect from him, because it was like, if he felt that I took his gun, he would think many other things of me. Then any other little thing that he thought that I did would trigger him for killing me. So I stayed away from him, because he was much older than me, much older than me. Him threatening me like that put me on point. That means I was aware of things. I knew he had the capability of killing me. That turned me around to deal with the killer instinct. When that man put the gun on me, when he pointed that gun at me, I became a shark eating the little fishes.

Having told the story of how it felt to be a frightened child in a killer's world, a little fish, Allan told of how he became an armed predator, a shark. After that, for the next year and a half, he never left home without a gun or two in his backpack. His story culminated in the shooting that placed him in the youth prison system at age thirteen. The day after an argument and an exchange of gunfire on the street, he and a friend walked out the front door of their apartment building only to find themselves confronting three armed kids bent on finishing the earlier conflict.

As Allan recounted details of the shoot-out, his body tensed, his face hardened, and his hands began chopping the air as he described it step by step. He seemed to be reliving every instant. Seeing the intruders, he and his friend pulled out their own guns—two each, one in each hand—and started shooting. There were nine shots. Allan slammed his fist against the table in front of him nine times for emphasis. All three of the enemy died.

After uttering the final word of his story, Allan put his thumb in his mouth and sucked it, as though he were completely oblivious to the fact that he was not alone, that there was someone there looking at him. For two minutes he who had described so dramatically by word and action his role in a fatal gunfight sat in this most eloquent of silences. Then, with weariness in his voice, he admitted something he had told no one else— that he cries in bed every night thinking about when he is going to die. He's afraid of dying before he has a chance to live his life, and he is afraid of what happens after death.

A boy once said to me, "If I join a gang I'm fifty percent safe. If I don't join a gang I'm zero percent safe." Adults don't enter into this equation. For some kids, this is the new *social math*.

In Chicago in 1993, I visited a school at the invitation of a social worker who wanted to show me her special program with a group of twelve- and thirteen-year-olds. It truly was a special program. She loved those kids, and they loved her. She spent money from her own pocket to buy things for the kids. When she left the room at one point, one of the kids said to me, "Mrs. Smith is a lovely lady, but you wouldn't put your life in her hands." Mrs. Smith was shocked to discover that two of those kids had guns in their lockers that day. They brought them not because they thought she wasn't committed to them and not because they felt she didn't love them, but because they didn't think she was powerful enough to protect them.

Personal experiences of trauma and betrayal don't occur in a vacuum. They occur in the larger American context of social poisons. One indication of that context is the declining trust found generally by kids in our country. According to the National Survey of Youth, 35 percent of the seventeen-year-olds in the United States in 1972 agreed that "most people can be trusted." By 1992, that figure was down to 19 percent. Similarly, 40 percent of the seventeen-year-olds in 1972 agreed that "you can't be too careful in dealing with people." By 1992 the proportion that agreed was up to 60 percent.

When I asked these same questions recently of students in an Iowa middle school and a Kansas social work program, I found the same results. But the vulnerable youth in prison have an extreme version of this condition of basic distrust. When Peter was asked what he would think if he picked up a newspaper and the headlines said, "Most people can be trusted," his response was, "What idiot wrote that?" This profound distrust of adult capacity and motivation is as striking as it is dangerous. It leads to kids on the street shooting first and asking questions later. It makes it difficult for kids to cooperate with adults in making schools and neighborhoods safer. It requires a wholesale effort to prove to kids that adults *can* be trusted and *are* powerful allies. We will look more closely at these perceptions in Chapter Seven.

ON THE DARK SIDE, ANYTHING IS POSSIBLE

During the Nazi period of the 1930s and 1940s, millions of people (particularly, but not exclusively, Jews) were systematically rounded up and shipped to concentration camps, where they were worked to death, starved to death, tortured to death, or simply executed. Three decades later, the Khmer Rouge Party, under the leadership of Pol Pot, did much the same thing to the people of Cambodia. Just after the turn of the century, the Turks attempted to exterminate the Armenian people. Where did the Turkish, Khmer Rouge, and Nazi leadership find enough evil or crazy people in their country to mount such ambitious programs of extermination? And what do these historical events have to do with kids who kill?

Yale University psychologist Stanley Milgram sought to find out. He conducted an experiment in which he brought psychologically normal individuals into a laboratory to play the role of teacher to a person identified as the "learner." This created a situation in which the experimental subject took on a role of authority with respect to the learner while still agreeing to work within the rules of the game set up by the experimenter. The experiment was designed to investigate the phenomenon of obedience in the face of authority (the teacher's willingness to do whatever the experimenter said to do in order to make the learner do what he was supposed to do). The learner was put in another room, and the teacher was supposed to administer electric shocks of increasing severity to him every time he made a mistake on an assigned task. Normal people complied and administered escalating shocks—even when they could hear the learner screaming in pain through the intercom that connected the two rooms. Some verbally abused the learner as they tortured him. They became the Turk, the Nazi, the Khmer Rouge. Milgram exposed a doorway to the dark side, where torture is possible. This is the lesson from Milgram's study: *When it comes to violence, anything is possible.* Anything is possible.

This lesson has important implications for understanding kids exposed to violent trauma, kids who live in an awful, surreal place where people follow orders and commit atrocities and where adults in charge of kids brutalize them to make sure they toe the line. It is so very real, this willingness we have to "do what we got to do." At age sixteen, Thomas killed on the orders of his twenty-one-year-old drug boss, who had promised to kill Thomas if he didn't follow orders. Thomas had learned from years of experience that such threats were not idle. In his world, people really do kill other people if they disobey orders.

I was in Cambodia in the wake of the Khmer Rouge genocide, and I've seen that anything is possible. But there is no need to go that far to discover this. You can learn it right here in our own society, where many violent and incarcerated youth know it firsthand. Sixteen-year-old Shawn told me how his nineteen-year-old "mentor" sat with the baby son of a drug dealer on his lap, holding a gun to the baby's head to force the baby's father to give up the drugs he had hidden somewhere in the apartment. When Shawn realized the nineteen-year-old was prepared to shoot the baby, he learned Milgram's lesson from the dark side. Anything is possible.

A film made at Cornell some years ago illustrates this harsh conclusion on the domestic front. The title is *I Still Can't Say It*. During the course of developing a child abuse prevention program, some of the teachers came forward to disclose that they themselves had been victims of abuse as children. The film has a chilling scene in which a teacher looks into the camera and tells her story. She says, "You know, when I was a little girl, my mother used to beat me. And one day somebody called the police, and the police came to our house. And the police asked me, "Is your mother beating you?" and I said no and the police went away. When my mother came home, she said, "Why didn't you tell the police that I've been beating you?" And I looked her in the eye and said, "— cause you could *kill* me."

Fortunately for this one little girl, and for the rest of us, knowledge of the dark side was not all she learned. Other relatives, teachers at school, the minister of her church, and eventually the man she married—all worked together to teach her about the light, about love, and about finding nonviolent ways to deal with her fear and her rage. Violent boys are not so fortunate. Usually, they get few, if any, of these advantages.

HOW IS VIOLENCE POSSIBLE ON THE DARK SIDE?

Depersonalization and desensitization open the door to unlimited possibilities for violence. When we depersonalize others, we fail to see their individuality, their humanity, and treat them in an impersonal way. If empathy is the enemy of violence, depersonalization is its ally. The more we are able to create psychological distance between us and others, the more likely we are to commit acts of violence and aggression against them. That's why all the various "isms" that dehumanize us play into the hands of violence and why racism and violence are linked. By depersonalizing them, good, caring people can support barbaric treatment of others; they put them outside their own circle, into the category of "the other."

Desensitization is another side of this principle. Even the most violent of the violent boys almost never go from the A to Z of violence in one step. A recent review of research by military psychologist David Grossman reveals something very disturbing about current youth socialization. Grossman points out that even as late as World War II, only about 20 percent of American soldiers (regular riflemen, not special forces) were able to point their weapon at the enemy and shoot them. Why? He believes it is because the fundamental human inhibition against violence toward other humans was operating even in soldiers who had already gone through basic training. Of course, from a technical point of view this was a problem for the military, which it set out to resolve. The military discovered that it was possible to overcome this inhibition by simply changing the training procedures.

Until World War II, the military trained soldiers to shoot at bull's-eye targets. Soldiers could get very good at this, but when a human being was put in a gun sight, many soldiers couldn't pull the trigger. In fact, 80 percent couldn't pull the trigger. The military changed the training after World War II, and by the time we were engaged in the Vietnam War, 90 percent of American soldiers were able to shoot their weapon at the enemy. How did the military do this? They did it through desensitization, that is, by training soldiers to shoot at human figures and not at abstract targets like the old-fashioned bull's-eye. How is this relevant to understanding violent youth? Grossman sees it this way:

With the advent of interactive point and shoot arcade and video games there is a significant concern that society is aping military conditioning but without the vital safeguard of discipline. There is strong evidence to indicate that the indiscriminate civilian application of combat conditioning techniques as entertainment may be a key factor in the worldwide skyrocketing violent crime rates, including a seven-fold increase in per capita aggravated assault.

Many parents, educators, and mental health professionals have discussed and debated the psychological significance of violent video games, but here is the clearest explanation of why this issue should concern us. We are teaching young people to have the same disinhibition that modern soldiers have but without the prosocial structure and discipline that soldiers are taught. As Grossman points out, the lasting influence of that structure and discipline is one reason that despite the massive prevalence of posttraumatic stress disorder among Vietnam era veterans and the fact that their suicide rates are very high, their homicide rate is, if anything, *lower* than that of their nonmilitarized peers. That is, military discipline serves as a kind of restraining force against this disinhibition. Similarly, although many youths grew up with guns in years gone by, they learned military-like discipline with respect to those guns and only used them to shoot at nonhuman targets. Both inhibitions may have served as protective factors. Today, the combination of ready access to real guns, videogame practice at shooting human beings, a general loosening of social controls, and increasingly frequent violent imagery on television and in movies poses a new danger.

NO ONE IS IMMUNE TO THE DARK SIDE

Brigadier General S. L. A. Marshall, the official U.S. military historian of World War II in Europe, commissioned a study of the psychological functioning of soldiers in conditions of chronic combat. His study revealed that among American soldiers who were in combat continuously for sixty days, the psychiatric casualty rate was 98 percent, meaning that when the experience of violent trauma is intense and chronic, virtually no one is immune. Those 98 percent of American soldiers who became psychiatric casualties had to be taken off the line and rehabilitated before they were able to go back into service. But what about the two percent who did not become psychiatric casualties? The researchers found out that these men were psychopaths. The lesson? Unless you are crazy to start with, you will go down emotionally if you move into a war zone. Very few people have immunity to this level of violence and human misery.

I think the results of this study are important in understanding senseless youth violence. As Malcolm says, "You place any one of them people outside, you put them in that predicament, and they are going to do the same thing." If you walk there, if you walk in his shoes, you will not be unaffected. You will not have the choices that perhaps you think you have now, unless you either have remarkable transcendent self-discipline and structure or are so profoundly psychologically damaged that you will enjoy killing a human being.

Another way of stating the lesson learned from Marshall's research is this: *Resilience is not absolute; some settings overwhelm human capacities.* Psychologist Pat Tolan at the University of Illinois studied fifteen-year-old kids in Chicago. His study answered the following question: What percent of kids are resilient if we measure resilience as neither being more than one year behind in school and requiring remedial education nor having mental health or developmental problems sufficient to require professional intervention to recover? Over a two-year period, Tolan studied fifteen-year-old African American kids who were living in disruptive families and growing up in the most afflicted war-zone neighborhoods of Chicago. The answer he found to his question was *zero percent.* None of the fifteen-year-olds were resilient in the sense that they escaped both significant academic deficit and mental health impairment. This is a kind of peacetime analogue to Marshall's study of American soldiers in World War II. The relentless pressure imposed on children exposed to the lethal combination of community violence, family disruption, racism, and personal experience of trauma is uniformly overwhelming. The accumulation of threat is too much for any of them to bear.

But let us not forget that even many boys from outside the confines of overtly abusive families and war-zone neighborhoods feel this pressure. As therapist Terrence Real makes clear in his book *I Don't Want to Talk*

About It, most boys feel an intense pressure, by virtue of the dictates of masculine socialization, to be tough, to suppress tender emotions, and to be powerful. This pressure often produces a false grandiosity when the allure of power and dominance becomes as addictive as a drug. Michael Carneal in Kentucky said what he really wanted was "more respect from the kids." Kip Kinkel in Oregon was smaller than many other kids, but he used his temper to compensate for his lack of size; he never backed down from a confrontation and was often the aggressive one, pushing and shoving.

Although the concept of resilience was developed by researchers and clinicians, it has increasingly become a kind of moral judgment, policy explanation, or excuse. After it was popularized in the 1970s and 1980s, it wasn't long before some policymakers started saying that we don't need to have intervention or prevention programs because children are resilient. For me this reached a kind of absurdly logical conclusion in a courtroom when a prosecutor asked a boy who was being tried for first-degree murder, "What's wrong with you that you weren't resilient growing up in this environment? Other kids seemed to survive without becoming criminals. What's wrong with you?"

The truth is, many kids in the same circumstances as the boy who was on trial for murder actually *are* becoming criminals. In their review of serious violent offenders, psychologist Rolf Loeber and criminologist David Farrington report that 85 percent of kids who commit serious, violent offenses as juveniles *don't* get caught. What is more, while some kids in difficult situations respond with criminal acts (with severe "externalizing behaviors," as the psychologists put it), other equally troubled kids respond with self-destructive acts and inner turmoil, with what psychologists call "internalizing" problems, that is, headaches, depression, self-loathing, bad dreams, and the like. Michael sits in jail awaiting a death sentence. His brother Robert has never committed a criminal act, but he is a very troubled young man, with no relationships, chronic nightmares, and stomachaches.

Overall, more and more kids are succumbing to the pressure of dealing with the dark side. Whereas in the mid-1970s psychologist Tom Achenbach and his colleagues found that 10 percent of all American kids were sufficiently troubled and developmentally disrupted to require professional mental health intervention, today his research indicates that the number is about 20 percent.

ON THE DARK SIDE THE FUTURE ENDS

Psychiatrist Lenore Terr reports on the deterioration of what is called future orientation in her study of the Chowchilla kidnapping, an incident in which a group of children were kidnapped and buried underground for two days before escaping. A year later, when asked how long they expected to live, these children reported answers that were on average six or seven years less than the answers given by children unaffected by that traumatic event. One of the things trauma does is undermine your sense of security in the future, your future orientation. At the extreme, trauma produces something we call terminal thinking. Ask a lost fifteen-year-old, "What do you expect to be when you are thirty?" And he says, "Dead."

Terminal thinking is a major impediment to everything positive we would want teenagers to do, because almost everything positive depends upon their having a future orientation. If you were a traumatized adolescent, why would you study? Why would you stay in school? Would you drive carefully or avoid drugs? Why would you have safe sex—or, better still, no sex at all? Why would you do anything that adults want teenagers to do if you didn't envision yourself in the future? This is what Malcolm was talking about on my fiftieth birthday when he looked at me wistfully and said, "Wow, fifty years old! I might make it to thirty, maybe." Then he said to me, "You know, if I wasn't here in prison, I'd be dead today." As we will see in Chapter Eight, that very recognition can become the starting point for finding a way back for violent boys, and the basis for reclaiming them.

YOUTH VIOLENCE MAKES SENSE FROM THE INSIDE OUT

Human beings are more simply human than otherwise. A boy's violence begins to make sense when we set aside our myths and look at the poisonous human experiences out of which it develops. His violence is an adaptation not only to the conditions of life around him but also to what's inside his head. It begins to make sense when we piece together the whole story. Our task is to look closely at the experience of violent boys to see what leads them down the path of violence. The next step in this process is to examine the peculiar moral universe in which violent boys live, to see it in its own terms, and to see its relation to society's code of moral values.

A BOY'S CODE OF HONOR

Frustrated Justice and Fractured Morality

MAKING MORAL SENSE IS DIFFICULT

Making moral sense of their behavior is probably the most difficult challenge in dealing with kids who kill. When I appeared on a radio talk show in the days after Kip Kinkel's shootings in Springfield, Oregon, one of the callers said, "Surely, by the time a child reaches the age of four years, he knows the difference between right and wrong!" How can we understand the acts of lethal violence committed by violent boys in a way that helps us not only help them but prevents other kids from doing the same in the years to come? Do these actions make *any* moral sense? Are these boys without moral sense? Are they simply immoral? We need answers to these questions if we are to complete our understanding of the chain of events that begins in the disrupted relationships and rejections experienced in infancy and early childhood, that includes the bad behavior and aggression we see in later childhood, and that culminates in lethal violence in adolescence.

Sixteen-year-old Taylor is in prison for stabbing a priest. How did it happen, and why did he do it? Generally, Taylor doesn't like to talk about it. Now, looking back on it during an interview with me, he seems a bit ashamed. When he is finally willing to tell me the story, it comes out like this: "I needed money. I used to go to the church—lot of good it did me—so I knew there was money in the church. So I went there to take it. You know, from the collection box. Anyway, I needed the money, and I was working on the box with a screwdriver, you know, opening it, when this priest comes in and yells at me to stop. I started to run and he came after me, so I stabbed him, you know, with the screwdriver. Then I ran."

It seems hard to fathom any moral framework in which stabbing a priest makes sense. But is it really any more or less sensible than killing your classmates? Or shooting a convenience store clerk because he stuttered and was slow to get the money out of the cash register? Or killing a stranger on the street who insulted you? Or shooting a cop to death because he stopped you on the street? The violent boys I know have done all these things and more. Do any of these acts make moral sense?

What strikes us about many of the kids who kill is that their actions don't seem to make any moral sense. And so we readily conclude that these boys *have* no moral sense. But things are not always as obvious upon reflection as they seem to be at first—both for the kids who kill and for all of us who judge them. To these boys and their peers, their acts often do make moral sense. Or perhaps they don't see their acts as either moral or immoral at all but, rather, as necessary for survival, or as simple entitlements. This latter point is worth reflecting upon.

Regardless of its origins, the action of many violent boys conveys a kind of arrogance, or what journalist Edward Helmore, writing in *The Guardian* in 1997, calls "deadly petulance." "I needed money," says Taylor, as if that is justification enough. "He insulted me," says Corneel, as if that is sufficient to warrant a death sentence. In this these two are not alone: many of the shooters in the small-town and suburban school attacks offer what appear to be similarly self-centered explanations. Luke Woodham feels like an outcast and reported, "I just couldn't take it anymore." Michael Carneal says he felt mad about the way other kids treated him. Mitchell Johnson says, "Everyone that hates me, everyone I don't like is going to die." Andrew Wurst says he hated his parents and his teachers and was mad about not being successful with girls.

Just hearing these few words from boys who kill does seem to cast their actions as grandiose, egotistical, and arrogant. Who the hell are they to take a human life because they feel insulted, frustrated, or teased or just because they need money? At this level they do sound like simply rotten kids. But there is much more to the story. The sense of their actions and the scope of their moral framework emerges from the details, rather than the headlines, of the story when we place these details in the larger context of their lives. It comes from their being lost in the world.

LOOKING IN THE MORAL MIRROR

Before we look closely at the boys, however, we must begin with ourselves. For starters, we need to recognize that most people accept killing as a necessity. The issue for most of us is not the wrongness of killing in general but killing outside the boundaries of society's rules and values. The critical point is how we define immoral killing.

Many of us can understand killing when we can see and sympathize with the moral justification behind it. There is no better example than the death penalty—judicially justified homicide. State governments throughout the United States impose the death penalty, and they do so with the support of a majority of the voters. Yet many Americans see this brand of killing as immoral, and once you get beyond our national borders, many more people are amazed that we condone it at all. In addition to our widespread acceptance of the death penalty, most of us accept as justifiable a killing committed in personal self-defense. Killing someone who attacks us is killing too, but it is accepted legally and morally as self-defense.

In recent years this moral and legal legitimacy has even been extended to include the actions of some battered women who kill their husbands after enduring years of extremely violent, nonlethal assault. This kind of killing has come to make moral sense to us after decades of public education about the psychological dynamics and cultural implications of domestic violence. But not so long ago, many men believed that a marriage license was a license to beat their wives and knew that institutions—police, courts, social services—accepted that right. Until recently, battered women who killed their abusive husbands could expect to be treated like eighteenth-century slaves in revolt: while the excessiveness of the victimizer's behavior was recognized, that behavior alone was not considered enough to justify radically violent action that challenged the status quo. It was particularly easy to apply this attitude to battered wives when it was assumed that they "asked for it" in the first place. Now, as we understand better what it means to live inside an abusive relationship, and as women have gained in status generally, we are beginning to see the moral sense when a woman sets her abusive husband's bed on fire or shoots him while he sleeps or poisons him at dinnertime. Again, we see this type of killing as justifiable homicide.

Most of us saw the moral sense in the killing of innocent civilians in Iraq. We saw it as a necessary side effect of prosecuting the Gulf War in 1992, and again in 1998 and 1999, as *politically justifiable* homicide. The same is true of our support for antigovernment forces in Nicaragua and elsewhere in the world throughout the 1980s. Killing seems to make some sense to people when it is politically sanctioned. Just how many absolute pacifists are there among us who would not justify almost any killing act when committed by a legally constituted government in pursuit of national security? Or, more broadly, how many pacifists are there when it comes to interpersonal violence on the streets, at school, or at home?

THE MORAL CIRCLE

All of us have a *moral circle* when it comes to violence; some acts are inside the circle of moral justification while other acts are outside that circle. Would you kill an intruder in your home? Would you kill a terminally ill relative? Would you abort a third-trimester pregnancy? Would you agree to the assassination of Saddam Hussein? Would you kill a relative if he were sexually abusing your child? Would you kill a raccoon that bit your son? What if there was a remote possibility the animal had rabies and killing it was the only way to find out for sure? Would you kill it? Killing a raccoon is not the same as killing a human being. Nor is killing Saddam Hussein the same as killing Martin Luther King. Stabbing an abuser is different from stabbing a stranger. Where does one draw the line, and how does one determine which killings make moral sense and which do not?

Cultures and societies set different standards for the morality of killing. Watching the film *Seven Years in Tibet* about the youthful Dalai Lama, many of us were amused to watch the lengths to which Tibetan Buddhists went to avoid killing worms while digging the foundation for a new building. Their reverence for life extends their moral circle very widely. Most of us would put worms *outside* our moral circle when it comes to killing. Does that make us immoral, or does it make much of the killing we do amoral (in the sense that few Americans can relate to the killing of worms as a *moral* issue at all)? Yet any four-year-old Tibetan Buddhist child knows the wrongness of killing any living being, worms included. How many Christian, Jewish, or Muslim children appreciate *this* moral distinction? Are worms inside the moral circle of these children?

What about dogs and cats? Most of us would put dogs and cats inside the circle, particularly if they are household pets (less so if they are strays). Thus, most Americans would have moral qualms about killing a dog or a cat but not a cow, a pig, or a chicken. How and where do we draw these lines? Is vegetarianism more moral than carnivorousness? Is cannibalism absolutely different from the killing and eating of our fellow mammals? Let us start by keeping these complicated moral distinctions in mind as we look deeper into the stories of young people who commit murder. Let's walk a bit in the lost boys' shoes before we judge them.

Most of us can morally justify some form of killing when it seems necessary. Most of us legitimize violence when we see no moral alternatives and denounce it when we believe alternatives are available. In this sense, necessity is the moral mother of murder. And that is the key to understanding boys who kill and their legitimization of violence. At the moment of crisis they don't see positive alternatives, because of who they are and their emotional history, and where they come from and how they see the world. They do what they have to do—*as they see it*. Understanding this horrible reality is very difficult; it requires a kind of openheartedness and openmindedness that is hard for anyone to achieve, particularly in today's political and emotional climate. But achieve it we must if we are to understand the motivations and experiences that drive boys to commit acts of lethal violence and then marshal our resources to prevent this from happening with other troubled boys.

STRUGGLING TO UNDERSTAND

I face my own personal struggle to understand when the incarcerated boys I interview talk about killing. It is my third interview with Conneel, and although the official topic of discussion is "his neighborhood," we end up talking about violence, specifically, his "first homicide." We are talking about girls, and Conneel says in passing, "They really started coming around after my first homicide." He says it so casually that I think it would be a good time to hear the whole story, particularly since other boys (such as Kip Kinkel) echo this theme; namely, that some girls find violent boys attractive.

Conneel tells his tale rather matter-of-factly, a narrative style common to the boys I have interviewed in prison. The discourse leading up to the description of the killing itself sounds rather chilling despite—or perhaps because of—the nature of the story. In this account, fifteen-year-old Conneel rounds a corner in his Brooklyn neighborhood and sees a nineteen-year-old standing on the street in front of his building; he is surrounded by other kids, most of whom Conneel knows from dealing drugs. Recognizing the gold chain around his neck as the one this youth had stolen from him at gunpoint two weeks earlier, Conneel approaches, gun drawn, and demands the chain back. The nineteen-year-old at first yells out that he doesn't know "what the fuck" Conneel is talking about, but then gives up the chain after seeing Conneel's gun. With the chain now in his left hand, Conneel puts the gun to the nineteen-year-old's head and pulls the trigger. The boy dies instantly.

Why on earth did he kill him when the chain was recovered? For Conneel it was simply, "I did what I had to do." What does that mean in moral terms? It means that this was a matter of retributive justice and an act of preemptive violence that made moral sense to Conneel because by robbing him in the first place the boy he killed had placed himself outside of Conneel's moral circle. Conneel calculated that if he didn't kill the other boy at that moment, he would be exposing himself to danger in the future, so he "did what he had to do." In Conneel's eyes, the boy deserved the death penalty for threatening him, and executing him was a morally justified act of punishment, deterrence, and self-preservation. The fact that in Conneel's eyes the shooting was morally justified doesn't mean it was right. I must say that I feel the same way about those who favor the execution of kids who kill. They offer a moral justification, but they are not right.

Consider Dennis, whose parents abused and then abandoned him to his grandmother when he was four years old. When his grandmother died only four years later, the perceived injustice of this abandonment and death was too great for Dennis to bear. And so he "declared war on the world" (his words), and we all know that "all's fair in love and war."

Violent boys operate in a particular moral universe. They often have moral circles much more circumscribed than those of other kids their age. Sometimes these moral circles shrink so as to virtually disappear, which produces what seems from the outside to be unlimited legitimization of aggression. However, all but those with the most profound psychological damage do have a moral circle.

The world that Dennis lives in is filled with violence, but it does have rules. In fact, it is highly moralistic in many ways. Malcolm lives in that same world. I learned this when he spoke of his response when he learned that his pregnant girlfriend had been shot. It was clear that in his moral system, the shooting of his girlfriend violated the rules. He perceived this act very differently from the way he saw what appeared to me to be similar acts in his world. As I sat with him, Malcolm was filled with outrage that someone would shoot *a girl*, even more so a pregnant one (with his male child). And he had some very clear ideas about how the shooting fit into the social life of his community. "Has to be outside people coming in. Has to be, 'cause you can't be in the same neighborhood and do something like that." "What is going to happen next?" I asked. Malcolm was pretty clear on that score, expecting that his friends and relatives would see to it that his son's death was avenged. And it was. Within two weeks, the boys who had done the shooting were identified, tracked down, and killed.

THE LURE OF THE DARK SIDE

There are individuals who are so profoundly damaged that they are literally amoral, that is, without any morality whatsoever when it comes to interpersonal aggression and violence. As Yale University psychiatrist Dorothy Otnow-Lewis reports in her book *Guilty by Reason of Insanity*, some of the most notorious serial killers are so psychologically damaged that they approximate this state of pure amorality. But such individuals are very, very few in number, and even most of them do have some small area of morality in which they suspend their lethal behavior—for a dog, a cat, a bird, a rat, a lizard, or even a child.

Complete amorality is extremely rare. We have encountered a couple of boys in our work who are so profoundly damaged that they seem to have no moral circle at all. The psychiatric term for these individuals is *psychopath*. Their psychopathy is chilling. Stanley, for example, speaks coolly and casually about sexual violence, about self-mutilation, about animals and people he has killed, and about his plans to continue killing when the opportunity arises. It is chilling to hear. It takes your breath away and it makes your skin crawl. It makes you glad there is someone observing through the interview room's window. When Stanley notices the reaction he is eliciting, he smiles and asks rhetorically, "Does this bother you?"

Few boys ever get to this point, where they are beyond morality. But some boys do come close to achieving this final state, particularly when they are operating in the war-zone mentality of a conventional youth prison, where honor and the preservation of some modicum of dignity is a constant battle. Some get there when they are immersed in some sort of negative ideology, such as Satanism, in which they adopt a profound nihilism, believing only in the darkest of the dark side.

A study done by psychologists Kelly Damphousse and Ben Crouch revealed that nearly 10 percent of juvenile offenders in the Texas system reported some level of involvement in Satanism. These boys were characterized by a low level of attachment to conventional society, as represented by parents and schools; a high level of attachment to peers; higher than average intelligence; and a sense of life being out of their control. The fourteen-year-old shooter in Edinboro, Pennsylvania, Andrew Wurst, was nicknamed Satan by his schoolmates. Kip Kinkel in Springfield, Oregon, was involved in the dark, violent imagery of "heavy metal" music. Luke Woodham, the sixteen-year-old shooter in Pearl, Mississippi, was part of an avowed Satanist group of boys in his community.

The culture of the dark side has a special draw for troubled boys, alienated boys, and boys who are outside the orbit of the positive features of American life. When this attraction combines with the power of negative peer groups, the result can be very dangerous. Social worker Ronald Feldman has studied the impact of peer group composition on adolescent behavior for decades. He finds that the tipping point in an adolescent peer group, from positive to negative, can come with only a minority of the individuals being predisposed to negative behavior. Once these negative peers take over the group, the positive boys either leave or are driven out or go along with the negative agenda. Today boys can become members of negative peer groups without even leaving home (e.g., through Internet chat groups).

PERCEIVED INJUSTICE AND THE MORAL CODE OF VIOLENCE

Malcolm spoke about his time in a youth prison that was out of adult control and that had deteriorated into a savage battle for physical and psychological survival. He reports, "I was fighting every day. If a person looked at me wrong, I'd reach across the table and hit him. If he touched something on my tray, I'd hit him. If he reached over at my food, I'd hit him. That's how it was. I had the mind of a savage. I didn't have self-discipline. I couldn't just let little stuff ride, because if I did I felt like nobody respected me. So I tried to inflict pain on them and serve justice. But it wasn't justice. I know that now."

Much more common than truly amoral boys are boys within whom a stunted or otherwise troubled emotional life combines with a narrow and intense personal need for justice. These impulses come to dominate a boy's moral thinking to the exclusion of other considerations, such as social conventions about right and wrong, consequences, empathy, and even personal survival.

I learned this lesson about the links between perceived injustice and the moral code of violence first from the work of psychiatrist James Gilligan. For many years Gilligan worked in the mental health system of the state prisons of Massachusetts, dealing with violent boys grown into full, psychologically impoverished manhood. Gilligan achieved the incredible openness of heart and mind required to understand men who commit lethal violence. He worked ceaselessly at knowing them, with an unprejudiced understanding of what violence is about in the lives of these highly criminal, highly dangerous men. As he did so, he came to understand that almost all acts of violence are related to perceived injustice, the subjective experience of frustrated justice, and an attempt to redress injustice. Deadly petulance usually hides some deep emotional wounds, a way of compensating through an exaggerated sense of grandeur for an inner sense of violation, victimization, and injustice.

When boys kill, they are seeking justice—*as they see it, through their eyes*. What makes these acts appear senseless to us is often the fact that we either don't see the connection between the original injustice and the eventual lethal act or don't understand why the boy perceived injustice in the first place. This latter point is sometimes easily dispelled if it results from our lack of understanding of the boy's experience.

Consider Stephen, for example, an eighteen-year-old who killed a police officer. Stephen is a polite young man with an engaging smile and a shy manner. Words don't come easy for him, but when they do come they often tell volumes about his desperate efforts to escape his physically and psychologically abusive mother in the years after his father died, when Stephen was eight years old.

I see little evidence in the reports of his social workers and psychologists that they recognized the injustice he experienced at home at the hands of a mother who rejected him while she accepted his brother, a mother who whipped his back raw while she rewarded his compliant brother and who told him that he was like his "no-good father" and that his brother "favored" her side of the family. Interestingly, what comes across in Stephen's records is just a boy who after losing his father grew into an ungrateful teenager who caused his mother embarrassment and inconvenience.

But I have had a chance to see and hear the real story, from the inside out. What did Stephen want more than anything in the world? He wanted to be loved and accepted by his mother. In this he is no different from any of us. Is there any greater injustice for a child than to be unloved, rejected, and abused? Failing to receive, or perceive, that love and acceptance, what did he want? He wanted to be free of the imprisonment he felt at home, where, he told me, his greatest fear was that he would strike out at his abusive mother. And when I asked him if he thought God would forgive her for what she did to him, he responded, "I hope so."

Of course, not all the lost boys are so forgiving. Boys do commit parricide. In fact, kids kill their parents with alarming frequency, almost always in response to feeling they have been rejected and abused. In his book on the topic, *When a Child Kills*, lawyer Paul Mones presents numerous examples. Even when the initial story paints the child as an ungrateful or crazed monster, further investigation often (but, admittedly, not always) reveals that the killing took place as the culmination of years of deteriorating family relationships and, most often, abuse.

I met one boy from such a situation, a fifteen-year-old who had killed his abusive stepfather. Abandoned emotionally by his mother, Terry was left behind in the supposed care of her former husband. His humiliation of Terry was unceasing, but the boy had nowhere else to go. After nearly two years of escalating anger and sadness, Terry reached his limit when his stepfather casually slapped Terry's nephew across the face so hard that the two-year-old went sprawling across the floor. "I just wasn't going to take it any more," Terry told me. "I knew I would have to pay the price for what I did, but I didn't care. The man had to be stopped. So I went into the bedroom and got his shotgun. Both barrels. Then I called the cops."

Terry was sentenced to twenty-five years in prison. Killings such as Terry's are easier to make sense of than what Stephen did. Even if we think Terry's response was extreme and impulsive, most of us can at least imagine his moral framework: retributive justice, vengeance, and a desperate attempt to escape from an emotionally intolerable situation. But what about Stephen?

WHEN BEING WRONGED BECOMES INTOLERABLE

Stephen killed when he was stopped on the street by the police. Why was he out on the street? He needed to escape from home. Why did he kill that night on the street? He was carrying a gun and he was out on bail awaiting sentencing on a weapons charge; he was hoping for a brief sentence on that charge, but he knew that if he was picked up carrying a gun, the sentence would be lengthened substantially. At the moment he was stopped by police, he was caught by the injustice of his situation. Stephen needed freedom more than anything else (except love), and here was a threat to that freedom in the form of two cops who were stopping him on the street "for no good reason." As a result of this unfair action, he knew he would lose his freedom. He felt he had no choice but to prevent this injustice from going any further. He shot at the cops—he says to scare them so that he could run away. But after he shot twice, they started shooting at *him*. More injustice. Stephen returned the fire, and the result was a dead cop and his wounded partner—and one boy facing the death penalty.

In Paducah, Kentucky, fifteen-year-old Michael Carneal was tired of being teased and picked on by his schoolmates. Luke Woodham of Pearl, Mississippi, said, "No one truly loved me." Overweight and bespectacled, he had been picked on since kindergarten. His note said, "I killed because people like me are mistreated every day." Perceived injustice. No, make that real injustice.

This intolerability is an important aspect of the psychological situation faced by kids who kill. It often reflects their sense of honor and dishonor. This is a very American attitude. New Hampshire's state motto is "Live free or die." Soldiers are taught the code of "death before dishonor." Boys incorporate this code. Evidence of this is their belief in divine punishment and their frequent recourse to suicide as a means of escaping. James Gilligan reminds us that adult killers are much more likely to kill themselves than to be killed by the state.

Kids see death as a way out, too. One of the two brave schoolmates who wrestled Kip Kinkel to the ground and put a stop to his shooting spree reported that he heard the boy plead, "Shoot me." According to the classmate who wrestled Michael Carneal to the ground as he stopped shooting momentarily to reload, the boy said, "Kill me now." Stephen has said that he wants the death penalty if the alternative is life in prison, and Malcolm told me he would rather die than submit to any more abuse.

DEATH BEFORE DISHONOR: SHAME AND VIOLENCE

While there is an inner circle of compassion in Malcolm's life, outside that circle it is all tooth and claw. For example, he once nearly killed a man who molested his younger cousin. The crime for which he is presently serving time is another example:

As his sister opened the door of a neighborhood convenience store, a young man named Clifton burst out the door, knocking her and her two-year-old son to the ground, causing the little boy to suffer a concussion. Without apologizing, Clifton laughed and walked off. Malcolm tracked him down to demand an apology for the insult and blatant disrespect of his sister and her child. First he studied Clifton's movements, waiting until he was sure he could confront him one-on-one. Then he arranged for Clifton's girlfriend to set him up for a meeting. Then he had his brother pull his car in behind Clifton's car in the girl's driveway so that there would be no possibility of escape. Having made these preparations, Malcolm confronted Clifton, gun in hand, and gave him an opportunity to apologize. Clifton laughed in his face. This response was intolerable. Malcolm hit him in the head with his fist and again demanded an apology. Clifton declined and reached down for his own gun. When he did, Malcolm opened fire. Two shots. Luckily for both of them, neither was fatal.

Many of the acts of lethal violence committed by boys are deliberate and sometimes even meticulously planned, rather than spur-of-the-moment explosions of rage. I think this is significant, because it highlights the importance of understanding that boys think about violence as a solution to their problems. More than just the result of an uncontrollable urge, these violent acts are related to Gilligan's idea of frustrated justice. This is particularly true of the boys who committed the school shootings in the 1997–1998 school year:

In Kentucky, Michael Carneal timed his assault so that it would occur during the regular morning prayer meeting at his high school. In Arkansas, thirteen-year-old Mitchell Johnson and eleven-year-old Andrew Golden developed an elaborate plan involving a false fire alarm to draw students out into the line of fire they had set up, like soldiers preparing an ambush; they succeeded in killing students and a teacher. In Oregon, Kip Kinkel carried his arsenal into the school cafeteria at just the right time in the morning and was able to shoot twenty-four classmates, two fatally.

What produces this intolerable state of being in which violent boys live? James Gilligan believes that injustice produces shame, and it is shame that generates the intolerability of existence. Shame imposes the fear that one will cease to exist, the prospect of psychic annihilation. Nothing seems to threaten the human spirit more than rejection, brutalization, and lack of love. Nothing—not physical deformity, not debilitating illness, not financial ruin, not academic failure—can equal insults to the soul. Nothing compares with the trauma of this profound assault on the psyche.

Those who are shamed are vulnerable to committing violence and aggression, because they know that acts of violence against self or others are a reliable method for reasserting existence when life experience has denied it. "I hurt, therefore I am." A colleague of mine reports that an adult prisoner once told her, "I'd rather be wanted for murder than not wanted at all." A grim assessment but ringing with truth. Acts of violence and aggression confirm existence. And, paradoxically, acts of violence against the self may serve the same purpose, particularly for children; as they contemplate suicide or actually engage in a suicide attempt, many youth seem to think, "That will show them. They'll be sorry when I'm gone."

Remember that adolescents are theatrical, viewing the world as a stage, with themselves playing the leading roles. And their plays are often melodramas and, on occasion, even tragedies. Many of us can recall thinking suicidal thoughts, but most of us had the inner resources and outer supports to leave it at that. Of course, tens of thousands of kids each year can't leave it at that and do attempt suicide.

The greatest danger comes when the crisis of perceived impending psychic annihilation is melodramatically merged with the idea of addressing intolerable injustice with violence. The two go together, because in our society the idea of retribution through violence is a basic article of faith. Vengeance is not confined to some small group of psychologically devastated individuals. It is normal for us, a fact of value in our culture.

It isn't surprising that those of us who feel unjustly treated—by our mother or father, a spouse or lover, a friend or acquaintance, even a child or society itself—resort to violence to redress that sense of injustice. The most vulnerable members of our community show us where the negative values in our culture lead, show us how things really look at the extremes. The actions of violent boys show us what comes of our society's poisonous belief that "revenge is sweet." We would all do better to heed the ancient proverb "When you begin a journey of revenge, start by digging two graves, one for your enemy and one for yourself."

The links between injustice and shame operate inside families in their most devastating forms, but they also operate outside the family in the larger community, particularly at the intersection of race and class. Ethologist Desmond Morris said many years ago, "The viciousness with which children are treated is a measure of the dominant pressures imposed upon their tormentors." It is a message worth repeating today: If you want peace, work for justice—in the world and on the playground.

MAKING MORAL MISTAKES

Illuminating the role of shame and perceived injustice in the lives of violent boys provides a good beginning to making some moral sense of their violent actions. But there is more to tell. One of the most difficult things to understand about the lost boys is their use of the word *mistake* to describe what others define as an immoral act. Few aspects of youth violence elicit such a negative response as this one does. As Stanton Samenow, a psychologist who has worked with criminals for many years, puts it, "They may have left a long trail of injury behind them, may even admit that they have done harm, caused horrible problems, but if you ask if they think they are bad people, they will say no. A rapist will say, 'I'm basically a good guy, though I have made some mistakes'—imagine calling rape a mistake!"

I've heard it, too. Lost boys use the term *mistake* to refer to deliberate, intentional acts of violence that achieve their conscious goal. Is there any way to understand how they can regard these immoral acts as mistakes without resorting to explanations that hinge upon the assumption that they are simply lying or engaging in self-protective denial?

Studies of moral reasoning generally focus on the development of sophisticated thinking as the hallmark of moral development, yet sophisticated thinking is but one side of a triangle. The other two are sophisticated feelings and behavior. Thus, the moral person is one who does more than reason about dilemmas. Such a person has moral character. As character education expert Tom Lickona puts it, being a moral person involves "knowing the good, desiring the good, and doing the good."

The standard for efforts to assess the thinking part of morality or moral reasoning grew out of the work of Harvard psychologist Lawrence Kohlberg. Kohlberg's approach has been adopted and adapted by many investigators as a strategy for identifying how well kids are doing in applying their intellect to the task of figuring out moral dilemmas. His system has three levels, each of which contains two stages representing more sophisticated reasoning and more abstract principles than the levels and stages that come before it. The three main levels are "preconventional moral reasoning," "conventional moral reasoning," and "postconventional moral reasoning." At the preconventional level, the emphasis is on fear of punishment, desire for rewards, and the trade-offs between the two that alternative courses of action will produce. At the conventional level, the focus is on doing what "good people" do and respecting family and society's rules. At the postconventional level, the key is an attempt to live by more universal principles, that is, principles that go beyond specific times and places and people.

Most violent boys stand mostly at Level 1 in Kohlberg's classification system, preconventional moral reasoning. Systematic studies of juvenile delinquents responding to moral dilemmas of the type used by Kohlberg also identify such kids as primitive thinkers. For example, psychologists James Nelson, Deborah Smith, and John Dodd have reported that juvenile delinquents in general tend to operate at Level 1, where the concern is with the pragmatics of reward and punishment and getting what one wants. A boy at this level responds to the rightness and wrongness of alternative courses of action on the basis of what and how each possibility will cost and benefit him. Few violent youths are at Level 2, where right and wrong are couched in terms of what helps people meet their legitimate needs. For these boys, "wrong" equals "mistake." Thus, when they say they made a mistake in committing their crimes, often this is an indication of unsophisticated moral reasoning, not amorality per se.

In the wake of the Jonesboro shootings, in the spring of 1998, I ask Conneel about the two boys who committed the murders. Conneel has already admitted to me that he himself was responsible for several deaths and has amassed a substantial arsenal that is hidden in the basement of his apartment building. When I ask him to tell me what he thinks about an appropriate punishment for Mitchell Johnson and Andrew Golden, he starts out with the thought that they might deserve the death penalty. But then he quickly pulls back from that position, reminding me that he is concerned that the death penalty may be imposed upon *him* for *his* lethal acts. He thinks for a while, and then continues. "They're responsible for what they did," he says. "They shot innocent victims—girls," he reasons, "and they should go to prison for that. I'd say at least fifteen years in jail so they can change." When it comes to judging *others*, Conneel is about normal for an American. Of course, like many of us, he has trouble applying those standards to himself. His killings were not of innocent people, he is quick to point out. But isn't that always the point? Do any violent offenders see the target of their lethal violence as innocent?

To an outsider, the violence that lost boys commit often seems to make no sense or to evidence a total breakdown in morality. But this is not the case when we see the world through their eyes. These boys often commit acts of violence on the basis of a "moral" idea in their heads, usually something to do with revenge or injustice or wounded pride or glory. Pressures build as they ruminate on the injustice done to them, usually some specific insult or disappointment set within a bigger picture of resentment. In this way, there is no such thing as a "senseless act of violence." This does not mean that we simply accept their analysis as legitimate, of course, but it does force us to look beyond our shock, horror, and indignation to see the roots of the problem.

MORALITY DEVELOPS IF NURTURED

Boys who kill tend to operate at a low level of sophistication in their moral judgments. But these levels of reasoning are not fixed. They reflect how a boy has adapted to date, not what is possible for him in the future. Indeed, one of the goals for any program to succeed with them is its ability to elevate their moral thinking and help them believe that they can live in a world where something other than survival ethics rules. More on that later.

Another way of looking at moral development is through the development of conscience. Psychologist Barbara Stilwell and her colleagues have explored this process, and they, too, offer a system of levels to convey the progression through which children move morally. Conscience is an individual's sense of listening to a moral voice (the image of Pinocchio's Jiminy Cricket comes to my mind). Stilwell reports two findings particularly useful to understanding the lost boys.

First, the average fifteen-year-old exhibits a "confused conscience," meaning that he is trying to deal with competing and sometimes incompatible moral messages coming from inside and outside his head. This is relevant because it highlights the idea that the confusion lost boys display is to some degree normal; it is the nature of the issues they face that is abnormal. It is one thing to be a fifteen-year-old confused about cheating on a math exam and quite another to be confused about killing someone who threatens you with violence. I can recall the first from my adolescence, but I had no experience with the latter. This is not a demonstration of my moral and developmental superiority but, rather, of the relative social health of my childhood environment. I will return to this issue of social health and its relation to moral development later, when I address violence prevention in Chapter Seven.

Second, Stilwell and her colleagues report that conscience development is a big problem for children with Conduct Disorder, which we have seen afflicts the majority of violent boys. As one nine-year-old boy in her study put it, "a conscience is a little guy inside you that tells you right from wrong, but I ain't got one of them." Interestingly, at this stage of what Stilwell calls external conscience, what the child needs to progress developmentally is "emotional attachment, supervision, clarity of rules, and limit setting"—just what most violent boys don't receive most of the time.

CONSCIENCE UNDER CONSTRUCTION

Eleven-to-fifteen-year-olds are as much children as they are adolescents, and their ability to engage in reality-based moral thinking is still very much "under construction." Some children have erected a solid internal monitor, a prosocial conscience, by the time they enter adolescence. But, again, as psychologist Barbara Stilwell's research shows, most teens actually have to deal with a "confused conscience." Some are still mainly responding to external messages about what is right and what is wrong. And some have a great emotional emptiness inside that drives them to seek extreme solutions to their problems. Some of this emptiness is personal, as we see from the individual life histories, but some of it is social and cultural in its origins.

But whether they exhibit conscience or not, boys are not yet adults, and their ability to appreciate the consequences of their behavior is often quite limited. This has a bearing on what we should do with juvenile killers. The fact that they are capable of committing lethal, adult-like crimes does not mean that they *are* adults. The two things are quite separate and distinct. The common belief that "if you can do the crime, you can do the time" is offered to justify the prosecution and incarceration of kids as if they were adults, but this approach has no basis in the realities of child development.

FEELING FOR YOURSELF IS THE FOUNDATION OF FEELING FOR OTHERS

When it comes to the feeling part of morality, boys who kill are at a special disadvantage. The key to moral feeling is empathy, which is an openness to the feelings of others that allows a person to appreciate what an action means emotionally to someone else. But when a boy's own emotional life is closed off and locked away, when he can't accurately and openly feel his own feelings, it is unlikely that he has much of a basis for being empathic with others. Of course, this is a problem for males generally in our society, as Terrence Real's work so vividly demonstrates. In this sense, the emotional blockage so characteristic of violent boys is partly a result of their maleness in American culture.

But added to this generic problem is the fact that most violent boys have specific unresolved issues of trauma from experiences of abuse and rejection at home, in addition to their exposure to violence and victimization in the community, on the streets, and through the mass media. In psychological terms, this means many have a history of dissociation, the emotionally self-protective strategy of choice for children facing trauma. As we saw in Chapter Three, this adaptation shuts off and compartmentalizes feelings, and very likely inhibits empathy.

Twenty years ago, a study by Gregory Jurkovic and his colleagues found that the most dangerous violent juvenile delinquents display very little empathy. In his widely read book *Emotional Intelligence*, Daniel Goleman defines emotional intelligence as the ability to read emotions in others, to communicate effectively in the nonverbal realm, to manage the ups and downs of day-to-day life, and to have appropriate expectations for relationships. Empathy is one of the foundations for emotional intelligence, and emotional intelligence is at least as important for life success as intellectual intelligence. Goleman puts it this way: "The empathic attitude is engaged again and again in moral judgments, for moral dilemmas involve potential victims." A boy who has organized his inner life around the need to protect himself from his feelings of victimization and unworthiness is unlikely to pay attention effectively to the feelings of others, especially to their feelings as victims. This psychological defense mechanism is an important source of deadly petulance, that arrogant stance in which an individual feels justified in responding to insult with lethal violence. Violent boys are so desperately defensive that they overcompensate with arrogance. It's not because deep down they really feel superior to everyone else that they assume the prerogative of deciding who lives and who dies, but because deep down they feel so empty and worthless.

In talking with violent boys, I find validation for this interpretation. For example, although the youth prisons program offers "victim awareness" programs, the boys find it hard to make use of these programs because their own victimization remains largely unacknowledged and certainly unaddressed. Conneel says, "What about me, man? What about what I have gone through? I mean, I want to talk about what hurts me, and all they want to talk about is the people I hurt. I won't do it. The whole program stinks."

A WORLD WHERE MORALITY IS IRRELEVANT?

Perhaps one clue to the moral universe of violent boys comes from listening to someone like Kareem talk at length about the personal characteristics and attributes required to become a successful architect versus a successful gangster. He says, "You got to be smart for both, you know. It don't come easy. You got to work hard and be tough. You got to take advantage of your opportunities and figure out the best way to get what you want. You need knowledge, lots of knowledge; it's just different kinds of knowledge. You got to be ambitious and go for it. Nobody's going to hand it to you, you got to take it."

As he elaborates on this theme, the focus of his discussion is the similarities. You need to be intelligent. You need to be emotionally controlled. You need to work hard. You need to be competitive. You need to be able to "read" people. When I ask him if there is any moral difference between the two careers, he seems at first puzzled, then replies, "No. That's not the point."

Of course, for most everyone else that would be the point; being an architect is socially acceptable whereas being a gangster is immoral and illegal. Of course, there is a large measure of hypocrisy and duplicity on both sides of this equation. *Kareem* knows that being a gangster is different from being an architect, and *we* know that there is a lot of immoral behavior committed by people in the legally legitimate world.

Before he killed his classmates in Oregon, Kip Kinkel telegraphed his intentions to friends at school the day before he did the shooting. He reportedly said, "I am going to do something stupid tomorrow." Notice that he didn't say, "I am going to do something *wrong* tomorrow." He said "stupid." His choice of words is consistent with how these boys see the world.

I think what he said relates to the sense of inevitability that some boys have about their violent actions. It flows from the conclusions they have drawn about the nature of morality as they have come to know it.

Boys often see the pure exercise of power. This is a particular problem for boys who develop patterns of bad behavior and aggression early in their lives. Maltreated boys are likely to develop a "hypervigilance" to negative social cues and a relative inability to see the positive social cues. They *do* live in a different world from those of us fortunate enough to have grown up loved, accepted, and treated well. Their social maps chart the same physical territory, but it is as if they are color-blind—not because they were born that way but because their early experiences stunted the development of color vision. They see the negative but not the positive. They learn early that power is what counts and that conventional morality often masks and justifies abuse. For example, the values espoused by Stephen's abusive mother look good on paper but not on his back. I believe these early lessons are one important reason why the morality of violent boys often appears as primitive and "truncated" (usually Level 1 in Kohlberg's scheme). It is primitive because it reflects the lessons they have learned from their experiences in the world.

ADOLESCENT MELODRAMA HAS MORAL IMPLICATIONS

As children pass into adolescence they are particularly vulnerable to melodrama and sentimentality. This finds benign expression in their attraction to stories of doomed lovers. This is why so many adolescents saw the movie *Titanic* over and over again and why Shakespeare's *Romeo and Juliet* is a perennial favorite among teenagers. Thirty years ago when I taught in a junior high school, we took the entire ninth-grade class to see the Zeffirelli version. The tears flowed, even among the most delinquent kids in the class—in fact, *particularly* among the most delinquent kids in the class. And this melodramatic sentimentality can actually be a resource in dealing with children. More than one child therapist of my acquaintance has reported that they found their work with girls enhanced when they were able to make use of *Titanic* as a parable, as a reference point in discussing their client's own life. Boys like *Titanic*, too, but they are much more likely to find their parables in *Rambo*, *Blade*, *Boyz in the Hood*, *Terminator*, and *Dirty Harry*.

Impulsiveness and self-centered thinking are the other hallmarks of adolescence. Teenagers do act rashly, and they do see the world as if it revolved around them. By and large, they do believe, with Shakespeare, that "all the world's a stage." But teenagers more than adults tend to believe that they are always the star of the show. This is why teenagers find it nearly impossible to leave home for school in the morning without carefully considering their appearance. After all, *everyone* will be looking at them. Sociologist Erving Goffman identified this "imaginary audience" as an important influence in adolescent behavior. Most of the time, in most teenagers, this self-centeredness ranges from cute to exasperating, but when the script of the play in which the teenager is a star is a violent tragedy, people die. The lost boys are teenagers, but they are starring in a horror show while more fortunate teens are starring in situation comedies or championship games. Television shows and movies play a role in providing teenagers with the scenarios for their performances.

BOYS NEED PROTECTION AND MORAL TEACHING

Once youngsters get melodramatic moral ideas into their heads, they need the moderating influence of adults to bring them back to moral reality. Many American kids, troubled or healthy, don't receive that protection. As we saw in Chapter Four, there is a breakdown in childhood protection all around us, a breakdown that hits violent boys hardest because they are most in need of protection.

In some cases this breakdown takes the form of adults who care for kids by training them to shoot down living beings—albeit usually with the intention that they limit their shooting to animals. The breakdown also comes when adults saturate kids with vivid media images glorifying violence as the legitimate solution to all problems and provide them with point-and-shoot video games that desensitize them to the act of killing. It comes when adults fail to take seriously and respond effectively to early signs of trouble that often are quite dramatic—for example, threatening statements, revenge fantasies, and acts of cruelty to animals. And finally, the breakdown in childhood protection comes when adults leave children too much to their own devices—home alone, either literally or figuratively. All this leads to a breakdown of adult authority and greater reliance by kids on peer influences and the violent culture of the mass media, a recipe for moral retardation. When this happens to boys in general the result is sad, taking the form of alienation, aggression, and the obnoxiousness that we so commonly refer to as disrespect for one's elders. But, most dangerously, when it happens to vulnerable boys, it exposes them to a do-it-yourself morality. And when it occurs in the context of shame and existential crisis, killing becomes the right thing to do "on stage" for such a boy's imaginary audience, no matter how big a mistake it may be offstage, where the real-world consequences must be faced.

Moral development is the process through which children learn the rules of conduct in their society and learn to act upon these rules. But this learning must take place in the heart as well as in the head. Without adequate adult buffering and limit setting, the moral behavior of children is left in the hands of children themselves, where their own feelings and thoughts are the last line of defense.

What can adults do to protect boys from negative moral development and teach them good moral sense? Let me outline a few positive steps here (I return to this issue in more detail later, in Chapter Seven):

• First, adults can *stimulate the development of empathy*. To behave morally, children need to develop empathy, the ability to feel what others are feeling. Empathy helps them to connect abstract principles of morality with real-life situations and feelings. Without empathy there is always the danger that morality will become moralistic, a caricature of caring in which an individual's distorted perspective on what is right and wrong becomes a self-justifying rationale for violence. After the shooting stops, the fallacy of their moral reasoning often becomes clear to kids who kill, but by then it is too late.

• Second, adults can *protect boys from degrading, dehumanizing, and desensitizing images*. Go to almost any movie theater showing an R-rated film full of horrible violence and aggressive sexuality, and you can see young boys entering the theater. This exposure is a corrupting influence on the foundations of moral development.

• Third, adults can *stimulate and support the spiritual development of boys*. While going to a church or synagogue is no guarantee of receiving caring moral instruction designed to increase empathy, a boy's involvement in a nonpunitive religious institution does help. Psychologist Andrew Weaver at the University of Hawaii has reviewed the evidence linking religious and spiritual experience to adolescent behavior and development, and he has found that this experience does buffer children from the cultural and social poisons of modern life. It is important that the religious experience be nonpunitive, that is, that it put the message of love center stage.

I remember as a teenager reading something that the great humanitarian Albert Schweitzer wrote about morality. Schweitzer said that if a farmer is plowing his fields to raise food to feed his family and destroys ten thousand flowers, that's morally acceptable. But if on the way home he gratuitously destroys one flower, that's a moral crime. I think there is something very important in this idea, something that is critical to an understanding of the moral calculus of violent boys, whose imperatives of necessity are driven by very primitive forces because their basic emotional needs are so grievously unmet. Caring is the basis for expanding their moral circles.

EXPANDING THE MORAL CIRCLE THROUGH THE EXPERIENCE OF CARING

Over the months that I interviewed Malcolm, his moral calculus began to change concerning the pit bulls he used in the dogfights he staged for profit. When we started, there were very clear boundaries about which dogs were inside and which were outside his circle of caring. He didn't use all his pit bulls, he used only those he had included in his world of expediency. He held back the few that were his pets, including them in his circle of caring. The change was this: after five months of our conversations, Malcolm volunteered the information that he had decided he could no longer put *any* of his dogs in the ring and was giving them up. He had opened up to the emotional meaning of his relationship with the dogs. Nevertheless, he was ambivalent about this course of action: on the one hand, he sounded proud of himself for making this decision, but he was sad about giving up the money and the status that came with his position as owner of the fighting dogs.

In my own life I have undergone a similar development. As I began to explore the links between animal abuse and child abuse, I found myself befriending a bird, a lizard, and a rat, adding them to my circle of caring, which already included a dog and a cat. Eventually I had to give up my childhood hobby of fishing—I became morally incapable of it (though I miss it sometimes). That same expanding circle of caring moved me toward vegetarianism. I do occasionally miss veal and hamburgers. Sometimes morality is inconvenient.

But where does caring stop? Violent boys experience the world as a dangerous place, often because they face physical threats, but always because they feel psychologically beleaguered. Can they afford to expand their circles of caring beyond what they bring with them into adolescence? For some, the dangers of expansion are physical: on the mean streets of the most socially poisoned environments, those who care may appear weak and thus invite exploitation. The same is true of life in a conventional prison. The boys speak of this often, when given a chance.

Sixteen-year-old Arnell gives me a short course in how to act on the street and in the prison beyond the privacy of the interview room. He demonstrates how to walk tough, how to look tough, and how to talk tough. "You take any crap from anyone," he says, "and you get marked as a pussy. Know what I mean? And if you get marked as a pussy, your life is hell. Man, you could get to a point where you rather die than live that way."

How do the ethics of survival and the circle of caring negotiate a settlement? For some boys the danger is purely psychological. They feel so very vulnerable because of rejection and shame that they come to fear anything that lowers their guard. They may feel they cannot afford the risk of stretching, of reaching beyond what survival ethics demand. It is their psychological vulnerability that keeps them at Kohlberg's Level 1.

All of us operate in two moral systems: one set of ethical principles for the people we consider insiders, a second set for outsiders. But troubled, violence-prone boys differ from most of us in how they decide who is inside and who is outside the circle, in where they draw the line. Where they draw the line is a matter of personal history and circumstances as much as, or perhaps more than, it is a matter of choice. Incarcerated boys often remark that when they were on the streets, they lived to survive and behaved accordingly but that now they are (safely) institutionalized, they can afford to consider other moral options. They may find it scary to switch moral systems, because doing so requires that they have trust and faith. Though often in short supply, neither is totally absent. Building trust and faith in the first place is the foundation for preventing youth violence. Finding ways to nurture it in boys who have already killed is the key to their moral rehabilitation.

Now that we understand the pathways that lead a boy to lethal violence, we can discuss with some assurance the kinds of programs and policies we will need to prevent boys from becoming violent and for reclaiming and redirecting those who have already stood over a victim, weapon in hand. The task of Part Two of this book is to explore ways of preventing youth violence and rehabilitating the perpetrators when prevention fails.

Part Two

WHAT BOYS NEED

Amazing grace, how sweet the sound,
That saved a wretch like me.
I once was lost,
But now am found,
Was blind but now I see.

—Shaker hymn

THE POWER OF SPIRITUAL, PSYCHOLOGICAL, AND SOCIAL ANCHORS

ANCHORS IN A STORMY SEA

As a little boy, I was a terror. While my *behavior* was under control by the time I was ten, my thoughts and feelings took a lot longer to tame. Few people were aware of these feelings, because I kept them to myself and my outward behavior was exemplary. Despite outward appearances of being organized and responsible in doing my homework, I was impulsive. Despite fitting in and being a good citizen at school, I was prone to fits of intense rage. As do many boys, I had grandiose thoughts about my powers and rights, coupled with dark doubts about myself.

At age twelve, I would sometimes ride my bicycle around other people's neighborhoods imagining what it would be like to commit a perfect crime, perhaps a murder (much like the main character in Dostoyevsky's novel *Crime and Punishment*). But what I still lacked in inner controls and emotional resources was more than made up for by my talents and abilities and the social environment I inhabited: a world filled with people who cared for me, with opportunities to become involved in positive activities at school and in the community, and with cultural messages of stability and moral responsibility. And I believed in God. In other words, while I was still living with a stormy sea inside, I was solidly anchored.

We can save our sons, even our temperamentally vulnerable sons, from turning violent by connecting them to positive values and embedding them in positive relationships. These values and relationships help boys compensate for early experiences of emotional deprivation and trauma and protect them from the influences of social toxicity, negative peer groups, mass media violence, and the crass materialism of our culture. Understanding these spiritual, psychological, and social anchors provides the basis for programs and policies to claim boys before they are lost. And these same positive influences help us understand what can be done to reclaim boys after they commit violent crimes and are incarcerated.

We can find such anchors for boys in many places. We find spiritual anchors in organized religion and in other institutions of the soul that connect children and teenagers to the deeper meanings of life and provide solid answers to the existential questions, Who am I? and What is the meaning of life?

The psychological anchors, which underlie resilience in children and youth, include strong attachment (having someone who is crazy about you), the capacity to actively respond to events rather than passively react to them, intellectual ability, authentic self-esteem, constructive coping strategies, and an ability to seek out social support from outside the family. And they include efforts to combine traditionally masculine traits with traditionally feminine attributes (a combination termed "androgyny").

The social anchors are to be found in those elements of social health in families, schools, and communities that stand as a counterweight to social toxicity. One important anchor is the adults who commit themselves unconditionally to meeting the developmental needs of kids. Social health comes from stability, security, affirmation, time for socialization, economic equality, a good home for the spirit, a whole community, and democratic public institutions that protect human rights. But it all starts with basic hope for the future.

LIVING IN THE MOMENT FOR THE FUTURE

One of the paradoxes of childhood is that while children live in the present, they are required to do things that build a foundation for the future. Living a good life in each present moment depends in part upon living with an eye to the future. This comes naturally to children unless they face some challenge that leads them to question their future existence. In 1937, my mother was a ten-year-old girl growing up in a working-class neighborhood of London in the midst of a diphtheria epidemic. She recalls that the reality of death hit her hard when a close friend of hers died of the dreaded disease. She and her healthy friends gathered soberly to consider what this death meant for them. "I wonder if I will live to 1950!" she remembers crying out to her friends. Unexpected and premature death shakes kids' confidence in the future. Those who have an extreme lack of confidence in the future, terminal thinking, feel that the future is over for them.

A psychiatrist colleague of mine, who provides mental health services to troubled adolescents, shared a sad but fascinating story that illustrates the importance of having a future orientation. One Monday morning she received a call from a friend telling her that she had just come from the doctor and that he had diagnosed her with a fast-acting cancer that likely would kill her within six months. "You know what I am doing today?" she asked my colleague. "I am going to the bank, and I'm withdrawing all my money. And this afternoon I am going out to buy a sports car and mink coat and devote my remaining time to indulging myself and nothing else. After all, what am I saving for?" Her comment provides sad testimony to the role of trauma in dislodging a person's sense of the future. Later that day, my colleague was still thinking about her friend's phone call when one of her patients showed up for his regular appointment. A seventeen-year-old drug dealer, he was driving a sports car and wearing a mink coat. It struck her that this young man had the same terminal thinking as her terminally ill friend and the same response—short-term materialistic striving. The irony was not lost on her.

But the story does not end here. At a recent lecture to a professional criminal justice group, I mentioned this very example of terminal thinking. As I recounted the cancer patient's response to her diagnosis—her decision to use her life savings to buy a sports car and a mink coat—my eyes fell upon an old friend in the audience. He, too, has inoperable cancer and is within half a year of death. He knows it, and yet he is not rushing out to buy a sports car or a mink coat. Instead, he has used some of his last precious time on this planet to organize the meeting I was addressing.

Why? Because he cares about kids, because he wants to leave behind something more than possessions or bank accounts, and because, in short, he is in touch with his soul.

Right there in front of me was a shining example of what psychoanalyst Erik Erikson called generativity, the human impulse to focus on the legacy we leave behind for future generations. Looking at my friend in the audience, I appreciated more than ever before the critical role that having a higher purpose plays in human development and saw how weak the reed that material affluence is when compared to generativity. Materialism cannot anchor boys, but a sense of meaningfulness rooted in higher purpose and a more enduring reality can.

The need to find positive anchors is a big issue for troubled and violent boys, and for all those adults who are responsible for their behavior. When we deal with teenage boys who are positively embedded in life, thriving, and grounded in parental acceptance, we easily take for granted their future orientation. They bubble with confidence about the future— their future and the future of their world. They look forward (sometimes impatiently) to a time when they will be adults, with all the privileges that come with that status. They do their homework, help with household chores, and take seriously advice about taking care of themselves. They think about what they will do and become after high school. They position themselves for relationships, knowing that at some point they will meet someone to love forever. Anchored in the future, these boys live in the present in a responsible way.

Those who work with boys who have a history of psychological and social impoverishment, the lost boys, come to expect a different attitude, a different orientation toward the future. Many of these boys come to prison with a foreshortened sense of the future, with terminal thinking. But in every challenge there is an opportunity, and the experience of prison provides some violent boys with an extraordinary opportunity to reexamine their lives. Some incarcerated boys begin to see that having survived offers them a new chance at living and the beginning of wisdom. "If I hadn't been arrested and sent here, I would be dead by now. Being in prison is the pits, man, but it's better than being dead," says Alfred.

Like the epidemic of youth violence itself, problems with future orientation are not limited to kids who live in inner-city war zones or who are in prison. A 1992 Harris survey of sixth-to-twelfth-graders living in cities across the country found that 35 percent said they worried that they will not live to old age because they fear they will be shot.

MEANING IS WHAT MATTERS

If a boy has a strong sense of future orientation, the present tends to take care of itself: I do what I need to do today to prepare for the good things available to me in the years to come. Meaningfulness is implicit in the routines of day-to-day life. But boys whose future is far from secure need a strong explicit sense of meaningfulness to counterbalance that threat.

Early in the twentieth century, psychoanalyst Carl Jung wrote that "neurosis must be understood as the suffering of a human being who has not discovered what life means for him." This may help explain why some troubled boys try to change their lives after fathering a child. A child can be an anchor to help a boy discover what life means for him. I see this when I talk with young men facing the death penalty. Often they are tempted to accept death if the only alternative is life imprisonment. What usually dissuades a young man from this choice is the prospect of not being around for his children, even if "being around" means being locked up for the rest of his life.

Psychologist Viktor Frankl survived Nazi concentration camps and out of that experience came his classic work *Man's Search for Meaning*. More recently, University of Chicago psychologist Bert Cohler wrote that having a coherent and *meaningful* account of one's life is one of the crucial factors predicting life success in the face of adversity. The views of Jung, Frankl, and Cohler are part of a long and distinguished tradition in psychology and psychoanalysis that maintains that the foundation for feeling good about oneself, thinking clearly about the world, and leading a morally responsible life is having a purpose in life that provides a strong sense of meaningfulness. And this is all the more true when the going gets tough.

Kids feel a sense of purposefulness when they are rooted in a world that makes sense. It makes sense to follow the rules if you feel the authority that makes the rules has your interests at heart. It makes sense to respect your elders if you see them as powerful, well-intentioned, in charge of the world in which you live, and benevolent toward you. It makes sense to work hard if you see hard work rewarded. It makes sense to be loving if you know what it feels like to be loved. And it makes sense to take care of others if you know that you and the people you care for are all connected to a positive spiritual order within the world.

But a boy who is cut off from this feeling of belonging to a world that makes sense is set adrift. He lives in a world without purpose and faces a crisis of meaninglessness. As a result, he has no guides, no transcendent models for knowing what classical philosophy dating from Plato has always called "The Good." I see this crisis of meaninglessness in boys from all walks of life, from all classes and races, who have not yet found any meaningful anchors. What sense of purpose do they bring with them to high school, to the workplace, to jail? Often, it is simply to finish high school, to get out of their neighborhood, to get out of jail.

But none of these goals anchor them in the positive life of the larger society. Many rootless boys are instead led down a renegade pathway to lethal violence. Many incarcerated boys are doubly at risk because they have already demonstrated resistance to prevention programs that might offer the very anchors they have gone without for so long. As we will see later, harnessing spiritual forces may be the key to reclaiming troubled boys even after they are established on the path of lethal violence. But first we need to understand how these forces play a role in anchoring boys in the first place.

SPIRITUAL ANCHORS

In the storm of his life, Dennis becomes a devout Christian, and it brings him peace and direction. Facing ten years of imprisonment, Kevin embraces Islam and finds in its teachings ways to deal with his anger and fear. Allan becomes a practicing Buddhist, and it brings him peace. Each of these boys was forced to look for something more than simple and superficial answers of his previous life.

What tools does a boy have to make sense of his life if he has no sense of being loved and appreciated? Without these feelings of affirmation, there is only biological reality as a basis for telling the story of one's life: "I am born. I live. I die." If one goes beyond this but only as far as material success, there are only two basic alternative narratives that describe the psychological quality of that life. One is "I am born. Have a nice day. Then I die." The other is "I am born. Life sucks. Then I die."

For many violent boys, life mostly sucks. Those are Tommy's exact words as he sits on death row for killing a police officer. I ask him, "What have you learned from life?" "Life sucks," is his answer. This comes from a violent boy who describes himself as "emotionally defenseless" because of his early experiences and the intense loneliness he feels every day. This core sense of meaninglessness is common enough in our society; many people feel that way in a socially toxic environment like ours. But when this feeling occurs in the life of a boy whose temperament and experiences put him at high risk for displaying violent behavior, it can become a fatal condition—for the boy and for everyone who comes in contact with him.

Spirituality and love can fill in the holes left in the story of a boy's life and help him develop both a strong positive sense of self and healthy limits, thus forestalling the need to compensate with grandiose posturing and deadly petulance. This is the story Andrew tells as he sits on death row for killing two gang rivals. Ten years have passed since the murders, and during that time Andrew has undergone an important transition while the wheels of the legal system turn slowly, processing his appeals: he has connected with the deep spirituality of Christianity. Andrew now wears a cross around his neck and a locket; in the locket are pictures of his two sons. "I live for them," he says, "and for God. All I ask now is the opportunity to live to see my boys grow to be men and for time to make my peace with eternity." Andrew's Christianity is a religion of love.

When it is grounded in spirituality and love, religion infuses life with purpose by connecting the ups and down of everyday life to something permanent and beyond the reach of day-to-day experiences. Of course, religion is not automatically the source of spirituality and love. For some lost boys, religion is just more of the same empty, punitive power assertion, shallow materialism, violence, and rejection they encounter at home. I hear this often in the accounts violent boys offer of their religious experiences. They speak of rote prayer, hypocritical sermonizing, and rationalizations for injustice and abuse and of the sheer irrelevance of churchgoing to their own inner life and need for purposefulness. Many lost boys grow up with their parents' contradictory impulses and activities: Michael's mother went to church twice a week and then came home and beat him; Conneel's father went to church every Sunday and then came home and beat Conneel's mother.

Religion can be much more than materialism and punitiveness, of course. Psychologist Lloyd Wright and his colleagues are among a growing number of researchers focusing on the role of religion and spirituality in helping adolescents and adults navigate through life. They find that an individual who believes that his life has a religious purpose has a source of spiritual support that buffers against depression. A sense of purpose is vital in countering depression, because as therapist Terrence Real found in his studies, covert depression in boys and men plays an important role in generating violence against self and others. In their research, Wright's group assessed the extent of their subjects' spiritual support by determining whether they attended church at least twice a month and agreed with the following statements: "Religion is especially important to me because it answers many questions about the meaning of my life" and "I try hard to carry my religion into my other dealings in life because my religious beliefs are what really lie behind my whole approach to life."

When spiritually grounded, and supportive rather than punitive, religion can make a big difference, particularly in adolescence. This is the conclusion of a group of psychologists and other mental health professionals organized by pastoral counselor and psychologist Andrew Weaver. Weaver's group reviewed research in major research journals dealing with adolescent issues and found many studies documenting the fact that spirituality (in the form of nonpunitive religion) exerts an anchoring effect on kids. These effects include the following:

• *Reduced suicide:* Teenagers who are involved in religious institutions are less likely to attempt suicide and less likely to think about doing so.

• *Less depression:* Teenagers who are involved in religious institutions and feel they experience a high level of support for their spirituality report less depression overall and are less likely to experience depression that is at a clinically significant level when they are depressed.

• *Less casual sex:* Teenagers involved in religious institutions are less likely to favor casual sex and more likely to wait longer before they become sexually active.

• *Better response to trauma:* Traumatized teens involved in religious institutions feel more social support, are more likely to find meaning in the traumatic event, and experience lower distress and faster recovery than other teens.

• *Less substance abuse:* Teenagers involved in religious institutions and beliefs are less likely to use drugs and alcohol.

TROUBLED BOYS NEED MORE THAN A TRIP TO THE MALL

Troubled boys in today's America are likely to face the double whammy of both terminal thinking and a crisis of purposefulness. A boy who loses touch with himself as a participant in the future but who retains a sense of purposefulness of life can continue to lead a normal life in society. A boy who believes in his future can get through periods when he loses sight of his purposes. His alienation is counterbalanced by his hope. But with neither hope nor a sense of purpose, troubled boys are psychologically adrift and are prone to seek any harbor in their storm of alienation and fear. These are the boys who are drawn to nihilism, Satanism, and all the other isms of the dark side.

The materialism of American culture does little to sustain children in times of crisis. Leather running shoes, jewelry, and designer clothes are not enough. The inherent weakness of superficial materialism may not be apparent when things are going well. But during challenging times the spiritual emptiness of shallow materialism is exposed for what it is, and crisis ensues. Violent boys who turn to robbery to feed their addiction to materialism load up their lives with fancy clothes, expensive shoes, cars, and jewelry. But it doesn't work. They are still in deep emotional trouble, and trauma intensifies this crisis.

Psychiatrist Bessel van der Kolk asks incoming psychiatric patients, "Have you given up all hope of finding meaning in your life?" I have asked this question of thousands of individuals in my lectures, and I find that about one in a hundred people responds yes. I encourage honest answers by asking the entire audience to close their eyes while people respond by raising their hands.

What happens when van der Kolk asks this question of those who have experienced trauma? Among those who experienced major trauma prior to age five, 74 percent answer yes. Among those who experienced major trauma after age twenty the figure is only 10 percent. Why is the experience of trauma associated with a loss of meaningfulness, and why is the relationship so strong for children? While trauma represent an enormous challenge to any individual's understanding of the meaning and purpose of life, the crisis is particularly difficult for children.

If the crisis of meaning and purpose inherent in the experience of trauma is not acknowledged and resolved, it can result in psychological and physiological symptoms that can become debilitating, often to the point of requiring psychiatric care. Remember that van der Kolk asked this question of people who, although having trouble just getting through the day (or night), managed to find their way to his psychiatric clinic for professional help. By and large, lost boys are traumatized boys. They do many things in a failing attempt to cope with their trauma, but rarely do they have the resources or knowledge to cope effectively and in a socially acceptable way. They take drugs. They engage in violence. They steal. They gorge themselves on sex. They join gangs and cults. And when no one is watching or listening to them, they suck their thumbs and cry themselves to sleep.

Most people who have experienced trauma and who may even have the symptoms of Posttraumatic Stress Disorder (PTSD) are able to cope without resorting to violence, either self-inflicted or against others. Why? The answer lies in the fact that trauma can produce two kinds of wounds. The first are the psychological and emotional problems mental health professionals know as PTSD, the package of symptoms that includes heightened sensitivity to events that mimic the traumatic situation, emotional numbing, and a tendency to relive the traumatic event. But the second traumatic wound is philosophical in that it poses a threat to a person's sense of the meaningfulness of life. I think van der Kolk's results support the idea that if one can heal from or avoid the second wound, the wound to meaningfulness, one can likely deal with the first wound, which is more narrowly psychological.

An understanding of the relation of a sense of meaninglessness to age at which trauma is experienced is an important contribution to our efforts to understand and help troubled and violent boys. Psychologists know that there are critical periods in the growth of many human attributes, when positive experiences strongly promote development and negative experiences strongly impede it. This is also true of the child's sense that the world is meaningful. These structures of meaning, upon which children and youth depend to make sense of the world in a positive way, are most efficiently and effectively established in early childhood.

Trauma is a challenge to a child's sense of meaningfulness coupled with the experience of overwhelming feelings of terror. Dealing with this two-part assault on the psyche is greatest for the youngest victims, whose framework of meaningfulness and capacity for dealing with feelings of terror are not well developed. Psychologists Jonathan Davidson and Rebecca Smith report that when faced with potentially traumatic experiences, children under the age of ten are three times more likely than teenagers and adults to develop PTSD—56 percent versus 18 percent.

COPING WITH TRAUMA: THE ULTIMATE RESILIENCE LIES IN THE SPIRITUAL LIFE

We have seen how spiritual anchors lead to a sense of purpose, to meaningfulness, and to future orientation where there might otherwise be purposelessness, meaninglessness, and terminal thinking. Psychiatrist Robert Coles finds these philosophical developments in the experience of children who are resilient in the face of terminal illness. Like my friend who used his last months organizing a conference on juvenile justice, some of the kids Coles interviewed confronted their immortality with a sense that every moment is precious and purposeful. They met the challenge though religious belief grounded in spirituality and through deep relationships with the people around them. They combined spiritual with psychological and social anchors.

When faced with the prospect of death or prolonged isolation or imprisonment, kids need enduring and deep relationships, with God and with human beings who can help ground them. With such a relationship in place, be it faith in God or an unshakable sense of warmth, stability, and affirmation from people in his life, a kid can hold on to a sense of purposefulness, as did Dennis, who was serving time in prison:

> Since I've been in here, in a sense I have taken up a Biblical, spiritual belief. I believe in . . . in Jesus Christ and in . . . in God. And I count on God to help me through this thing. I shared that with my grandparents, that I've become a Christian, and that I'd accepted Jesus Christ into my life, that I believe in the power of the Holy Spirit. And my grandparents, they liked that. My grandma was supposedly a Catholic; my grandfather was supposedly a Christian. [Laughs] So I told them about myself, and

they were happy. It took me a while to get to that, it took me a while. I had fear of God, 'cause I always thought he was somebody who punished, not somebody who loves and cares, as you read in the Bible. That's why I was praying for God to keep his hand in my case and have people come and help me. And he did.

As we shall see in Chapter Eight, the impulse to look for something deeper and bigger can be the starting point for prevention and early intervention, before boys get into big trouble, and for rehabilitation, after they do.

SPIRITUAL ANSWERS TO THE CHALLENGE OF BEING A MAN

As Terrence Real points out in his book *I Don't Want to Talk About It*, being a boy is inherently traumatic in our culture. It requires that a boy cut himself off from the sources of softness, comfort, intimacy, expressiveness, and positive dependency and "be a man." One important function of religion and spirituality for troubled and violent boys is to help them cope with the challenging issues of life to which they have fallen prey.

While most violent boys have had to cope with major traumas in their lives—such as witnessing or being the victim of violence at home or in the community or encountering severe rejection—most of the available research on the positive role of religion in the lives of children and teenagers deals with the more common but less severe traumas and challenges of growing up in America, such as divorce. Nonetheless, this research does shed light on the role of spiritual anchors. For example, psychologist Joianne Shortz has looked at the way adolescents cope with parental divorce. She found that spiritually based coping activities, such as "trusting God for protection and turning to him for guidance," were most significantly related to positive coping behaviors. These included keeping a "positive focus" on life and making connection with "interpersonal support." When life threatens to wash a boy away into the maelstrom of violence, spirituality can provide the needed rock of ages. Stephen tells me he hopes God will forgive his mother for what she did to him, and that he also hopes God will forgive his violent sins.

When a boy's need for something enduring and good is deeply violated, he may seek out a negative universe on the grounds that anything is better than nothing. John Douglas and Mark Olshaker find that this deep violation is one of the origins of the extreme behavior exhibited by serial killers; they believe that brutal child abuse leads to a descent into evil to provide *some* structure of meaning for the child. Deep violation also has implications for identity. Everyone needs to be someone. When a boy sees no positive alternatives available to him, he may opt for the identity of the dark side. This explains the research, reported in Chapter Five, indicating that Satanism often finds a home among lost boys.

Many of the boys and men I know found the starting point for that path back from violence through spiritual exploration. Each replaced the ugliness in his life with spiritual beauty. Each of these individuals began seeking answers to the psychological challenges of traumatic experiences in human development. Their path led to and through the unconscious to the spiritual, and ultimately to the light of spiritual freedom.

As we shall see in Chapter Eight, the success of spiritual exploration in the lives of lost boys is one reason why spiritual literacy should be a part of educational programs for boys at risk. Once this spiritual foundation is in place, *then* educational programs, counseling, vocational experiences, and regular psychotherapy can help a boy move to a positive path in his life. Psychotherapist Ronnie Bulof-Janoff puts it this way, based on her work with trauma survivors: "It may seem remarkable, yet it is not unusual for survivors, over time, to wholly reevaluate their traumatic experience by altering the positive value and meaningfulness of the event itself. The victimization certainly would not have been chosen, but it is ultimately seen by many as a powerful, even to some extent worthwhile, teacher of life's most important lessons." Until they undergo spiritual transformation, violent boys cannot learn these lessons and are stuck in their self-defeating patterns of behavior and belief.

PSYCHOLOGICAL ANCHORS: RESILIENCE

Psychologists call the ability to bounce back from crisis and overcome stress and injury *resilience*. The ultimate fate of vulnerable young boys is very much wrapped up in issues of resilience. Can they overcome being rejected and abused, abandoned and terrorized? Can kids bounce back from the threats they face in school and in the community? Can they redirect their energies away from the patterns of thinking and acting that lead to Conduct Disorder? Can they rise up to meet life's challenges without degenerating into violence against others or themselves?

Everyone knows someone whose life is a testament to resilience. A close friend of mine overcame multiple forms of abuse and deprivation in childhood to become a brilliant, caring psychologist and researcher who deals with abused children. The concept of resilience rests on the research finding that while there is a correlation between specific negative experiences and specific negative outcomes, in most situations the majority of children and youth do *not* display that negative outcome. Violent boys are not part of this majority. They face an accumulation of negative experiences and their temperaments and their early experiences deprive them of crucial psychological resilience resources. What is more, we must always remember that studies and assessments that only focus on external behavior and accomplishments may obscure the costs of negative experiences to the individual's emotional well-being.

True, research shows that about one-third of kids who display chronic bad behavior and aggression at age ten go on to become chronic violent juvenile offenders. But a majority of these ten-year-olds face many other difficulties, but short of criminal behavior, in later life, difficulties of equal importance in human terms. My friend who deals with abused children has managed to avoid succumbing to the risk of *social* failure, as defined by poverty and criminality, but she experiences real harm from her diminished capacity for successful intimate relationships (three divorces and two children she never sees). Thus, even apparent social success—performing well in the job market, avoiding criminal activity, creating a family—is not the whole story. Success on the outside may obscure damage on the inside.

Julio, the young Cornell student I mentioned in Chapter One, triumphed over the odds to move from the inner city to the Ivy League. He is a model of resilience to the extent that he turned away from bad behavior and aggression and became an academic success story. But Julio carries survivor's guilt and traumatic symptoms that plague him to this day. The inner life of individuals who overcome pernicious environments may be fraught with damage to their self-worth and to their capacity for intimacy. Resilient in social terms, these individuals are severely wounded souls.

This observation of external success coupled with internal damage may parallel what has long been evident in comparing the resilience of boys versus girls. Boys who succumb to the accumulation of risk factors in their life are prone to act out with explicit antisocial behavior, such as violent juvenile delinquency, thereby grabbing the attention and concern of adults around them. Girls, on the other hand, are more likely to respond with internalized problems, such as eating disorders, overt depression, and self-destructive behavior. Does this mean girls are more resilient than boys? A simple accounting of social success variables might lead us to think so. However, if we take into account the full range of manifestations of harm, we can see that such an answer would be wrong. At-risk kids adapt—for better *and* worse. Even when they succeed socially, they still need psychological and spiritual anchors.

Resiliency is more than outside success, more than graduating from high school, staying out of jail, holding a job. It also means developing a positive sense of self, a capacity for intimacy, and a feeling that life is meaningful. Researchers find many conditions and characteristics that promote in children the resilience to which this expanded concept refers. I see six of these characteristics and conditions that are directly relevant to saving boys from a life of violence. Just as religion is the key to spiritual anchors, these factors are critical to psychological anchors. As you read on, think about the boys you know intimately or those in your neighborhood or in your child's school. How many of them seem to be missing one or more of these key psychological anchors?

Stable Positive Emotional Relationships: Someone Who Loves Me

The first resilience factor is a stable positive emotional relationship with at least one person, someone absolutely committed to the child and to whom the child feels a strong positive attachment. This alone injects purpose into young lives. In March of 1997, I was on a panel in New York City with a group of high-risk inner-city teenagers. Several of the girls said that having a baby was the thing that turned around their lives—or, rather, what motivated them to turn their lives around. Having a baby meant there was someone who was crazy about them; motherhood brought out the best in them by giving some purpose to a life that had previously been experienced as meaningless.

I've seen the same result in some of the boys I have worked with in prison. When Conneel talks about the future, he keeps coming back to his son's love and what he can do to straighten out his life so he can be there for his sixteen-month-old son. After reflecting on his own childhood, Conneel sees that there was no one there who loved him absolutely. Now, with the benefit of reflection forced upon him by his time in prison, he hopes to prevent in the next generation the absence of love he himself experienced as a young child. He says, "The thing that keeps me going, sometimes it's the only thing, is my son. I feel if I can show him a better way than I took, my life will be worth something. I don't want him to be alone the way I was. I want to be there for him, like my father wasn't there for me." There is hope here, this goal of providing love to a child is an anchor, even for a boy who has suffered from its absence in his own life.

A positive and stable emotional relationship provides a concrete image for a child. It shows that child that the world is grounded and rooted in being loved, and therefore in being lovable. Being the center of someone's universe is hard to beat as a resilience factor. And the greater the number of people who feel that way about a child, the better it is for that child. I grew up knowing that my Italian grandfather was buried with a picture of me in his hands. I knew that my mother thought the sun rose and set around me. These things sustained me.

The Ability to Actively Cope with Stress

The second condition for resilience is the ability to actively cope with stress, rather than just reacting to it. Some kids seem to have this drive to master their environment, to make it meet their needs. Others are dominated by their social environment, conforming to what it offers rather than creating it anew. Troubled, violence-prone boys usually present a mixed picture. They combine active and passive efforts to deal with stress. On the one hand, they are survivors—and oftentimes are very aware of this. Dennis carries with him at all times an index card with the names of his friends who are dead. On the other hand, violent and troubled boys often have a fatalism about them, a dread that things are beyond their control.

Are violent boys passive or active? Except for their violence, when we scratch the surface and dig more deeply into their lives, we discover that these boys are often quite passive when it comes to interpreting their place in the world. As many of them see it, they are simply victims of "the system." This is one reason so much of the programming designed to rehabilitate them focuses on issues of personal responsibility. It's easy to see why those who design programs for violent boys zoom in on this issue: the boys tend to see the faults around them (e.g., they often speak of how they fell in with "bad company" when they were youngsters); they speak of the injustices they have experienced, the humiliations they have endured; and their accounts are usually in the passive voice ("This was done to me"; "I was affected by that"). All these are danger signals.

Active coping means finding a way to make something positive out of life, for example, by developing special talents and skills or simply by working extra hard at being a good person worthy of public praise and reward. Resilient kids find positive ways to cope with difficult situations; confused, troubled boys find other, less positive, ways of responding; and lost boys use violence in an attempt to make the world meet their needs.

As second-born children with high-achieving, popular older sisters, Kip Kinkel and Andrew Wurst faced the challenge of getting the attention of their parents and their peers. They may have resorted to violence as a way to get the attention they craved. This is common to violent, troubled boys, just as active, positive coping is the hallmark of resilient youth. Where does this response come from? Each case is different, of course, but we find the roots of this resort to violence in early temperament and in what boys learn from their encounters with the world in their early years.

Intelligence

The third foundation for resilience is intelligence. What seems to matter most is that a boy test at least at an average level of academic intelligence. While IQ tests are never the whole story when it comes to intelligence, particularly for kids who have not had good access to education, they do tell part of the story. When combined with other assessments of a boy's reasoning skill and problem-solving ability, measures of intelligence reveal a child's capacity to think about complex realities and make sense of the world.

Kids who are substantially below average on broadly based assessments of intellectual ability face a disadvantage in sorting things out. They make mistakes in assessing causes and consequences. It is as if they face life's challenges with one hand tied behind their back. Many, but not all, troubled and violent boys reveal these limitations. But the apparent intellectual deficits of violent boys can be deceiving. I was struck by the slow, simplistic answers James gave to my questions during our interviews, and yet he won all the awards for mathematics achievement in the prison school. Antoine flunked out of high school, but he impressed me with his analyses of the books I brought him.

We must be careful to avoid jumping to conclusions about lost boys' intellectual capacity on the basis of their dumb behavior and their academic difficulties. For some of them, the biggest issue is a lack of emotional intelligence, as Daniel Goleman calls it. Indeed, one reason many academically delayed kids *don't* get into trouble is that they have adequate emotional and social intelligence and are therefore able to deal with people effectively. The inability to be emotionally smart, a kind of emotional retardation, and the inability to read nonverbal information effectively is what psychologists Stephen Nowicki and Marshal Duke call "dyssemia" in their book *Helping the Child Who Doesn't Fit In*.

While resilient boys find the positive in the social environment around them, other boys often seem to have an acute ability to pick up only negative emotional signals—to detect threat, fear, and anger. Thus, they tend to see every glass as being half empty. Sometimes this apparent lack of integration is temperamental. But more often we can trace these deficiencies to what is learned from being maltreated as we saw in Chapter Four. And, as psychiatrist Dorothy Otnow-Lewis reports in her book *Guilty by Reason of Insanity*, there may be a neurological basis too. Many of the most violent boys in prison have experienced trauma to their brains, trauma in the form of blows to the head, falls, car accidents, and illnesses that diminish their capacity to think clearly. Otnow-Lewis reports that the kind of brain damage evident in some boys is the kind that leads to grave difficulties in connecting emotions and impulses with the parts of the brain that control thinking and reasoning. These deficits may play a role in their inability to recognize emotional cues effectively, for example, in being hypervigilant to negative cues and oblivious to positive cues.

There is a big difference between resilience and survival. The former implies an ability to maintain healthy functioning or at least return to healthy functioning in the wake of threat or crisis. The latter subsumes distorted development and negative behavior. Lost boys survive, but they do not exhibit resilience as I am defining that term.

In addition to their violent behavior, lost boys often show other signs of what it has cost them to survive: diminished enjoyment of life, emotional disabilities, and physical impairment. Vincent survived, but he finds little meaning in life and experiences his day-to-day life as profoundly boring. Darnell cannot respond to any emotion beyond anger. Stephen's back is so deeply scarred he refuses to take his shirt off, and his psyche carries the scars of the humiliation he ran away from home to escape. Dennis accepted the risk of life on the streets as preferable to the sexual abuse he experienced at home.

Authentic Self-Esteem

The fourth condition underlying resilience is the possession of authentic self-esteem, a sense a person has about his own intrinsic value. Authentic self-esteem gives boys positive psychological momentum; with it a boy can deal with the ups and downs of life without panicking or concluding that each down signals impending disaster and rejection. So many boys seem to lack self-esteem that psychotherapist Terrence Real has identified it as one of the major sources of covert depression in males.

The competitiveness of American life means there are always more losers than winners. All boys eventually must experience being on the losing end of some competition, be it at school, on the playground, on the athletic field, or on the street. If a boy does not have internal reservoirs of authentic self-esteem, he is in deep trouble once this happens. One response to feeling like a loser is to mask the feelings of failure and rejection and put forward in their place self-aggrandizing behavior. What lies behind the bravado, the posturing, and the macho presentation of manhood so common to violent boys is doubt, confusion, and a negative definition of self. So much of what violent boys do seems designed to compensate for emptiness, to divert attention from the holes inside, from the fear of failure common to the lost boys.

Barry Loukaitis, the fourteen-year-old who shot two students and a teacher in Moses Lake, Washington, in 1996 exemplifies this. He modeled himself on the young murderer in Oliver Stone's film *Natural Born Killers* and told friends he thought it would be "pretty cool" to go on a killing spree. In Jonesboro, Arkansas, Mitchell Johnson made up stories of being in a gang and adopted a threatening demeanor when he could get away with it. One adult who knew him said, "He swore he was with the Bloods, wore red all the time, and talked about killing animals. He was always threatening and getting into fights." Behind this bravado is something else: profound doubts about oneself and one's place in the world. When I first ask Malcolm about being afraid, he says, "I'm not afraid." Week after week we return to this topic; I ask the question again every time he tells me of another harrowing experience. Finally, he admits that he has been "posturing." "I talk so much to hide my fear," he says.

Positive Social Support from Persons Outside the Family

The fifth foundation for resilience is social support from persons or institutions outside the family. Social support has at least two distinct dimensions. The first is its role in simply making the individual feel connected to people beyond the confines of the family. The second is its role in promoting prosocial behavior, in representing the core values of the community and, more broadly, society. Kids who live in abusive families within dysfunctional communities are in double jeopardy. They may have nowhere to turn to receive positive messages about themselves and learn about mainstream values. And schools—potentially the one place to provide the warm, firm embrace the child needs—often are part of the problem. All too often, they reject rather than accept difficult children, in effect pushing them deeper into trouble.

Emotionally needy boys who are rejected by teachers and parents are prime targets for antisocial older youth and adults. These negative role models recruit vulnerable boys, and they exchange self-affirmation for loyalty to the antisocial cause. Many violent and troubled boys have stories of how they were befriended by older boys who accepted them in return for their involvement in criminal enterprises.

When I asked Stephen about his motivation for joining a gang, he said, "They were like a family, but a hell of a lot better than the family I had." Luke Woodham was offered membership in a Satanic peer group that promoted violence, alienation, and experimentation with torturing animals. Malcolm was offered a gun at age ten "for protection" by his older brother's twenty-one-year-old best friend. Dennis was recruited for a robbery ring at age nine by the twenty-three-year-old ringleader. Conneel, at age nine, was offered fifty dollars to be a look out for a twenty-five-year-old drug dealer.

Androgyny

A sixth foundation for resilience lies in a person's ability to incorporate both traditionally feminine and traditionally masculine characteristics, what psychologists call androgyny. It is well understood in breeding plants and domestic animals that combining different strains and bloodlines produces better offspring and results in what biologists call "hybrid vigor." The same can be said for children when it comes to social development. Believing in narrowly sex-typed views of what a man is and can do and what a woman is and can do makes boys vulnerable.

Tommy and I are discussing the prison's anger management and conflict resolution program. "What do you think of it?" I ask. "It's okay," he replies. "Does it make sense to you?" I ask. "Sure," he responds. "But could you use it on the outside in the world?" "Not really," he responds. "Maybe if you were a girl. But guys are different. A man's got to do what a man's got to do." Tommy is trapped in a narrow definition of masculinity. Some of his friends have died from it, but he sees no options beyond more of the same: "A man's got to do what a man's got to do."

Psychologist Emmy Werner's research reveals that in cultures all over the world, including ours, androgyny is adaptive and thus an element in resilience. The more successfully people incorporate both traditionally masculine and traditionally feminine attributes, the more likely they are to master the situations they face. This is often a big hurdle for boys in general, but particularly for boys who live in a very macho world that rejects as second class everything that is feminine.

Where and how do boys learn what it means to be a man? They seem to learn it all too often from the mass media and from the most visible males in their community, particularly their peers. Boys' friends are the arbitrators of what is masculine and what is feminine, so resilience among the boys in a community depends upon changing macho attitudes among male peer groups and broadening their concept of what a real man is and does. This takes involving caring real men in the lives of boys, as individuals and as members of a group.

One aspect of traditional masculinity is often a sentimental view of women in the abstract: "I honor my woman." But this sentimentality casts women in a subordinate role, dependent upon masculine goodwill to keep the peace. It often translates into disdain and disrespect for women in practice. Conneel says to be a man means to take care of "your women," but he does admit that he has hit his girlfriend a few times.

SOCIAL ANCHORS IN A HEALTHY COMMUNITY

The six psychological anchors of resilience complement the core function of spiritual anchors and are important in generating ideas for programs to save boys before they become troubled and violent. But there can be still other anchors in the lives of boys. These are the social anchors, the characteristics of a healthy community that holds and protects boys as they grow.

How do we measure social health? Some researchers string together measures of the social environment that tap the presence or absence of specific social problems and resources. For instance, Fordham University's Institute for Social Policy produces an Index of Social Health for the United States that is based on measures of sixteen factors, including infant mortality, teenage suicide, school dropout, drug abuse, homicide, food stamp use, unemployment, traffic deaths, and poverty among the elderly. The index ranges between 0 and 100, with 100 being defined as the most socially healthy. After increasing during the 1950s and 1960s, the index reported a decline from 1970 to 1992: from 74 to 41. This means that the overall well-being of our society has decreased significantly. Other studies have compiled lists of social assets and liabilities.

All these measures are useful, but I would add some measure for the role of spirituality in an assessment of a community's health. A study by sociologists Dale Blyth and Nancy Leffert measured community health by the relative absence of sixteen problem behaviors among youth, including tobacco use, alcohol use, illicit drug use, sexual activity, depression, suicide, antisocial problems, and school problems. They found social support for religion and spirituality to be one of the defining characteristics of a healthy community. Communities with a majority of high school students attending religious services at least once a month were twice as likely to be among the communities with the fewest problem behaviors among youth than were communities in which a majority of kids did not participate in religious experiences.

Stability

Children are fundamentally conservative. They thrive in situations of stability. Whether it is continuity in child care arrangements, family residence, or day-to-day routine, children need stability. What were the social environments like in which the human capacity to be a parent evolved? Sociologist Alice Rossi answered this fundamental question by reviewing anthropological evidence dealing with cultures and societies all over the world. On the basis of her review, she concluded that the answer is "small, stable groups with a lot of shared child rearing." To the extent that environments offer stability, they increase social health. Yet more and more boys in the United States feel uprooted or rootless. The growing instability of life in communities around the country is creating just the right conditions for the epidemic of youth violence to take root.

AFFIRMATION

Affirmation means receiving messages of one's value and worth. All of us need to be affirmed. This is documented in child development research on the positive effects of acceptance and the negative effects of rejection. Psychiatrist James Comer wrote a biography of his family entitled *Maggie's American Dream*. In it he asked, "Why, as poor, Black kids in racist America, did I and all my siblings succeed?" His answer focuses on the affirmation he received at home that counteracted the rejecting messages he received in the larger community. In a revealing passage, he quotes his mother Maggie telling him about his long-dead father: "They don't make men like that anymore," she says, "except his sons, of course." The message of affirmation is clear: He was a valuable man. You are like him. You are a valuable person. (Compare this experience to Calvin's: he was told that he was just like his dead father—"a no-good bum.")

Security

A healthy community feels safe. Security is a delightful state of being. Securely attached babies crawl away from their mothers to explore the world around them, confident in the knowledge that she will be there when they need her. Insecurely attached babies are paralyzed with anxiety, afraid to crawl too far from their mothers. Accordingly, some kids grow up believing the world is a safe place while others see danger all around them. There was a time when children were taught, "If you need help in the community, ask an adult." Once upon a time, kids were taught that if they needed help crossing the street, they should go to the corner and ask an adult, "Would you cross me, please?" Today kids are taught to fear and distrust strangers. In a study conducted in Toledo, Ohio, nearly half of the elementary school children surveyed in 1985 reported that they thought it was likely or very likely that they would be kidnapped. Nationwide a third of kids in Grades 6 to 12 said they feared they would not live to old age because they would be shot.

There are still communities in our country where children feel safe and secure, but we should not discount the widespread impact of television news and "entertainment" programs in communicating the possibility of harm to all children, no matter where they live. When a child is kidnapped in California, children in Illinois feel vulnerable. When a boy opens fire at a school in Springfield, Oregon, kids in my daughter's school in Ithaca, New York, wonder if they are going to be next.

Time

Who has time for kids these days? In a healthy social environment, adults are encouraged and rewarded for investing time in engaging in cooperative activities with children. As my mentor used to say, "A kids doesn't end up a chip off the old block because he was knocked off it, but because he knocked around with it." What else of real value do adults have to offer children except their time? A healthy social environment recognizes that and provides opportunities to fulfill it. What matters is not just that adults are physically present, of course, but that they are psychologically present and available to kids. Research on the early days of television reveals that the most common reason given for buying a television was "to bring the family together." What a bitter irony that is!

Without adults, particularly men, to spend time with them, boys wander confused in the world and are drawn to the caricatured hypermasculinity of the mass media. One thing a healthy social environment does for boys is show them how to be a good man. Lee May's book *In My Father's Garden* chronicles the central role in his life of his father's absence and speaks eloquently of the way in which finally coming face-to-face with his father allowed him to face up to what it means to be a man.

A socially healthy environment promotes this coming to terms with absent fathers.

Troubled and violent boys often speak of parents who were not psychologically available to them. Today many parents and children fail to engage in constructive activities together. I have visited many homes where the television is a constant presence, clearly taking the place of active interaction. Children need adults' investment of time in them. Few things are more important to them. Some kids will even put up with being sexually molested if the perpetrator spends time with them in return. A violent and troubled boy may speak of adults or older kids who took an interest in him, but they clearly were socializing him into negative behavior. A healthy social environment does not force children into these dilemmas. It offers mentors who represent the best of the community.

ECONOMIC EQUALITY

The seven-year-old daughter of a colleague of mine once wrote in a composition for school that she was the "poorest kid on the block" because she lived in the smallest house. Indeed, she *did* live in the smallest house on the block. However, it was a seven-bedroom house on a block of even larger mansions! What does it mean about our children when they define being poor as having less than others—no matter how much they have?

When most of the people of the world live on incomes measured in hundreds, not thousands, of dollars a year, what does it mean when we in the United States define the poverty level at $14,000 dollars a year? India defines poverty as having access to less than 2,100 calories per day, and using that yardstick it estimates that 20 percent of the population is poor (in what we in North America would consider a *predominantly* poor society). But if poor children around the world are shoeless, how do we make sense of North American "poor" kids who wear $150 running shoes?

While traveling in China in the early 1980s, I spoke with a man living in a rural village who reported to me that "before the 1948 Revolution very few people were rich, but now many people are rich." As evidence, he pointed to the fact that he himself owned a wristwatch, a radio, and a bicycle. By that standard, poverty is virtually absent in the United States, and we North Americans are universally rich. But, of course, in the new China of the 1990s, mobilized around the slogan "It is glorious to get rich," more and more Chinese are rich in North American terms. To a growing number of Chinese today, when cellular phones, cars, and designer jeans have taken their place as desirable, attainable commodities, defining wealth in terms of owning a wristwatch, a bicycle, and a radio seems quaint and naive.

Thus, analyzing the meaning of wealth to a child is not simple, because poverty is a judgment a child makes about his circumstances in life in relation to other kids and what his society defines as normal. A child's measure of poverty has to do with how he feels he compares with others in terms of what he and his family own. *Feeling* poor is the issue, more than *being* poor. At the end of an interview, Warren, a fifteen-year-old who had witnessed a murder, asked me, "When you were growing up, were you poor or regular?" That is it precisely—are you poor or regular?

Being poor means not meeting the basic standards set by society. When you are poor, it is not so much a matter of what you have but what you *don't* have. It is a matter of being different from the "regular" members of your society. And it is the message that that difference sends to kids that matters. If being poor means being consigned to second-class citizenship, is it any wonder that it leads to feelings of shame in kids and that in a violent society such as ours those feelings of shame lead to aggression?

Data from the Luxembourg Income Study of eighteen different countries, comparing the difference, for each country, of the income, after taxes and income transfers, of families in the lowest 10 percent of the population with those in the highest 10 percent, reveal that the United States has the largest gap between rich and poor of any of the countries studied. Whereas in Sweden, for example, the rich end up with about twice what the poor make, for the United States the differential is a factor of six!

A socially healthy environment seeks economic equality. It generates social policies that recognize the value of "We are all in this together," as opposed to "Every man for himself." It's partly a matter of dignity. The bigger the gap between rich and poor, the more likely those at the top are to feel either entitled by privilege or incapacitated by guilt, while those at the bottom feel some mixture of rage and shame. That's not a healthy situation. Low-income kids see that. They see what they have and don't have in relation to other kids in our society, other kids they see on television and in the movies particularly. In a healthy social environment, all children have a sense of being included, no matter what they have or don't have relative to others.

DEMOCRATIC PUBLIC INSTITUTIONS THAT NURTURE HUMAN RIGHTS

A healthy social environment is committed to democratic public institutions that foster universal human rights. Do we care about other people's kids? Should they have access to child care? Should every kid have access to high quality education? Health care? A healthy social environment commits public institutions to all these goals. And it commits to public institutions—schools, government agencies, libraries—that will foster democratic values and virtues for everyone, not just for the affluent elite. Troubled and violent boys often speak with cynicism about public institutions. During the course of my interviews I have had occasion to hear their views on presidents and congresses, mayors, governors, and senators.

One measure of our society's commitment to human rights is our relation to the United Nations Convention on the Rights of the Child. The United States stands nearly alone now among the nations of the world in *failing* to ratify this important document. Human rights issues often seem to be outside the scope of public debate in the United States where children are concerned, despite the fact that our national history began in a revolution to assert the primacy of human rights. A healthy social environment places democratic institutions in the service of human rights at the core of its public policy agenda.

SOCIAL HEALTH ANCHORS KIDS IN CHILDHOOD, WHERE THEY BELONG

The sum total of a community's social anchors is its social health. Adding these social anchors to the psychological and spiritual anchors I discussed earlier sets the stage for a plan of action. It leads to a comprehensive approach to the epidemic of youth violence, a comprehensive approach that places the responsibility for raising and protecting boys where it belongs—in the hands of adults in families, schools, and communities.

Looking back at my childhood and adolescence with the benefit and bias of hindsight, I realize that adults shielded me and my peers from some of life's nasty realities. We had a social contract. Children knew their place in the scheme of things, which was to experience child-hood—to play, to learn, to do what they were told, to stay within the rules. And adults were in charge. Their job was to take care of kids—to teach them, to play with them, to guide them, to protect them, and to support them. Adults held up their end of the social contract, and their commitment to it increased the moral basis for expecting that kids would do the same.

One sign of how much things have changed was the release of sexu-ally explicit material about President Clinton in September 1998. With-out regard for its possibly corrupting and disillusioning effects on children, Congress voted to release transcripts and videotapes of testi-mony with graphic descriptions of various sex acts between the President and his young mistress. Those in government and out who protested that this material was entirely inappropriate for family consumption (i.e., for children and teenagers, who would have easy access to it) were dismissed as fuddy-duddies. It does not matter that kids can have access to the same material on cable and broadcast television and on videocassettes. The fact is that these lurid accounts and images put them in another category because they deal with the president. In a healthy social environment that fact alone would be enough to keep the matter within adult circles and out of the consciousness of kids. In today's society that is a very tall order because television, the Internet, movies, and easily available books and magazines "tell all." Changing this would require a high level of so-cial conscience and control measures.

When I visited a third-grade classroom in a school located in subur-ban Illinois in 1994, I thought of how the adult conspiracy to prolong childhood and protect children had eroded. I was there to talk with the kids about violence, but after listening to them for a while I took a some-what different tack. I asked them to close their eyes and tell me what words came to mind when I said, "Mr. Rogers." All of them were familiar with Fred Rogers from his long-running television program *Mr. Rogers' Neighborhood*. When given a chance to free-associate, their responses in-cluded "kind," "nice," "good," "helpful," "loves kids," and other positive sentiments. A few minutes later I asked them to repeat the word association exercise, only this time we started with *Beavis and Butthead*, an adolescent-oriented cartoon depicting every adult's worst nightmare of obnoxious teenagers. Now the words that came from the kids' mouths included "mean," "bad," "nasty," "cruel," and "sets fires." When the children opened their eyes, one of the boys spoke up this way: "Come on, Dr. G., Mr. Rogers was part of our childhood; Beavis and Butthead are today." Eight years old, and childhood was but a memory! This is an important point because the life accounts of incarcerated youth are filled with evidence that they, too, were children exposed too soon to too much.

As I sat in the classroom in Illinois, I stifled my impulse to respond, "Excuse me. Mr. Eight-Year-Old, but why are you speaking of childhood in the past tense?" because I knew that in a very unfortunate way he was right: for many eight-year-olds childhood *is* in the past, for it is adolescent culture with which they are dealing. Of course, it is worth remembering that they are not alone in the view that they are already adolescents. Many adults seem to share it, and that is the real breakdown in the traditional social contract. For example, in recent years many states have lowered the age at which children can be tried as adults to fourteen or thirteen, and some states have no age limit. There are currently 300-plus young men on death row who committed their offenses while they were teenagers too young to legally drink or vote. Although this legal trend seems quite consistent with the fact that younger and younger children are leaving childhood to enter adolescence, with all its special issues and challenges, it highlights the importance of preserving childhood for at-risk boys as a strategy for saving them from violence.

SAVING VIOLENT BOYS
ISN'T EASY

In January 1998, I sat in a room with thirty professionals at a children's psychiatric center in New York City. We gathered together to compare notes about the persistent Conduct Disorder and aggressive behavior of one eleven-year-old boy. One by one these competent and well-meaning professionals testified about little Malique and his problems. He attacked his brother. He attacked kids at school. In spite of the best efforts of these psychiatrists, psychologists, social workers, teachers, and counselors, Malique's behavior problems continued.

Malique's foster parents were present for the meeting, and they seemed as puzzled and frustrated as the rest of the group. Devoutly religious, they felt compelled to stick with Malique and his brother as a Christian mission. They knew he had been badly abused for several years before coming to them, so they were sympathetic to his plight. But they were frightened by his behavior and wondered what would happen when he became a teenager.

When Malique himself came in, I understood a bit more of the situation. He was a charming little boy. I could see why the staff still seemed to like him despite his being "a royal pain in the ass," as one counselor put it. As I listened to the staff talk about Malique, their efforts to work with him, and their expectations about his prognosis, I was sobered by the magnitude of the challenge faced by everyone in the room—including Malique.

What went wrong? Was Malique's situation hopeless? Is there anything we can do to prevent boys like him from entering the world of youth violence? Must they inevitably end up talking to me or Claire or a national newsmagazine reporter in a prison a few years hence? Obviously, it is not easy or we would be doing it so well already that there would be no headlines from Springfield, from Jonesboro, or from Paducah.

THE PARABLE OF THE LAMPPOST

Taking the easy way out in these matters is all too often the chosen path in America. Perhaps I can reinforce that point best by recalling the parable of the lamppost, which begins with George making his way home one night after a meeting. As he walks along the dark street, he comes upon his friend Joe, on his hands and knees on the street under a lamp post. George stops to ask his friend, "What's the problem?" "Well," says Joe, "I've lost my car keys and I live twenty miles away, so I can't go home until I find them." Being a good Samaritan, George joins Joe on his hands and knees under the lamppost to search for the keys.

Some time passes with no result, so George stands up and says, "Joe, maybe we are going about this all wrong. We need a *campaign* to find the keys." He reaches in his bag and pulls out some buttons that say FIND THE KEYS! and some balloons with the same slogan. He pins a button on Joe's shirt, and after he has blown up the balloons, he ties them to the lamp post and the two men begin to chant, "Find the keys! Find the keys! Find the keys!" That makes George and Joe feel good. Then George and Joe stand and wait. And wait.

After some times passes and nothing happens, George says, "Maybe we need a more systematic approach. Perhaps what we need is a public health approach." So from his pocket George pulls out a piece of chalk and draws a grid on the pavement under the lamppost, labeling each square from A to Z and from 1 to 26. Then he and Joe begin to search systematically—Box A1, Box A2, Box A3, and so on—until they reach box Z26. It's very systematic, but still they fail to find the car keys.

After thinking for a moment, George declares, "Maybe we need to try a behavioral approach." So he pulls from his other pocket a bag of M&M's chocolate candies and begins to feed the candy to Joe to get his searching behavior under control. Before long, George has Joe moving right and left under his complete control. It's quite impressive, but they still haven't found the car keys. "I know," says George, "maybe we need a psychoanalytic approach." So he proceeds to interview Joe about early experiences of loss in his life. After a while, Joe is achieving deep insights about his personality . . . but they still haven't found the car keys.

"Maybe we should try a literary-historical approach," says George, a bit concerned at their lack of progress. So he pulls from his briefcase a book titled *"The History of the Key in Western Civilization,"* and he and Joe sit down to discuss the symbolism of keys in Ingmar Bergman's films. Fascinating, but still no keys. Finally, in desperation, George says, "Joe, perhaps we need a really radical approach to this problem. Now, where exactly were you when you lost your keys?" "Oh," says Joe, "I was about a hundred yards up the road when I lost the keys." Not surprisingly, George's eyes widen and with exasperation he says to Joe, "If you lost the keys a hundred yards up the road why are we looking here?" "Well," responds Joe, "the light is much better here."

There are always forces at work pushing us to look where the light is better when it comes to dealing with human problems like youth violence. But if the keys to the problem lie elsewhere, in the dark places in our society, in the dark secrets of our culture, working where the light is good will yield few results beyond the appearance of action. We have seen too many programs that don't rock the boat or require us to change ourselves or our institutions in any major way. Based on politically fashionable themes, these are well-meaning but ineffectual programs for which funding is readily available from donors who wish to appear responsible.

Pinning ribbons to our shirts or putting bumper stickers on our cars that say STOP THE KILLING! will not make a difference. Lecturing kids about drugs and violence has had no measurable impact. Bemoaning the "decline of the American family" will do little to save one troubled child's life. And executing teenagers or trying them as adults surely is not a good answer to youth violence.

What will it take? I see preventive possibilities at each step along a boy's path, along the way that leads from birth to jail or morgue. I see everywhere around us opportunities to create and support the spiritual, psychological, and social anchors our children need. The agenda includes effective ways to prevent child maltreatment, to prevent rejection, and to prevent temperamentally difficult boys from being mishandled at home and in school. The agenda includes ridding our neighborhoods of the social toxins that poison our sons. It includes policies and programs that provide the support needed to make the world safer for boys—and thus safer from boys

INITIATING AND SUSTAINING POSITIVE CHANGES

British psychiatrist Michael Rutter asks us to imagine the life of a human being as a journey along a pathway. At various points, the traveler confronts a set of gates that lead to different routes. Some of these routes are simply alternatives to the same destination. Others represent completely different and distinct pathways, leading either to places of great danger or to desirable destinations or to dead ends. Once the traveler opens and then passes through a gate, his fate is limited to the options available along the path chosen.

Young boys are on a journey. They repeatedly encounter such diverging paths. Do I join this peer group or that one? Do I use drugs or not? Do I side with adults? Each time they turn down one path rather than another, they change the odds that they will arrive at a particular destination, for example, high school graduation or incarceration, college or the morgue. In this chapter the emphasis is on claiming boys before they make choices that lead to lethal violence. In the next chapter we will explore the possibilities of reclaiming the unfortunate boys whom we, as their parents, teachers, and counselors, were unable to rescue from lethal violence.

Identifying preventive measures and then acting on them is the core of our agenda. However, in fulfilling this agenda, there are at least two forces at work with which we must be familiar. The first derives from the fact that over a period of time, human behavior comes to reflect what is stimulated, encouraged, rewarded, and successful in a particular social context, be it home, school, or peer group. Malcolm spoke to this when he said, "You put anyone in this environment, and they are going to behave the same as we do." Community psychologist Rudolph Moos calls this phenomenon *progressive conformity*, and it can work for better or for worse, depending upon what that home, school, or peer group represents and encourages. But it is not that simple. There are individual differences in behavior in any situation, whether healthy or poisoned. In any situation, some boys become caring, prosocial teenagers while others are sucked into the worst kind of behavior. Progressive conformity is real, but it is not absolute. There is a competing force.

In addition to being shaped by the force of social conformity, human behavior develops a kind of psychological and social momentum of its own. Behavior that initially needs reinforcement to sustain it can become self-sustaining and attain what psychologists call *functional autonomy*. We often call these behaviors habits. One way of looking at a boy's conscience is to see it as internalized moral reasoning that has achieved the state of functional autonomy. The boy with a strong conscience no longer needs continual reinforcement to maintain his good behavior. Achieving functional autonomy for good behavior is the goal of every moral teacher.

In a sense, then, our goal is to put confused, lonely, or depressed boys in situations of healthy progressive conformity and build patterns of positive functional autonomy, as opposed to negative environments and negative patterns of thinking, feeling, and acting. This was the successful intervention of my early life. Various elements of the social environment of my childhood conspired to guide and protect me. I responded with positive behavior in school and in the community, positive behavior that became a good habit.

LINES OF DEFENSE AGAINST LETHAL YOUTH VIOLENCE

Defending at the Beginning: Before Birth

The place to begin to prevent lethal youth violence is at the beginning, before a boy is even born. The goal is twofold: to prevent boys from coming into the world at a biological disadvantage and to prevent them from being maltreated by their parents. How do we accomplish this? Fortunately, some of the same programmatic efforts that reduce the likelihood of biological damage before birth can also reduce the likelihood of damage after birth, at the hands of parents. Chief among these is home health visiting that begins prenatally and continues through the first several years of life.

When Mary became pregnant, she was lonely and afraid. Her rela-

tionship with her husband Bob was rocky. In fact, they had decided to separate just after Mary found out she was pregnant. When Bob moved out,
Mary moved in with her mother so she wouldn't be alone. Young and
scared, Mary was relieved when the clinic told her she could enroll in the
home visiting program. Week after week Marilyn, the nurse, came to visit
with Mary, teaching her how to prepare for the baby and listening as Mary
expressed her feelings and thoughts about the future. Marilyn continued
to see Mary on a weekly basis for the first six months after John was born.
Then, when she saw that Mary had things well under control, Marilyn
began to increase the amount of time between her visits. When John cel-
ebrated his second birthday, Mary was "graduated" from the program.

Home visiting programs introduce a caring person who represents the
community into the life of a child before he is even born. At their best,
these programs make contact with families soon after conception, and a
caring, competent woman enters into a long-term, supportive relationship
with the mother-to-be. The home visitor comes to the family's residence
on a regular basis and continues to do so for the first two years of the
child's life. She provides information and a sense of caring that prospective parents in general need but that prospective parents with an accumulation of risk factors in their lives particularly need. The home visitor
establishes a relationship in which the needs of the mother-to-be, the
needs of the unborn child, and the interests of the community are all met.

The premier researcher studying home visiting is psychologist David
Olds at the University of Colorado Medical Center. His research shows
that the biggest positive effects of home visiting occur when the program
serves high-risk, single young women in their first pregnancy. Olds has
worked with psychologist John Eckenrode at Cornell University and followed the progress of families and children who received nurse home visiting. They find very positive and durable results that can extend into
adulthood. Babies whose mothers received nurse home visiting were
born with fewer health problems (e.g., less prematurity and higher birth
weight). And in the first years of life there is dramatically less child maltreatment. Babies in a comparison group of "unvisited" families among
an identified high-risk population had four times as much child maltreatment in the first two years of life. Child maltreatment is believed to be
the major cause of neurological impairment in boys who are especially
vulnerable to learning patterns of aggressive behavior in the home.

These are the boys who go on to act out in school and in the community the aggression they learn at home. Home visiting stabilizes and supports families so that they can develop positive momentum and positive functional autonomy. Follow-up studies report that even fifteen years later the effects are still apparent, including less involvement of the teens in the criminal justice and welfare systems.

The first line of defense, then, is a healthy baby and a positive parent–infant relationship—and keeping it that way. Unfortunately, most high-risk families do not receive home visiting. This is a serious social error, but one that is not going unaddressed. The National Committee to Prevent Child Abuse (NCPCA) has an initiative, called Healthy Families America, that is seeking to promote home visiting programs throughout the United States. (Note: Information for contacting the NCPCA and other organizations mentioned in this chapter is included in the Appendix.) The Committee's success in accomplishing that goal ultimately will play a significant role in preventing youth violence: it is estimated that every 1,000 cases of child abuse and neglect prevented leads to 250 fewer cases of juvenile delinquency.

PROMOTING POSITIVE PARENTING PRACTICES

Our second line of defense lies in programs that promote positive parenting practices, practices that stimulate healthy child development. In her book *The Nurture Assumption,* Judith Harris dismisses the importance of parents in child development and emphasizes the role of peers (in combination with genetically based temperament). There are many ways in which the influence of peers is critical in the development of children, particularly in the case of violent boys who link up with peer groups that encourage their aggression. However, this does not mean that parents cannot and do not play a significant role. One of the most effective challenges to Harris's book comes from studies of intervention programs aimed at increasing effective parenting. Commenting on Harris's view, University of Washington psychologist John Gottman puts it this way, "These studies show that if you change the behavior of the parents you change the behavior of the kids, with effects outside the home. When parents learn how to talk to and listen to kids with the worst aggression and behavior problems, and to deal with the kids' emotions, the kid becomes less impulsive, less aggressive, and does better in school. There is a very strong relationship between parenting style and the social competence of their children."

This strong relationship is why efforts to improve parental competence, particularly parents' ability to respond effectively to aggressive and troubled boys, are vital in preventing youth violence.

I spoke with Lorraine just after she had completed such a program. Participating in the ten weekly sessions had increased both her skill in managing her four-year-old son, Tom, and his nine-month-old sister, Tanya, and her satisfaction with family life. She said that before the program she never knew how smart babies and young children could be. Now she read to her children every night, took them to the library every Saturday, and was more confident that she could handle them without resorting to hitting. Lorraine is a success story common to effective parent education programs.

Parent education should start early. One good example is Parents as Teachers, an innovative program, begun in Missouri, that involves parents and their infants in guided interactions designed to promote both the relationship between the two and the overall intellectual and emotional development of the child. For example, parents are shown how to engage their infants in age-appropriate interactions using toys, games, and books. They see and learn effective strategies for responding to their children that stimulate their development.

Programs like Parents as Teachers reflect sound child development theory, such as that developed by the Russian developmentalist Lev Vygotsky. Vygotsky understood that child development is fundamentally social: it proceeds through relationships. He recognized that children are capable of one level of competence on their own and a higher level of competence in the company of teachers, a broad category that includes parents, other adults, and older children. The difference between what children can do alone and what they can do in relation to the teacher is called the *zone of proximal development* (ZPD). Effective parents operate in their child's zone of proximal development as much of the time as possible by responding to the child in ways that are emotionally validating and developmentally challenging. Programs such as Parents as Teachers help parents understand the ZPD. And these programs work: kids in such programs evidence enhanced overall development.

One critical goal for such programs is to improve the social prospects of temperamentally difficult children. Every child contains the potential to develop into any one of numerous different personalities, depending upon how he or she is treated. If children are not handled expertly, odds are that the difficult ones will behave badly and will eventually be rejected by their parents. Rejection by parents and others is the primary route through which nonabused children develop Conduct Disorder. And it is not just an issue between children and their parents: teachers and well-behaved peers may reject such difficult children because their behavior is so aversive. When children are rejected, they begin to gravitate to antisocial peers, some of whom may have been rejected themselves or may be victims of maltreatment at home. We must always remember that it is impossible to understand a child out of context. A child's development only makes sense *in context,* when peers and culture are taken into account.

Peers matter in how a boy behaves outside the home. We can see this in the conformity of kids to their peers in styles of clothing, slang, and taste in music. Peer influence operates, as well, in matters of aggressive behavior. Many of the boys I have interviewed have spoken of the intense pressure they felt to be part of a peer group, membership in which stimulated increasingly aggressive behavior in them. Sometimes, this peer effect can result in an event more violent than a boy would produce on his own. For example, it may well be that neither of the boys who did the shooting in the Jonesboro murders would have committed the crime alone. But together they had a terrible synergy.

It is easy to see how parents and teachers come to reject difficult children. Rejection is almost inevitable. That's why widespread availability of ZPD-based parent support and educational programs is a critical piece of a comprehensive violence prevention program. By showing parents and teachers how to accept these children *and* how to get their negative behavior under better, nonabusive control, everyone benefits.

What is more, psychological maltreatment is always a risk when parents regularly operate outside the ZPD, when they treat their children in ways that are emotionally invalidating and developmentally stunting. As we have seen, psychological maltreatment, particularly rejection, is a primary cause of the developmental problems that result in violent acts on the part of children and youth. While much media attention focuses on physical and sexual abuse, there are few organized efforts in our society to understand, recognize, and deal with the psychological maltreatment and rejection of children. Programs such as Just "For Kids!" exist to increase public awareness and improve professional response.

Intervention to Deal with Attachment Problems

The third line of defense is early intervention programs that deal with the attachment-related problems that were discussed in Chapter Two. As we have seen, many of the boys who get lost are disconnected or detached from the earliest months and years of life. Yet one of the anchors for resilience is at least one strong, secure attachment. Throughout this book we have seen what poor or nonexistent attachment means in psychological and social terms. Day-care providers, early education teachers, pediatricians, nurses—all are on the front lines of prevention and early intervention.

Each morning when twenty-month-old Tyrel and his mother came into the child care center located in the building where she worked, it was obvious that there was something wrong in their relationship. Other children Tyrel's age were dealing with the daily separation smoothly or perhaps with only a short period of distress followed by a quick integration into the center's activities. Tyrel would cling to his mother and then scream and cry when she tried to leave. When she tried to comfort him, he would cry even louder, breaking down inconsolably after struggling in her arms. It seemed that no matter what his mother did, it wasn't what Tyrel needed. Finally, he would wear himself out and lie down on a mat in a corner of the room. When he recovered, Tyrel would seek out staff members and demand attention in every way a little boy can—pulling at their clothing, poking them, knocking things over, attacking other children. It seemed that the very effort of demanding attention itself was overwhelming to Tyrel, for eventually he would end up crying again, just as he had when his mother left. This pattern was repeated day after day.

When parents or other adults notice evidence of an impaired attachment relationship in a young child, they can help the child repair the relationship and develop the capacity to sustain effective relationships. Child psychiatrist Stanley Greenspan has developed one of the strongest approaches to understanding and dealing with these fragile relationships. Greenspan focuses on the way a challenging and difficult temperament paradoxically causes an infant to seek attention and to then become overwhelmed when he succeeds in getting it. Both child and parent are primed for trouble, because the parent typically does not understand what the child needs. What the child does need—and what may take professional intervention to teach the parent or caregiver how to provide—is a blend of soothing and structure. For young children this means soothing physical contact—patting and stroking the back, for example—and repetitive soothing words spoken in a soft, gentle voice in combination with firm and clear limit setting. As the child develops language, it may be necessary to teach him how to describe his own behavior in words, so that he can use language as a means of practicing self-regulation. For example, the therapist may say to the child, "Let's do fast walking and then let's do slow walking," while concretely showing the child what these words mean in terms of his own actions.

These interventions become the basis for regulating the child's relationships by helping him get his negative behaviors under conscious control. When they do not receive this crucial double dose of special attention, difficult children begin to get offtrack developmentally. Returning them to a normal developmental path usually requires professional support and assistance, including efforts to help the parent understand the special needs of the child and the strategies that are effective in meeting those needs. The happy result can be a child who is restored to a more positive pattern of behavior.

Early Childhood Education

High-quality early childhood education programs—such as well-run preschools, high-quality Head Start centers, enriching nursery schools, and developmentally oriented day-care centers—are the fourth line of defense. These programs play a leading role in ensuring that boys are turned away from violence, because they improve intellectual development, which, as we have seen, contributes to resilience. Moreover, early childhood education programs not only serve as focal points for parent education and support programs, which improve the ability of parents to care for children in a nurturing and accepting way, but also serve the community as an early warning system for identifying and helping boys who are developing problems with aggressive behavior.

Four-year-old John was such a boy. He started in the Head Start program in his church's basement on his fourth birthday. Three weeks later he was on everyone's list of troubled children. He took other children's toys; he pushed and shoved in line waiting for snack; he was always eager to play violent fantasy games, and he was always the first to break these games down into real fighting. Hardly a day went by without some incident involving John that left another child crying. One day it was throwing a block, another it was biting. After one such incident, John became the focal point for the Head Start staff's weekly meeting. After sharing their views of him and his behavior, staff members agreed that the center's social worker would contact John's mother to arrange a home visit.

A week later, the social worker reported to the group the results of her visit. She found that John's mother was overwhelmed with his behavior and didn't seem to have any ideas for getting it under control other than spanking him each time he misbehaved. Although she expressed love for her son, she clearly was at the end of her rope and reported that she spent most evenings just trying to avoid John, often by letting him watch television. The social worker was able to formulate a plan with the rest of the staff to provide more structure for John during the day and to work with his mother to carry through on this approach at home. With the support of the center staff, John's mother was able to cut down on his television time, involve him in cooperative games with her, and reduce her reliance on spanking. Within four weeks everyone, including John's mother, noticed a major improvement in his behavior— less aggression and more cooperation.

These educational, monitoring, and supportive roles are vital for families at risk for maltreating and rejecting their sons. Indeed, research on the Perry Preschool Project, one of the most famous long-term follow-ups of high-quality early childhood education, shows that for every dollar spent on the program during early childhood, seven or eight dollars were saved years later as a result of less involvement of the program's graduates in the criminal justice system, as compared to peers who did not attend such an early childhood education program.

The National Association for the Education of Young Children has spent years developing standards to define quality when it comes to these programs. Making these standards a reality for every young child is an important violence prevention measure in its own right. Beyond that, the National Birth to Three Center has put together useful materials on how to deal with issues of trauma in the life of very young children. Recently, a new resource has become available: Safe Havens, a set of materials designed to prepare teachers and child care providers to support children and families who witness violence in their communities.

Early Intervention in Response to Bad Behavior and Aggression

The fifth line of defense is early recognition of cases of Conduct Disorder and effective responses to redirect behavior and reshape the social maps of vulnerable children. What does it take to rehabilitate children with Conduct Disorder? As Malique showed us, it is never easy or simple. Psychologists Robert Wahler, Gerald Patterson, John Gottman, and Rolph Loeber are leaders in this field. Their programs focus on training parents and other adults to redirect their interaction with difficult children away from the entrapped, coercive, and rejecting patterns that seem to arise so naturally in real life. When there is support for the goals of these interventions in the social environment of the parents and child, they can be quite successful.

Ricky was such a child, and Juleen and Bill such parents. They were referred to their local child guidance clinic by Ricky's elementary school guidance counselor. The counselor saw all the signs of Conduct Disorder in Ricky's file—a pattern of being sent to the principal for fighting and stealing, two one-day suspensions for hurting other children, and a report from the third-grade teacher stating her suspicion that Ricky was responsible for the death of the class's pet rabbit. At the clinic, Juleen and Bill received instruction in how to analyze the connections between their behavior and Ricky's problems. With the help of the therapist, they came to see how they were actually unwitting accomplices to Ricky's bad behavior by responding to him only when he misbehaved and by taking any positive behavior of his for granted. It took several months of work, but eventually Juleen and Bill were able to maintain a new pattern of responses to Ricky. As they did so, his behavior began to shift, and the number of aggressive incidents decreased. The parents cooperated with each other and supported each other through some very difficult days and nights, but as their hard work began to pay off, they could see that it was worth the effort. This kind of clinical help is necessary to turn around a troubled boy in time to save him, his family, and the whole community from grief later on.

Of course, simultaneously with all these efforts there must be a vigilant child protection system that identifies and responds to child maltreatment whenever it occurs. This includes a strong commitment to deal with psychological maltreatment, especially rejection, and provide treatment for the children affected. Unfortunately, the reality is that in most communities the most abused and neglected children receive no mental health services after being identified as victims of maltreatment.

During the summer of 1998, as I was writing this chapter, I interviewed three young men on death row in Illinois who had been sentenced to the gas chamber. Each of these men had been subjected to extreme child maltreatment, yet none had received mental health treatment once that victimization was substantiated by the state child protective services agency. I could not help but think that if any one of these young men had been taken hostage by a terrorist group and tortured for years, there would have been no question about their need for and entitlement to mental health services upon their release. Yet we did not provide the same services to these "hostages" once they were released from their tormentors. And now we intend to execute them.

Many child protection agencies and individual workers feel inadequately prepared and supported for the task of recognizing psychological maltreatment and providing treatment for child victims of abuse. To help deal with this challenge, Just "For Kids!" has supported efforts at Cornell University's Family Life Development Center to develop a special training curriculum for protective service workers to improve their capacity to deal with the core issues of psychological maltreatment. This curriculum builds upon years of effort to define the special developmental dangers posed by psychological maltreatment in the forms of rejecting, ignoring, isolating, terrorizing, and corrupting.

Violence Prevention Programs in the Schools and in the Community

The sixth developmental line of defense is violence prevention and reduction programs at the elementary school level. There are growing numbers of such programs in communities all over the country, programs that grow out of research showing that patterns of aggressive behavior and belief are becoming so entrenched in children by age eight that without intervention problems with aggression in adulthood are predicted. As the appendix shows, there are growing numbers of program models to choose from. How does a community choose which programs to use? One good guide is the work done by sociologist Del Elliott at the University of Colorado Center for the Study and Prevention of Violence.

After analyzing violence prevention and reduction programs across the country on behalf of the Colorado Center, psychologists Patrick Tolan and Nancy Guerra at the University of Illinois in Chicago found that the most effective strategy is one that begins in childhood and combines changing a boy's ideas about aggression (*cognitive restructuring*) with experiences practicing alternatives to violence (*behavioral rehearsal*). Cognitive restructuring refers to reframing a child's attitudes, values, expectations, and attributions concerning aggression and, in particular, the legitimization of aggression. Behavioral rehearsal refers to actual practice in nonaggressive behavior—conflict resolution, mediation, choosing alternative behavioral settings, and so on.

Two programs worth considering for use at the elementary school level are the Good Behavior Game, developed by Sheppard Kellam at Johns Hopkins University, and Let's Talk About Living in a World with Violence, developed by my colleagues and me at the Erikson Institute in Chicago. Both reduce aggression in elementary-school-age boys.

We developed Let's Talk About Living in a World with Violence in 1993 as a workbook-based program to stimulate child–adult and child–child dialogue about the meaning, rationale, and effects of and the alternatives to violence in all domains of the child's life, including the family. During its developmental phase at the Erikson Institute, Let's Talk About Living in a World with Violence was field-tested at fifty-four sites in twenty-five cities across the country, with nearly one thousand children from ages four to sixteen from diverse racial and socioeconomic backgrounds. Subsequently, it was evaluated in schools in small towns in New York State and in Chicago. The results indicate that when used by a motivated teacher, this program results in significant reductions of aggressive behavior by elementary school children. Moreover, the behavior changes are observable six months after use of the program.

Sheppard Kellam's program builds upon his finding that when first-grade teachers exert effective classroom management, aggression declines among boys who enter their classroom with higher than average aggression. To create this pattern of effective management for aggressive boys, Kellam focuses on mobilizing children in groups to control and redirect aggressive behavior on the part of their elementary school peers through the Good Behavior Game. Groups are formed and are offered rewards for being able to maintain increasingly long periods of "aggression-free" time. Using the Good Behavior Game during first grade reduced aggression *among the most aggressive children*, an effect that was still observable five years later, during sixth grade. Kellam's research also shows that nonaggressive children can be mobilized to control aggression in their peers and that the effects of this mobilization may extend for years beyond the immediate intervention.

All the Malcolms and Peters and Maliques I have interviewed could have profited from the Good Behavior Game and the Let's Talk About Living in a World with Violence program when they were little boys. Some boys are lucky enough to participate in these programs early enough to make a difference. I spoke with children in Chicago who had participated in the Let's Talk program. One boy told me, "I learned a lot about how to do things right, you know, not use violence all the time. There's too much violence in the world. Now I try to talk things out with people, not use my hands, use my head." His teacher reports that his behavior has improved to match his changed rhetoric.

A related effort is the growing number of programs designed to deal with bullies in elementary school. In their book *Bullies and Victims*, therapist Suellen Fried and psychologist Paula Fried outline a wide range of strategies designed to defuse bullying situations, redirect the behavior of bullies, and protect children from being victimized. Developing strategies like these is an important element of the overall violence prevention strategy, because many boys who end up committing acts of lethal violence in adolescence were recognized as bullies during childhood. Some boys bully to compensate for their experiences of victimization at home. Others develop the habit of bullying in school when their aggressive temperament is inadvertently rewarded by kids who give in to them and by adults who either tolerate or actively encourage such behavior.

I hear many stories of bullying from the boys I interview. For example, Andre tells me how in third grade he found that he could get other kids to give him their lunch money just by threatening them. This became a well-grounded habit for Andre. Six years later, it was a small step for him to graduate to traveling with his friends across town, where they were not known, and strong-arming kids on their way home from school to give up their book bags, wallets, jackets, and hats and in some cases even their new running shoes.

Obviously, most schoolyard bullies don't graduate to acts of murder, but it may be telling that there are accounts of thirteen-year-old Mitchell Johnson in Jonesboro, fourteen-year-old Andrew Wurst in Edinboro, and fifteen-year-old Kip Kinkel bullying other kids at some point in their evolution toward become killers.

Character Education

The seventh line of defense is character education. Seventy years ago, pioneering researchers Hugh Hartshorne and Mark May investigated the conditions under which children resist the temptation to behave badly, lie, steal, and cheat. The results of their studies showed that the most important influence on how well kids resisted the temptation to be bad was the action of other kids. They concluded that "the normal unit for character education is the group or small community." It is an important lesson, one worth remembering today.

Modern character education programs involve the mobilization of schools and the rest of the community to endorse and promote a set of core values or "pillars of character," as they are called by some leaders in the field. The core values are trustworthiness, respect, responsibility, fairness, caring, and citizenship. Of course, put in such general terms, it is hard to imagine who could disagree with these values. The real challenge comes in applying them to actual situations. Such values provide a basis for organizing efforts to claim boys in a positive way, particularly in aligning child and adolescent peer groups in support of the effort.

Character education that mobilizes the entire range of community institutions seems to be the order of the day. I visited the town of Canandaigua, New York, in 1998 to speak at their annual character education community dinner. Everyone was represented at the dinner—kids and parents, professionals and ordinary citizens, civic leaders, business leaders, and clergy. And everyone had signed on to do all they could to put out a consistent message about the six values of the character education program. The two critical requirements of such efforts are that the programs must represent more than preaching at kids about values and that peer groups must be enlisted in the effort. Character education programs must provide concrete opportunities for kids to see the core values at work, alive in the minds and hearts of adults in their relationships with children and youth, and, most important, to see that they are valued in the context of the peer group.

Character education implies that every setting in which children find themselves involves recognition and encouragement of honorable behavior, integrity, and caring—in short, such settings are everything a socially toxic environment isn't. When the child goes to school, he finds that his behavior is judged by the standard of how well it conforms to the common code of values: trustworthiness, respect, responsibility, fairness, caring, and citizenship. His teachers expect such behavior of him, and he expects to be treated on the basis of these same principles. It becomes a common language for students and adults, used, for example, as the basis for discipline policies and practices. When a boy goes into a store, he finds the same commitment to live by the same core values. He can expect to be treated with dignity, and he is expected to behave responsibly. Thus, the agenda of character education offers a vehicle both for strengthening children and for detoxifying the social environment.

As a follow-up to his book promoting the character education model, educator Tom Lickona created materials and training programs to help schools and community leaders go forward with character education programs. Organizations like Character Counts! support these efforts, and it is a short step from character education to a focus on promoting spiritual development activities, such as meditation and caring. Surely, one of the ways to enhance spiritual development is to involve children and youth in caring for dependent beings—infants, the infirm elderly, growing plants, baby animals. The purpose of these activities is to provide a deeper and stronger anchor for kids than can be provided by the shallow "shopping mall materialism" of contemporary life.

There are programs that succeed in accomplishing this shift in values, but mostly they have been confined to alternative communities like the Buderhoff or special schools like the Waldorf schools. Religious schools aim for this same goal, and sometimes do succeed. The point is that it takes a special effort to resist the superficial materialism of mainstream American life and replace it with spiritually grounded activities that involve parents and children, home and peer group, school and community. Many religious traditions offer a basis for cultivating spirituality in children and youth. Starting from a Christian perspective and working with the support of Father Flanagan's Boys' Home, religious educator Thomas Everson developed a guided curriculum, called Pathways: Fostering Spiritual Growth Among At-Risk Youth, that is a good working model. It offers a wide range of activities designed to stimulate and support spiritual awareness and practice. Father Flanagan operated Boys Town on the principle "Every boy must learn to pray. How he prays is up to him." Having myself worked at Boys Town's Center for the Study of Youth Development in the 1970s, I am particularly pleased to see that Father Flanagan's vision is being disseminated broadly, through this new Pathways curriculum, to youth who need it desperately.

As is the case with character education generally, those who make efforts to promote spirituality and spiritual development among children in public institutions must be careful not to run afoul of the constitutional separation of church and state. I believe this can be done if our efforts focus on teaching guided meditation practices, offer purely spiritual guidance that does not invoke specific religions, and create activities that naturally evoke a reflective and reverent attitude toward life. I believe if each of us—man, woman, and child—began each day with a period of meditation and reflection, we would lose fewer boys. I can't stress too much that the issue is spirituality, not religion per se. There is certainly overlap between the two, but there is a difference.

What might the cultivation of spirituality look like in practice? It would mean starting off the institutional day at the school with a period of meditation, a calming of the mind and spirit, coupled with the reading of a short inspirational passage. It would mean that in the cafeteria, time would be set aside again for a period of meditation and for some statement of appreciation for the food. It would mean that each day each child would spend some time talking, reading, writing, and reflecting about the core values of the character education. It would mean that each school day would end with a period of meditation and reflection.

Harnessing the Positive Power of Peer Groups

The eighth line of defense is teaching mediation, conflict resolution, and peer counseling in programs for kids in middle school and junior high. An important element in these programs is that kids keep track of other kids. Shortly after the shootings in Jonesboro, Arkansas, a young boy in a New York City school who had participated in a peer counseling and conflict resolution program appeared on television. When asked how he would have handled the situation in Jonesboro, he replied confidently that if someone in his school had been saying the same things the boys in Jonesboro had been saying to their peers in the days before the shooting, an adult would have been notified immediately and preventive action would have been taken.

Suburban, small-town, and rural schools and communities can learn some things from the experiences of inner-city schools on this score. They already are. In their book *Waging Peace in Our Schools*, educators Linda Lantieri and Janet Patti describe the growth of the Resolving Conflict Creatively Program (RCCP) from a pilot effort in New York City in 1985 to a joint effort of Educators for Social Responsibility and the New York City Board of Education. The program has been the subject of extensive evaluation, and the results are very encouraging: less violence and more effective communication among kids and between kids and adults.

The content of the peer mediation and conflict resolution programs is important in its own right. But perhaps of equal, or even greater, importance is their role in linking kids to adults to validate the principle that kids who say troubling and troubled things need to receive adult help and should not be shielded by peers from adults. The whole culture of the peer group is at stake here. Junior high and middle school is the time of greatest peer orientation among kids, and so this redirection of the peer culture is vital. A peer mediation program requires a delicate balancing act for kids, for whom loyalty to friends usually comes before anything else. The Resolving Conflict Creatively Program accomplishes this redirection of the peer culture. The New York City boy who insisted that anyone in his school who had spoken the words of anger, revenge, and threat that were heard in Jonesboro in the days before the shooting would certainly have been reported to adults who could take some action was enrolled in the RCCP program.

YOU CAN CHANGE THE WORLD: THINK GLOBALLY, ACT LOCALLY

Even if we can establish all eight lines of defense against the development of aggression, it will not be enough, however. There will always be boys who remain unclaimed, boys who will slip through and be primed by their damaging experiences at home and their allegiance to negative peer groups to proceed from aggressive behavior to lethal violence. What about them? I think this is precisely why we must do more than address the psychological problems of vulnerable boys and the existence of negative peer groups. We must address the social health of the community directly.

Taking on the challenge of detoxifying the social environment is a job too big for parents and professionals alone. It is a job that requires us to act as members of a community and a nation. It is fundamentally political. What will it take to detoxify the social environment in ways that will prevent youth violence? Here, too, there is an agenda. But I hesitate to present it.

I hesitate even to list the items on this agenda because in our current political climate there is so much cynicism and distrust where government is concerned, and much of the detoxification agenda requires government action. In the early 1960s, surveys showed that more than 75 percent of American adults agreed with the statement "You can count on the government to do the right thing most of the time." By the mid-1990s this measure of confidence had dropped to about 25 percent. Ours is a tough social climate in which to propose any substantial public initiatives. This is why I hesitate. But the need is great, and that is why I go forward. I do so with the belief that we, knowing what we know, have no choice but to act.

PROTECTING CHILDREN FROM CORRUPTING VIOLENT INFLUENCES

The first item on the political agenda is to reduce the exposure of children to violent images. Televised violence increases the violent behavior of children, particularly troubled boys. After reviewing the evidence, an expert panel of the American Psychological Association concluded that *by itself* televised violence is responsible for up to 15 percent of all aggressive behavior by kids. Given that there are many influences on development and that one factor rarely, if ever, tells the whole story about the emergence of a problem, this is quite significant.

But how can we detoxify television and movies for children? One way to start is with stronger regulation of broadcasters. Action for Children's Television agitated for change on this issue for many years and ran up against the power of media lobbies and the general public's hunger for violence. Perhaps it is time for us as a people to "put up or shut up" about violence. Are we willing to accept tragedies like those in Jonesboro, Paducah, and Springfield as part of the cost of being an American, or are we willing to pay the price for a less violent society by depriving ourselves of violent imagery on television and in the movies, at least so far as children are concerned?

One positive step would be to strictly enforce regulations about movie ratings and perhaps expand them to keep young children out of theaters showing R-rated violent films even if parents agree to let their children see them. A second step would be to monitor and control the scheduling of violent television programs to limit child access. A third involves keeping vicious lyrics and music videos out of the hands of children and teenagers.

Doing all this would make a difference in detoxifying the social environment for children and youth. It would make a particular difference for troubled boys, who are most likely to act out violent scenarios when they reach the desperate point of no return—when they, depressed, angry, ashamed, and humiliated, are bent upon action to relieve their intolerable state of mind and heart through violent behavior at home, on the streets, or in school.

Beyond the general issue of media images, there is a special need to reduce the influence of what are called point-and-shoot video games. Military psychologist David Grossman has identified the danger. When playing these video games, a child actually holds a gun in his hand and points it at a screen to shoot the "enemy," thereby exactly mimicking the techniques used by military trainers to prepare soldiers for combat. Grossman worked on the development of these techniques for the military and therefore knows about them firsthand. The problem for military trainers, as we learned in Chapter Four, is that most normal human beings come equipped with an inhibition to shoot a fellow human being, and simply training soldiers to shoot at a bull's-eye target does not break down this inhibition. By using a target in the shape of a human figure, the military learned that it could break down a soldier's inhibition so that he is ready to fire his weapon at the enemy as soon as he enters the combat situation. Grossman has concluded that by exposing our kids to point-and-shoot video games, we are systematically training them to ignore their inhibition against shooting a fellow human, an inhibition that may be the last line of defense against lethal youth violence—for even a child who *wants* to shoot someone may be unable to do so if this normal inhibition is still in place.

What is a parent to do? In addition to supporting national efforts aimed at the big picture of public policy, parents can act locally to make a difference. One important arena for parental action is the parents organization of the local school. In some locations when students enter high school, their parents are asked to sign a contract indicating what they will and will not do (e.g., that they will check on homework assignments and that they will not allow unchaperoned parties). This helps individual parents resist the pressure of a child's entreaty "But, Mom! Everyone else is doing it!" Parents of younger children need the same support. This might take the form of a contract for early childhood education programs and elementary schools specifying that no parent will allow a child to watch R-rated videos or play point-and-shoot video games.

DISARMING CHILDREN AND YOUTH

The second task before us is to disarm children and youth to make sure they cannot access guns when the sense of intolerable shame, frustration, injustice, and melodrama gives rise to the impulses that result in lethal youth violence. The simplest way to do this would be for all adults to get rid of their guns so that children would neither have role models nor access. At this stage in our history—what with our history of fascination with guns, the lobbying efforts of the National Rifle Association, and the emotional attachment that many Americans feel toward their weapons— this seems unlikely. Nevertheless, it is critical to remember the role that easy access to firearms plays in youth violence and to keep our efforts at ending this easy access at the forefront of our child-positive agenda.

Kids in Canada get in as many fights as American teenagers do, but virtually no Canadian kid expects fights to lead to an armed response— and they don't. Some statistical analyses have revealed that the increase in lethal youth violence in the United States during the 1980s was primarily attributable to the increased use of guns by teens. Some countries, such as Japan and England, are virtually gun free and have almost no lethal youth violence. Does gun control matter? Do guns really play a role? To some people the answer is an obvious yes. But there are just as many people who seem to think the obvious answer is no. In the wake of the Springfield shootings, some people thought the clear implication was to "get rid of all the guns"; at the same time, a gun proponent was going on television to argue that the solution was to "arm the teachers." Others argue that "guns don't kill, criminals kill."

While it is true that guns require a human being to complete their lethal purpose, it is misleading to say guns are irrelevant to the life-and-death equation of youth violence. Evidence from international comparative studies proves that the presence of guns leads to more killing. The evidence is strongest when it comes to suicide. For example, ethnic Germans living in Switzerland have easy access to rifles (as do all Swiss men because of universal military training and reserve duty), but Germans in Germany do not. The suicide rate among ethnic Germans in Switzerland is four times what it is among Germans in Germany. When guns are available, people use them against themselves. That much is clear.

The relation between availability of guns and homicide leads to at least one important conclusion: It requires a highly controlled and healthy society to live with guns in its midst and not end up with people using those guns against other members of that society. The pervasive social toxicity of American life, coupled with our strong individualist impulse, makes us a bad risk when it comes to widespread availability of guns.

The efforts and small successes of some pilot youth disarmament programs around the country testify to the uphill nature of this struggle. Even in the face of the powerful gun lobby and the belief held by many Americans that it is their absolute right to own guns, it is possible to mobilize communities to concentrate on stopping youth gun violence. The Boston Gun Project has focused on active enforcement of existing gun control laws, which in many ways *do* limit youth access to guns in the "legitimate" market. In this program, guns are seized whenever possible. Kids are resocialized to avoid the arms race that occurs among adolescent groups when the excitement, prestige, and short-term sense of security of gun possession are invoked. Using this strategy, Boston was able to produce a dramatic decrease in youth gun violence; the city had no youth gun deaths for a two-year period. The Boston Gun Project is a wonderful and inspiring example, but it will probably take more than programs like this for a national campaign to reduce lethal youth violence to succeed.

While I don't own a gun and derive no particular satisfaction from the thought of target shooting, I recognize that not everyone feels the way I do. A significant minority of the population (predominantly but not exclusively men) derives great satisfaction from guns, hunting, and target shooting. Many of these same individuals feel peace of mind knowing that they have a gun in their homes, because they envision using it against an intruder. I was confronted by three such men after a lecture I recently gave at a community forum on violence reduction in a small city in Michigan. Each of these men opposed my recommendations about domestic arms reduction. One was trembling with rage at the thought that anyone would try to take his guns away from him, leaving him disarmed and thus at the mercy of the "criminal element." Another, more calm but equally unyielding, asked, "Why should I be held responsible for people who don't use their guns responsibly?" The third said he enjoys shooting and believes no one has the right to deprive him of that pleasure.

I acknowledged that it would be asking a lot for these men to give up their guns—too much, as they see it. All I could do was remind them that it is more likely that they or a member of their family will use the gun in a moment of rage or depression against themselves or some loved one than against an intruder or some other member of "the criminal element." Is disarmament asking too much? For some of us, the answer is yes. Making the world safer will take a great deal of basic work in transforming attitudes.

IF YOU WANT PEACE, WORK FOR JUSTICE

There are communities that are making progress in meeting the detoxification agenda. In collaboration with the Child Study Center at Yale University, the city of New Haven, Connecticut, is making great strides in moving toward a more peaceful world. Under the direction of psychiatrist Donald Cohen and psychologist Steve Marans, a variety of efforts are in place to mobilize local government in support of child development. These efforts include the Community Policing Program and a collaboration between child mental health professionals and police in which members of these groups work together to deal with issues of violence and trauma early in the lives of kids. The child mental health professionals offer seminars for law enforcement officers on a regular basis to share knowledge and information, and these same professionals ride along with police officers to get a firsthand view of what law enforcement looks like from the inside. As the program matures, the child mental health professionals carry beepers so that police officers can call upon them whenever they encounter a situation involving children.

As the New Haven experience shows, police officers can develop skills and sensitivity to augment the work of a community's child mental health professionals. And as such a collaboration continues, relationships grow and trust builds. I saw this myself one day in New Haven as I walked with one of the child mental health professionals to the university. As we came to a busy intersection, the police officer directing traffic noticed us and walked over to talk to my companion. He reported on a case he had responded to the previous week and indicated that the knowledge he had gained from one of the recent seminars had been instrumental in his ability to respond appropriately and effectively. The collegial feeling between the two men was clear and impressive.

Community policing and collaboration between police and mental health professionals are models that other cities are adopting (e.g., Newark, New Jersey). Such measures can be the basis for community-wide efforts to enhance the prosocial development of children and youth, and can thus decrease the risk of violence. Mutual respect and affirmation between police and mental health professionals are the keys, as they are for all human relations.

When and where kids feel they are affirmed and respected, they are less likely to turn to violence. This is one of the core principles anchoring a healthy society. Thus, one way to increase the safety and security of the worlds that boys inhabit is to eliminate discrimination based on race and class and replace it with affirmation based on the worth of each individual and group in every school and community. So long as we continue to permit prejudice in our institutional life and in our hearts and minds, we will be a violent society.

Of course, not all rejection that kids experience is based on racism and ethnocentrism. Some of it comes from the more generally alienating influences in our society. One example is a large student body in high school. Research dating back to the 1950s and 1960s demonstrates that small high schools encourage participation by teenage students—particularly those students who are at risk of dropping out because of their family background, personal characteristics, and prior school history. In a small school, these marginal students are needed to make school activities function. In a large school, such students are not needed because there are plenty of other, more socially and personally desirable, students to do what needs to be done to make a go of the sports teams, choirs, student government, publications, prom committee, clubs, and all the rest of the activities that constitute the social life of a high school. As a result of being needed, marginal students in a small school are more likely to feel that they belong and have a stake in the school and are more likely to care about the school. Thus, there is less delinquency and dropping out in small schools.

Moreover, kids can reasonably believe that adults are in charge in a small school. However, as the shootings in Jonesboro and Paducah unfortunately demonstrate, small school size alone will not prevent *all* youth violence, but it will make the social environment of the school more manageable and affirming to more students. Research on school size indicates that when a school has more than about five hundred students in Grades 9 through 12, it crosses the threshold into bigness. In 1950, the average size of American high schools was five hundred; by 1975 it was fifteen hundred. It is possible to limit the size of high schools by action of school boards and legislators, and I think it should be a high priority.

TO SECURE THESE RIGHTS, GOVERNMENTS ARE INSTITUTED

There is much to be done, but none of this agenda can come to pass so long as we are politically incapacitated by virtue of our distrust of public institutions. On one side of this debate are those who argue that a child's development is a private matter for his family. In this view, the role of government in the care and feeding of children and families must be minimal, limited perhaps to the most basic matters of child protection. Is this the appropriate foundation for government policies that affect the toxicity of the social environment for children and youth? Does the government stand outside the family, essentially as a bystander, only intervening when there is no other last resort in the "private sector"? Is there a position that justifies the government's role as more than that of a bystander? I believe there is. It lies with the original American political vision and is to be found in the Declaration of Independence.

The Declaration is the original contract with America, the touchstone for American public policy debate. In this document is found the essential and (for the time in which it was written) innovative premise of American political ideology. And what is this premise? It is not simply the assertion that "we hold these truths to be self-evident, that all men are created equal, that they are endowed by their creator with certain unalienable rights, that among these are life, liberty, and the pursuit of happiness." This assertion of human rights (at the time, the meaning of the word *men* was limited to white men) was wonderful, but not unique for its time. And as I understand it, Jefferson originally wrote "pursuit of *public* happiness," but he was persuaded by Benjamin Franklin that the word *public* was unnecessary because it would be clear to the reader that happiness is not a matter of individual indulgence but, rather, of the satisfaction that comes from being a positive member of society. We should remember this: The purpose of government is to promote not selfishness or a simply individual definition of happiness but, rather, the Good Society, public happiness.

This distinction is important, but what comes next in the Declaration is of vital importance. The most important ideological innovation of the Declaration is contained in the words that follow the statement of inherent, unalienable human rights: "That to secure these rights governments are instituted . . ." Here is the fundamental contract with America, the truly revolutionary principle that *governments exist to secure basic human rights*. The best of American history has been the refinement and application of this contract—including efforts to rectify the original omissions in the language of the Founding Fathers to include female and nonwhite citizens and to translate this basic commitment in light of changing social conditions and technology.

This is our political heritage, this revolutionary concept of government as the guarantor of human rights. It is quintessentially American to believe that government exists neither to protect the rich or any other elite group, nor to make the world safe for big business, nor to facilitate greed or self-interest, nor to promote a religious group's narrow agenda. The founders of our nation envisioned that the basic purpose of government is to secure basic human rights, unalienable rights. This is the foundation for our efforts to enhance social health in our communities. Every bit of progress we make in fulfilling this mission will reduce the likelihood that psychologically vulnerable boys will turn to lethal violence. But when they do, we still have to deal with them, and that leads us to the final topic of discussion in this book: reclaiming boys once they are lost.

8

RECLAIMING LOST BOYS

REVERSING NEGATIVE MOMENTUM IS TOUGH

Throughout the United States, juvenile detention systems are separate from the adult prison system. Each state has a graduated set of institutions in this system, starting with residential programs, which are almost indistinguishable from boarding schools and summer camps, and culminating in secure centers, which are more like prisons than anything else. Many terms have been used to identify the sites in this system such as *reform school* or *training school*.

Some boys who commit acts of lethal violence stay outside the system until the day they use a gun or a knife. Others slip from the normal orbits of teenage boys into lethal violence in a matter of weeks. A prime example of the latter is the case of three Fort Myers, Florida, seniors in high school who conspired with an older boy, Kevin Foster, to kill a teacher in April 1996. These three boys—Chris Black, Derrick Shields, and Peter Magnotti—had done well at school, were responsible workers at a fast food restaurant, and had no record of delinquency. The only apparent signs of trouble were that all three boys were described by classmates as "loners" or "geeks" or "nerds" and seemed to be drawn to the dark side of youth culture, most notably the nihilistic music of Marilyn Manson.

In the month preceding the April 1996 murder, these boys, who began identifying themselves as the Lords of Chaos, got caught in a negative spiral that took the form of a brief spree of vandalism, arson, and robbery. One night as they were about to break into their high school to continue their campaign of delinquency, they were seen by one of their teachers. The boys made a lame excuse and departed the school. But one of the boys worried that this teacher would report them to the authorities; as a result, he hatched a plan to kill him to prevent him from spoiling their fun and turning them over to the police. They carried through with the plan, with the leader, Kevin, doing the shooting. All four kids were tried as adults. Kevin received a death sentence. Pete received a sentence of thirty-three years, while Chris and Derrick received life imprisonment.

The lethal acts of boys who seem to descend precipitously into the world of lethal violence seem to be more likely to be either committed at school or school related, because school is still a potent setting for them, a place where what happens still matters to them—often excruciatingly so. This was true for the self-proclaimed Lords of Chaos. Other boys, the ones who have been getting into trouble and acting out aggressively since childhood, may already have left school (at least emotionally, if not physically) by the time they are adolescents. Therefore, the site of their lethal crimes is elsewhere—perhaps on the street, at a party, or in someone's home.

All in all, however, most troubled and violent boys follow a predictable pattern of escalating antisocial acts, acts that bring them to the attention of adults who try to stop their bad behavior. These boys typically start with the punishment system of their school: first, a warning from the classroom teacher, then an order to report to the principal's office, then a referral to the guidance counselor or school psychologist and perhaps being sent home from school, and, finally, short suspensions and then long-term suspensions or expulsion.

Along the way, these boys typically enter into the juvenile justice system when they first cross the line from aggressive acting out to violent crime *and get caught*. Remember, surveys of adolescents reveal that most teenagers commit some delinquent act and that 85 percent of those who admit to committing serious violent acts report that they have not been arrested for those acts. When a boy is apprehended, there is usually an initial appearance in a family or juvenile court that results in probation. In these situations, boys are not institutionalized but do come under the court's jurisdiction in the person of a probation officer who sets up a series of demands and conditions for the boy, and sometimes for his family.

Numerous youth advocates and treatment specialists have argued that most delinquent youth do not need to be institutionalized, that, in fact, they are more likely to improve if they are *not* institutionalized but, rather, are treated in the community. Among the treatment options most favored by the available research is multisystemic therapy (MST). In this approach, a wide range of therapeutic techniques are brought to bear on a boy and his family in an effort to guide his behavior in a more positive direction. These include family systems therapy, to assess and improve dynamics and relationships between the boy and his parents and siblings; efforts to change the way the boy thinks about his social relations, including peer relationships; and parent management training to improve the control and influence tactics of the parents.

Although it is not widely available in most communities, most evaluation studies give high grades to MST for its effectiveness in comparison with other approaches, such as individual therapy for the boy. The effects show up in lowered rates of rearrest and incarceration later on. For example, a study conducted by one of MST's proponents, psychologist Scott Henggeler, found that whereas only 22 percent of the boys who completed the program were rearrested after four years, 71 percent of the boys who completed conventional individual therapy were rearrested. In addition, Henggeler compared the cost-effectiveness of MST versus incarceration and concluded that MST costs about one-third as much per boy per year and is generally more successful in reducing negative behavior.

If home-based programs like MST are not available, or do not succeed, and a boy commits additional criminal or delinquent acts, he may be sent to spend time in some sort of juvenile institution. This residential placement may be an alternative school, a psychiatric hospital, or some other treatment center. Boys who eventually commit lethal acts of violence are often graduates or dropouts of these programs. Often they have developed a track record of negative behavior that conventional treatment programs cannot contain or reverse. It is as if they have built up so much negative momentum in their lives that regular programs are not strong enough to push them in a more positive direction.

Of course, some violent boys bypass the youth system and go directly to adult prison, having been tried and convicted as adults for their first violent offense. This happens, but it is rare. Andrew Wurst, the fourteen-year-old who shot a teacher at a school dance in Edinboro, Pennsylvania, is such a boy. Much more common is a pattern of escalating negative and aggressive behavior, with lethal violence being the culmination of a pattern of acting out that starts in childhood. Stephen and Thomas exemplify this pattern. The negative momentum in these boys' lives is evident in the size of their case files. Stephen's file is eighteen inches thick, Thomas's is two feet tall. In one case where I served as an expert witness, the youth's lawyers sent me two large cardboard boxes of records: school records, health records, child protective service records, family court records, juvenile court records, residential placement records, criminal court records. I sat for hours reconstructing his history of abuse and neglect—the acting out, suspensions from school, counseling, placement, psychiatric assessment and evaluation, and incarceration. It was exhausting just to witness his life through the records.

FAILURE UPON FAILURE: THE PROBLEM OF RECIDIVISM

Understanding a bit about how the juvenile justice system measures success is necessary to understand what needs to be done to improve it. National statistics reveal that most of the boys who are arrested for violent crimes and are sentenced to youth prisons will end up in trouble again in the months and years after they are released. That is, they become recidivists, to use the technical term. Most adult men in prison for a violent crime failed to be rehabilitated by their placement in a juvenile prison. Just what proportion "most" means is hard to say, because the number changes on the basis of how and when we measure success and failure.

Trying to obtain a firm estimate of recidivism rates for violent juveniles is impossible, because the numbers differ so much from decade to decade and from program to program and depend on whether the group of kids studied includes all delinquents and youth criminals or is limited to some subgroup, such as the most violent offenders. In their review of the evidence, criminologists Barry Krisberg and James Howell report rearrest rates of 55 percent for Florida juveniles within eighteen months of release in the mid-1980s, rearrest rates of 79 percent of Utah youth within twelve months of being released in the early 1980s, rearrest rates of 96 percent for California youth within fifteen years of being released in the 1960s, and 28 percent of youths from twenty states released in 1992. There are many questions and issues buried in these confusing data.

Are we to base our measurement of program success solely on rearrest data? Surveys reported by psychologist Rolf Loeber and criminologist David Farrington indicate, as I noted before, that 85 percent of serious and violent juveniles are not arrested for their violent crimes. Thus, if we simply look at whether or not a boy was rearrested, we may mistakenly conclude that a program was successful in redirecting him when in fact he may only have become more canny or may simply have lucked out and avoided detection. Several of the boys I have interviewed who were incarcerated for low-level offenses admitted to much more violent offenses for which they were never arrested. One boy had committed forty-eight armed robberies before he was arrested on an unrelated assault charge. Thus, the meaning of arrest rate as a true indicator of criminal activity is incomplete at best. But since arrest data are the easiest to obtain, most research does focus on this one measure of programmatic failure and success.

How long after they are released do we follow boys to find out if they become recidivists? The California study mentioned earlier found that if the measurement is made fifteen years after release, the recidivism rate is close to 100 percent. But many boys are rearrested within six months of their release. That was the case for Jose (a boy whose seventeenth-birthday wish was that he live to see twenty-five). As sweet as he was in the interviews and as sincerely as he insisted that he had learned his lesson, he was back in jail four months after his release, on a drug charge that sent him to adult corrections. Although Jose completed the program offered by the juvenile detention center where he was housed, he went right back to the world he had come from and soon was back with the same group of drug dealers he associated with before his initial arrest. It is important for understanding the needs of incarcerated boys and the challenges of reclaiming them to know that in the interviews completed just before he was released, Jose's love of material things had not changed. He went on at length to describe all the equipment he would need to adjust to being back in the world: expensive shoes and boots, new clothes, jewelry, and a car. It was clear that his mother would not be able to meet these needs. "Who will pay for all this?" he was asked. "My friends," he replied. They did. But the deal was that in return they expected him to rejoin the business of drug dealing. He did. To me, Jose's story indicates the importance of changing the basic materialistic values held by violent and troubled boys as the basis for detaching them from the call of the materialistic wild. It is certainly a tall order but one that is not out of reach if we know how to go about the process of deep personal transformation.

What is clear is that many boys fall back to their life of crime within six months of their release, but others manage to either stay straight or avoid detection until much later. A study conducted by Syracuse University psychologist Arnold Goldstein showed that overall about forty-five percent of the kids released from New York State juvenile prisons are rearrested within six months. The good news is that this number is not fixed. Boys who successfully completed a special program developed by Goldstein and designed to teach them how to control their anger and be more effective in common social situations evidenced a rearrest rate of 30 percent.

But even these numbers can be deceiving. Nowadays, the boys who commit the most serious violent crimes are usually sent to adult prison, having been tried as adults, or are sentenced to long terms in a secure center in the juvenile detention system, which means that they don't get released in time to be included in a study like Goldstein's (they are transferred to an adult correctional site when they reach the age of eighteen or twenty-one and still have time to serve on their sentence). When all is said and done, it is clear that the problem of recidivism is a big one, even with current state-of-the-art programming for kids. In fact, it is not uncommon to hear an estimated 85 percent recidivism rate offered, off the record, for the most troubled and aggressive boys by people inside the system, people who know that some of the published research reports overestimate program success because they only include boys who were positive enough to participate in and complete the program. Recidivism rates are very high for juvenile facilities housing violent boys, no matter how, when, and where you measure them.

High recidivism rates are testimony to the difficulty of reclaiming lost boys from the dark path and putting them on the right path. Knowing what we have learned in the preceding chapters about the development of troubled and violent boys, we confront with keen awareness of the enormity of the challenge the question, What *can* we do? The answers lie in solid, convincing research on the topics we have examined throughout this book: the influence of trauma on youth development, and the origins of bad behavior and severe aggression. This research provides some guidelines for rehabilitative programming for these boys, which begin with a commitment to nonresidential placement whenever possible.

The cost-effectiveness of treating as many boys as possible in their home communities with multisystemic therapy and other successful approaches is a powerful argument indeed. But often political considerations overrule this common sense, for example, when a boy's crime elicits community outrage or his background makes it difficult to justify the risk that he will commit another violent offense while in treatment but still free to roam the streets. When home-based treatment is not an option, for whatever reason, our focus must be on using the time in residential centers or prisons most productively.

PRINCIPLES FOR SUCCESSFUL PROGRAMS WITH VIOLENT BOYS

The first order of business for a residential center or prison is safety. Thus, we start with the immobilization of violent youth in settings that provide physical safety and prevent access to the temptations of drugs, sex, and the youth culture's materialism, which is conveyed and reinforced through advertising in the mass media. This setting of physical and cultural safety provides a context in which programming has a chance. Until adults are in control of the setting and can ensure the safety of the boys from each other and from themselves, nothing else positive will happen.

Heavy demands are placed on staff to maintain control but to do so in a way that avoids institutional abuse. The Family Life Development Center at Cornell University offers a program designed to help institutions do this: Therapeutic Crisis Intervention (TCI). TCI trains staff in residential facilities to adopt strategies and techniques that equip them to take charge but to do so without abuse. The program includes not only preventive measures to defuse violence when there is conflict but also techniques for safely restraining and immobilizing kids when they do act out. Programs like this are an essential element of a complete approach to creating a setting in which boys can be reclaimed. Without safety and security, there is no psychological space for the changes in behavior, thinking, and feeling that must come if a boy is to change for the better.

213

Once safety and security are established, boys need activities that promote psychological and social development. They need programs that build the psychological and social anchors I identified in Chapter Six. There is a growing body of evidence documenting how educational programs can provide these psychological and social supports for boys. Perhaps most notable among these efforts are the programs that work at changing the boys' ideas about violence and themselves by giving them practice in incorporating these new ideas into their behavior, first in the context of the institution and later in the world outside. Psychologists label such programs *cognitive–behavioral* to highlight their efforts to change both thinking (cognition) and action (behavior). University of Illinois psychologists Patrick Tolan and Nancy Guerra have looked at the effectiveness of a variety of violence-reduction programs aimed at teenagers and have concluded that cognitive–behavioral programs have the best success rate.

One prominent cognitive–behavioral program for youth in juvenile detention facilities was developed by Syracuse University psychologist Arnold Goldstein. It combines several elements in a structured ten-week sequence of lessons and activities. The first component focuses on teaching specific social skills to improve competence in the settings in which the youth must succeed in order to stay out of trouble, for example, school, work, neighborhood, and home. Goldstein calls this package Skillstreaming, and the skills include nonaggressive tactics for expressing a complaint, responding to the feelings of others, recovering from a stressful conversation, responding to anger, keeping out of fights, helping others, dealing with an accusation, dealing with group pressure, expressing affection, and responding to failure.

The second component involves activities designed to promote moral reasoning, in an effort to redirect boys' thinking as they consider what actions to take in everyday situations that provoke choices between prosocial and antisocial behavior. Each week, boys discuss moral dilemmas, including hypothetical situations, such as being on a sinking passenger ship in which there are not enough lifeboats for everyone on board, and real-life situations they are likely to encounter in the world, such as whether to inform on a drug dealer and cooperate with police if that cooperation could reduce their sentence but violate a friend's confidence.

The third element focuses on teaching boys techniques for recognizing the triggers for anger and for defusing and redirecting their anger so that it does not lead to violent behavior. The lessons include learning to pay attention to physiological cues and to use anger reducers such as deep breathing and peaceful imagery. The boys are encouraged to examine the hassles of daily life that arouse anger and practice, in extensive role-playing of such situations, various self-regulation techniques that can be effective in preventing aggression as a response to aroused anger.

Putting all three of these strategies together constitutes a treatment approach for violent boys that Goldstein calls Anger Replacement Training (ART). He and others who have applied this approach with delinquent, troubled, and violent boys report some success. In many cases, boys are able to learn the new skills, the new ways of reasoning, and the techniques for diffusing anger while they live in a residential center. When these new ways of thinking and behaving receive support from family members and others after a boy is released and returns home, the odds of success increase still further.

In one study, Goldstein found that after six months, fifteen percent of the thirteen boys who mastered the Anger Replacement Training and whose family members also completed the program had been arrested again, in comparison with thirty percent of the twenty boys whose family members did not participate in the program and forty-five percent of the 32 boys who did not participate in the ART program at all. In another study, ART was used with gang members in two neighborhoods in New York City: eight months after completing the program, thirteen percent of the group of 38 gang members who participated in the program had been rearrested while in the comparison group of twenty-seven boys, who did not receive the program, the rearrest figure was fifty-two percent.

GOING BEYOND BUSINESS AS USUAL WITH VIOLENT BOYS

Programs such as ART hold great promise for helping boys redirect their lives. But they are not enough, particularly for the most violent and troubled boys. For ART and other cognitive–behavioral programs to work, boys must be motivated to participate and learn. This is one of the principles of cognitive therapy. And boys must believe that they can apply the new knowledge and techniques in the world outside prison. The most troubled and violent boys often do not meet these criteria.

Claire and I have heard many boys talk about ART and other such programs in our one-on-one interviews. It is not always reassuring to listen to them. Some of the boys have memorized the lists of techniques and concepts but can do no more than parrot what is in the textbook. Others say they cannot imagine being able to apply these techniques in the situations they face in their world.

Claire is particularly good at exploring this issue with boys. Here is her interview with Lee, a sixteen-year-old boy who shot into a crowd of dancers one night because another boy insulted him:

"That's the most important thing I have to work on," Lee says, "controlling my anger."

"Suppose you were able to achieve your goal of graduating high school and going to college," says Claire. "Would you be able to live by the principles of Aggression Replacement Training out in the real world?"

"I think so."

"Let's imagine you are a student in college, and at lunch one day in the cafeteria you bump into the guy ahead of you in the line and he spills his drink on himself. What do you do then?"

"I use the ART techniques to defuse the situation," Lee replies. He explains how he would apply the concepts of anger management and de-escalation of conflict.

"What if next day you see this guy on campus and he comes over and shoves you and one of your books falls in a puddle? What do you do then?" Claire asks.

"I would say to him, 'Why did you do that? I apologized to you yesterday. What the hell are you doing, asshole!'"

"And then what if he says 'Fuck you!' and knocks your other book in the puddle?"

Lee thinks for minute and replies, "Then I would have to hit him, because if I didn't he wouldn't respect me and I wouldn't let anybody disrespect me. Never."

Lee has been through ART three times and has the catechism memorized, but it is clear that some of his core issues remain virtually untouched.

Maintaining order and physical safety and delivering cognitive–behavioral programs are not enough to initiate and sustain the deep changes necessary for rehabilitation in the long run. Conventional programs may succeed in providing some of the needed psychological and social anchors, but they are unlikely to provide the spiritual anchors that are required for success with the most traumatized, troubled, and violent boys. A complete rehabilitation program should adopt a broad understanding of the origins of youth violence and build on a foundation that is spiritual as well as psychological and social in nature. This complete approach rests on ten facts of life for violent boys, each of which implies principles to be used for rehabilitative programming in residential settings such as prisons and detention centers.

1. Child Maltreatment leads to survival strategies that are often antisocial and/or self-destructive.

Many violent boys were victims of child maltreatment. When maltreatment occurs as part of a more general accumulation of social and personal risk factors, it can lead to major developmental problems. Therefore, efforts to reclaim lost boys must deal with child maltreatment issues as part of the therapeutic program. This means using reading material and videos about child maltreatment and promoting a boy's efforts to identify incidents of child maltreatment in counseling sessions. This won't be easy, in part because boys often bury memories of child abuse deeply and in part because they are often reluctant to disclose experiences of victimization, no matter how much pain they have felt and sometimes no matter what hiding the fact of their victimization may cost them.

Some people in the legal system and in the larger society scoff at the idea that being abused as a child should play a role in evaluating and judging a boy who has committed a violent crime, and use the term "abuse excuse" to refer to this line of defense. They believe that boys and men will invent and exaggerate accounts of abuse to gain the undeserved sympathy of judges, juries, and the general public. There are two rather serious flaws in this reasoning. First, I doubt that anyone who has actually experienced the horror of being abused and who has come to terms with its effects would ever presume to discount its impact on their own development. Mostly, this dismissal of the developmental significance of abuse comes from people who do not really appreciate the psychological realities of abuse or who are suppressing those facts in an effort to protect themselves emotionally from confronting their own experience.

Second, rather than publicly parading their abuse in a self-serving effort to diminish their personal responsibility, most abused boys go to great lengths to hide their experience of abuse. When I interviewed seventeen-year-old James, he said he would rather take his chances in facing a first degree murder charge than admit in court that he had been sexually abused by his uncle. "I just don't want to put my family through that, you know?" he said. "I don't think my mother could take hearing about what her brother had done, after all she has been through with me." It was only after several sessions, and the intervention of his lawyer, that James reluctantly agreed to have his shameful secret spoken in open court. It is common for incarcerated boys to go through ten hours of interviews focusing on family and personal experiences of violence and never mention being abused, even when the scars are right there on their legs from whippings inflicted by extension cords or on their arms from burns resulting from cigarettes being ground out on their skin.

Also, kids often assume that whatever they experienced at home is normal; they may need to be taught directly about standards for the treatment of children and the meaning of child maltreatment. For example, Trinity College psychologist Sharon Hershberger found that abused kids thought, before such a program, that the treatment they received at home was normal, had no effect on their development, and was their fault. After treatment, they recognized certain behaviors of their parents as abusive, understood their potential for causing long-term psychological harm, and saw the responsibility for what happened as being in the hands of their parents.

I see this when I interview young men on death row, men who are appealing their death sentences. Sometimes it has been more than five years since their original trial. During the interim they have had time to reflect and read and often have been interviewed numerous times by psychologists, social workers, psychiatrists, and lawyers about their background and their childhood experiences. Sometimes they have even had some psychotherapy. It is sometimes only after all this focusing on their experience, all the years of processing what happened to them (as well as what they did) that these scarred men will acknowledge that they were victims of child maltreatment. The least of my concerns is an over-reliance on abuse as an excuse. Usually, it takes all of our efforts just to bring it out as an explanation at all.

2. The experience of early trauma leads boys to become hypersensitive to arousal in the face of threat and to respond to such threats by disconnecting emotionally or acting out aggressively.

The experience of trauma produces dramatic and hidden emotional responses in a child. These responses include emotional numbing and withdrawal. Traumatized children try to escape feeling the pain even when they cannot physically escape the situation or the people who cause that pain. This becomes a habit. According to psychiatrist Bruce Perry, this pattern often is diagnosed as Attention Deficit Disorder (ADD), rather than as a trauma-related adaptation, by adults who are not aware of the trauma.

Of course, Attention Deficit Disorder itself is a major problem of troubled and aggressive boys. It occurs often in these boys and is a constant irritant to them and to those around them in school, in the community, at home, and in residential placement. While medication has proved useful in suppressing some of the negative behavior associated with ADD, the effects tend to be short-lived and do not sustain themselves when the medication is discontinued or later refused.

Traumatized boys whose behavior resembles ADD are often powder kegs waiting to explode. In a situation in which they feel powerless, like a prison, these boys will initially seek to withdraw when threatened. When pushed too far, however, this attempt to reduce the overstimulation through withdrawal can give way to aggressive responses. Adults working with these boys need to understand that this response can make a youth appear emotionless when in fact these boys are actually filled with intense emotions.

A staff member in a secure facility for violent boys tells it this way.

> I see this boy sitting in the back of the group, with his hands pulled up into his sleeves and his shoulders hunched over. So I say to him, "Hey, Darrell, I want you to pay attention to what I am saying." He ignores me. So I say a bit louder, "Darrell! I told you to pay attention." Nothing. No reaction. So I go back to him and say, "Darrell, if you can't pay attention, I am going to have to put you on report, and you know what that means." Still nothing. So I reach out to grab his shoulder to get his attention, and before I know it he is out of the chair and swinging at me. And I'm thinking, "Where the hell did that come from?"

Trauma-related powerful emotions under the surface in a boy can trigger severe aggression in response to upsets that seem minor or trivial to an outsider. Therefore, adults dealing with these kids should avoid power assertion whenever possible to reduce the experience of threat and thus maintain the youth in an emotionally engaged and nonaggressive state. "Gentle but firm, always kind" should be the watchwords. It takes a lot of preparation and support for staff to live by this credo, but the more they can do so, the more they permit the rehabilitative aspects of the program to influence the thinking and behavior of violent boys without being sabotaged by their emotions. Of course, healing the emotional wounds of violent boys is necessary for eventual rehabilitation, and the overall emotional climate of the facility can help on that score.

3. Traumatized kids require a calming and soothing environment to increase the level at which they are functioning.

One of the effects of living a traumatic life is that it affects a boy's emotional temperature, in the sense that he becomes very reactive to stimulation. Trauma can even affect the development of a child's brain. A boy's brain may even get into the habit of being so reactive that it takes less and less to set him off. Neurologists call this process by which it takes less and less external stimulation to set off an internal reaction *kindling*. This phenomenon has been observed in the development of depression. Initial episodes are triggered by external events of loss and stress, but as kindling proceeds, the individual needs less and less of an external cause to set off another episode of depression.

When a boy with a traumatic history is triggered, his functioning descends from the higher parts of the brain (the cortex), where he can think clearly, to the lower parts of his brain (the limbic and midbrain regions), where primitive thoughts and emotions directed toward survival predominate. It is when boys are responding with their cortex that they can participate in rehabilitative programs. When they are responding from their primitive reptilian brain regions, they are just struggling to survive. The question for staff members of a rehabilitative program is thus always, Which is it to be, the thinker or the lizard?

Therefore, adults caring for violent boys should provide an environment that encourages calmness and reflection. This should include soothing classical music, meditation, and a generally low-key, rather than overstimulating, daily pattern of activities. The last thing these boys need is provocative music and arousing videos—no Marilyn Manson and no "gangsta rap." What these boys most need is an environment that is quiet and calm, one that promotes reflection rather than distracting attention from reflection. Playing classical music stimulates the higher parts of the brain and can set a positive tone for the rest of the activities in a facility housing troubled and violent boys. Also helpful are videos that promote calm reflection, rather than stimulate primitive emotions, and participation in such creative arts as painting, drawing, photography, and fiction writing.

One interesting innovation has been to have Tibetan monks come to a juvenile correction facility to demonstrate the art of the sand mandela, an elaborate work of art made out of various colored sands and including symbols of positive cultural significance (for the monks, of course, the key symbols are Buddhist). The creation of a sand mandela offers extended periods of calm focus for boys, an opportunity to create something of great symbolic significance to them, and a chance to communicate with holy men. An added benefit in a prison setting stems from the fact that many of the Tibetan monks themselves were imprisoned by the Chinese government occupying their homeland; there is, therefore, a natural bond between the inmates and the monks. The Samaya Foundation in New York City has pioneered in this approach and has produced a video introducing the process.

Another effort directed toward the creation of a calm environment for traumatized violent boys is the teaching and encouragement of meditation practices. Perhaps more than anything else, meditation practices can help soothe, calm, and focus troubled and violent boys and put them in a state of mind in which educational efforts can succeed. Incarcerated boys face the prospect of years of enforced solitude. When faced with this enormous human challenge, some boys survive either by nurturing rage and hate inside, awaiting their chance to wreak havoc on the world later, or by simply deteriorating into madness.

Meditation is one of the few strategies for converting the danger posed by enforced solitude and immobilization into an opportunity for personal growth and development. One fine example is Vipassana meditation, a technique originating in India that combines efforts to focus on the experience of the present moment with reflection on one's contribution to one's suffering and pain. It has found a place in Indian prisons as a result of the work of Kiran Bedi, inspector general of prisons in New Delhi, a remarkable social reformer and law enforcement officer who is well-known in India for her unorthodox methods to achieve the rehabilitation of criminals. At the time she took charge, the standard model for the Indian prison was described by the superintendent of Tihar prison, Tarsem Kumar, in terms that sound even bleaker than descriptions of many American institutions:

> To add to the acute problems of overcrowding, inadequate sanitation, insufficient breathing space, etc., the jail staff were trained under the old rules where the outlook was to oppress, deprive, isolate and punish. The staff believed that oppression and imposing maximum restrictions on the inmates would make them suffer, so that once a prisoner was released he would not commit crimes again for fear of being sent back to this hell. But they were mistaken. After their release, many prisoners did return, and some prisoners who were incarcerated for petty crimes resorted to more serious crimes after their release, having learned in Tihar how to become bigger and better criminals. One of the members of the Planning Commission of India correctly remarked that the prisoners at Tihar were doing their Ph.D. in crime. Tihar was breeding criminals, not reformed citizens.

The first ten-day Vipassana course was taught with Dr. Bedi's support, and the events leading up to and following this experience are documented in the award-winning film *Doing Time, Doing Vipassana*." Today there is a permanent meditation center within the walls of Tihar Jail, as well as in several other Indian prisons, at which regular Vipassana courses are conducted. Following the establishment of this technique in the prisons of India, Vipassana courses have been successfully conducted in prison facilities in Taiwan as well as in the United States as part of a program to reduce recidivism.

Vipassana courses have been conducted in the United States in the North Rehabilitation Facility (N.R.F.) of the King County jail system in Seattle, Washington. One very common result from the practice of this meditation by prison inmates is their reduced desire for revenge. Relations among prisoners and jail staff become much more harmonious, and self-discipline dramatically improves, thus decreasing the need for ag-gressive supervision and punishment by jail officials.

Seventeen-year-old Alan said this of his experience with meditation in the youth prison where he is in the third year of a ten-year sentence for attempted murder:

> Each day I find time for my meditation. At first it wasn't easy. So many thoughts flooded through my mind I was impatient to stop. But I worked at it, every day. The books you gave me on meditation helped me under-stand better how to do it. It took a lot of time to get it right, but hey, I've got plenty of time. That's about all I have is time. Now that I have been doing it for four months, I don't feel right if for some reason I miss my morning and evening meditation time. It's like I am hungry for it if I miss it, so I try not to miss it. In my mediation I am learning about peace for the first time in my life. I feel different in myself and with the other residents. I'm calmer and when things get tense on my unit, I try to pro-ject my own inner peace all around me. Thank you for getting me started. It makes all the difference in the world. Bless you.

4. Traumatized youth are likely to evidence an absence of future orientation.

Without future orientation there is no motivation to invest time in preparatory activities—going to school, learning new skills, delaying gratification. With a strong sense of the future, motivation to participate in educational and personal change programs increases. Without it, the prospect of being incarcerated can be fatal. It is not uncommon for boys to think about suicide or even to take action to end their lives once they begin to realize that by conventional measures their lives may be over. This is one reason some boys call out to be killed when apprehended, as did Kip Kinkel. Sometimes when I speak with a boy who is on trial and whose probable sentence is life imprisonment, he will say simply, "If they sentence me to life, I am going to kill myself." As psychiatrist James Gilli-gan points out, on the basis of his years of work in adult prisons, men all too often fulfill this vow.

Therefore, institutions that care for violent boys should provide ac-tivities to promote future orientation. To my knowledge, this is not the explicit goal of any program, but I think it can and does take place when boys are involved in caring for plants, animals, and other human beings. Taking care is one of the few reliable tactics for stimulating future orientation. Once violent boys are safe and secure, they need opportunities to see the future concretely in front of them in the form of something or someone to take care of.

Of course, there must be a lot of supervision for caregiving activities. The risk of putting violent boys into relationships with others when they may be aggressive and hurtful is self-evident. And since many violent boys have a history of troubled, even cruel, relationships with animals, there is a need for caution in any potential caregiving situation. Starting with plants and then moving to animals, and eventually to human beings, may be the most prudent strategy.

In stimulating future orientation, it is useful to make use of literary materials to provide role models. Biographies of boys who seemed mired in terminal thinking but who found a way to rebuild a concept of the future are very important. Jarvis Masters's *Finding Freedom: Writings from Death Row* is a fine example. *The Autobiography of Malcolm X* is another.

5. *Youth exposed to violence at home and in the community are likely to develop juvenile vigilantism, in which they do not trust an adult's capacity and motivation to ensure safety, and as a result believe they must take matters into their own hands.*

By and large, kids who are institutionalized for committing acts of lethal violence have learned that adults cannot protect them and have experienced years of being on their own without adult protection—in fact or in their perception of things. Therefore, an important element in institutional programming and management must be efforts to promote trust in adult authority.

Doing so requires creating a highly controlled environment in which youth conclude *rationally* that they are safe and thus can afford to relinquish their defensive posture. Boys need to be able to relax and let down their guard. They will only do this if they can look around them and see that the adults *are* in charge, that the adults *are* fair, that the adults *will* protect them. Only then can violent boys divert their energies from hypervigilance toward learning and personal transformation. It is a matter of trust, and for these boys trust is a very precious commodity, one that is in short supply.

Soon after he arrives and before he has had a chance to learn the special character of the facility in which we are sitting, Tommy tells me, "I been around, you know what I mean. I been in every single facility in this state, and I know how to take care of myself. You're on your own in here, let me tell you. I got shivs hidden everywhere I need them, you know what I mean. I got one in my room they ain't never going to find. I got one in the classroom and in the shop. I am prepared to defend myself, you know what I mean? You can't trust nobody. Not the staff, not the other residents, nobody but yourself."

A couple of months later, after he has had a chance to see that things are different in this facility than in the others he has been in, Tommy changes his tune a bit when I ask him, "Do you feel safe here now?"

"Yeah," he says, "this place is different, man. You can breathe a bit and relax a little, you know what I mean? The staff here are in control, you know what I mean?"

"What do you mean?" I ask.

"I mean, like they know who's who and what's what. You understand. It's different here."

"What about those shivs?"

"I still got them hid. I got no need for them right now, but a person got to be ready—you know what I mean?—in case the situation changes here. You know what I mean?"

6. *Youth who have participated in the violent drug economy or chronic theft are likely to have distorted materialistic values.*

Many violent boys have come up through the illicit drug economy or have been involved in chronic theft, robbery, burglary, and extortion. This means they have had firsthand exposure to the corrupting influence of "big money" in our shallow materialistic culture. These boys are used to having lots of pocket money, used to buying jewelry, used to treating their friends to opulent purchases, used to all the many other ways modern kids participate in the lavish economy that surrounds most of us.

Therefore, it is necessary to promote spiritual values that transcend the materialistic culture. But this will not happen as a matter of "do as I say, not as I do"—when adults tout the need for "higher values" but manifest love of worldly material success. Many boys have bought into the idea that the size of one's bankroll defines one's worth as a person. Adults may inadvertently encourage this thinking in boys when they extol life success stories that emphasize material worth. I recall sitting painfully through an inspirational lecture delivered by a facility director who went to great lengths to describe the success of some of the facility's graduates. Rather than focusing on the strength of character these boys showed in growing into responsible men, he chose to highlight the fact that they now own cars and houses, in some cases more than one of each.

This kind of rhetoric is hardly the path to transformation for violent and troubled boys who are already hooked on material acquisitions and the goal of making big money. Quite the contrary, the kind of transformation needed for these boys requires concerted effort by staff to model more noble values and to involve boys in directed reading, spiritual practice, and discussion designed to expose them to these values. This process of transformation includes wearing simple uniforms, practicing guided meditation, participating in the creative arts, performing service to others, and engaging in spiritually oriented instruction such as tai chi and yoga to increase self-discipline.

I think all of our children—indeed, all of us—would benefit from intensive spiritual development to counter the insidious influences of our culture, but vulnerable boys certainly cannot tolerate that culture. In this, as in so many other areas, violent, lost boys need a rehabilitation program that takes them beyond the usual existence for American kids. Violent and troubled boys need to undergo a powerful transformation and redirection, so that they can be inoculated against the seductions of materialism. Remember, we are talking about reclaiming boys who are otherwise lost. Left to their own impulses at this point in their lives, odds are that they will end up dying early or serving decades in prison and being the focal point of enormous grief as perpetrators and victims of future crimes.

7. Traumatized youth who have experienced abandonment are likely to feel life is meaningless.

Connection is crucial. Human beings are fundamentally social beings. This insight has ancient roots in philosophy, from Aristotle to Spinoza. It finds scientific documentation in psychologist Lev Vygotsky's *Language and Thought,* in which he recognizes human development as proceeding through social experience.

Having some identity in relation to peers is so important to most children and youth that even a negative definition of self is better than nothing at all. This insight is vital in understanding violent and troubled boys. They *will* achieve an identity, whatever the cost of doing so to themselves and their communities. Feeling like he is a nobody is emotionally intolerable for a boy.

Desperation pushes boys into signing on with the dark side. Typically, they are defined as loners or outsiders by their more positive peers. Chris Black, Derrick Shields, and Peter Magnotti in Fort Myers, Florida, created an anti-universe as the Lords of Chaos rather than live as nobodies in their high school. The eventual result was a dead teacher. Luke Woodham in Pearl, Mississippi, gravitated to a Satanic cult in his community rather than live as an isolated outcast. When theologian Reinhold Niebuhr wrote of the permanent contest between "the children of light and the children of darkness," he identified some of the issues we face in reclaiming troubled and violent boys. These include the fact that sometimes trust will be abused and that some boys are too lost to be saved at all.

Often, a lack of positive purpose is one of the consequences of early abandonment. Stewart's beloved grandmother died when he was eight. Taking him in four years earlier, when his parents abandoned him, she had promised him, "I will take care of you. You are safe now." But when she died, Stewart "declared war on the world." Within months he was part of a petty theft ring led by a nineteen-year-old. Four years later, he was carrying a gun as a soldier for a drug ring in his neighborhood. A couple of years after that he committed his first shooting, and a year later his first murder.

As representatives of Niebuhr's "children of light," we must help violent boys create the basis for new lives by exposing them to novels, biographies, and relationships with adults that provide good examples of positive meaningfulness in the face of loss and abandonment. We are in a struggle for the souls of these boys, and literacy is one of the important resources in this struggle. The research of psychologist James Pennebaker documents that writing is more therapeutic for traumatized individuals than just talking. Literacy and literature are vitally important in the process of reclaiming violent and troubled boys, because they can find new alternative models for themselves in the positive lives of others.

Lost boys need new working models that concretely show them how they can become someone other than the person they have been. This implies that adults who work with and care for these boys must bring to this work a strong positive sense of purpose themselves. They should share with the boys their own personal narratives of hope and redemption in the face of adversity and loss and be mentors in the biggest, broadest, deepest sense.

8. Issues of shame are paramount among violent youth.

Violent boys are plagued by issues of humiliation and shame. Be they poor, minority, abused children from inner-city war zones or alienated middle-class majority kids from "normal" families, they share these issues. These two groups of boys are connected in their participation in violence, in their troubled inner lives, and in their seduction by the dark side. But they are differentiated by the circumstances of their backgrounds. We face a paradox in seeing both groups of boys clearly, however. In the case of inner-city victims of child abuse, it is often easier to see the origins of their violence in economic inequality and racism and in families overwhelmed by stress, but it is harder to see their hurt and the disillusionment, because these boys often present a macho, tough, belligerent exterior that frightens adults. In the case of middle-class kids, it is easier to see them as troubled and depressed—because they often seem so pathetic, particularly after the shooting is over—but it is harder to see the causes of their inner turmoil and their violence when their families and communities appear so "normal" on the surface.

But when we look deeply, we can see the fundamental human similarity between the violent boys from the inner-city war zones and the lost boys from "good families" and "good communities." All violent boys share a common sense of inner crisis, a crisis of shame and emptiness. These boys are ashamed of who they are inside, and their efforts to compensate for that shame drive their violence. It may be buried under layer after layer of protective bravado or it may be worn like a badge on their sleeves, but it is there. It may take hours of listening to a brash, tough inner-city kid to finally hear him admit, "I'm afraid of God's judgment" or "Nobody really cares about me" or "I want to be somebody." It may only take one short conversation with a killer from the American heartland to hear the pathetic quality of his voice and recognize the shallowness of his posturing.

Watching the Lords of Chaos interviewed on NBC's *Dateline* in September 1998, after they had been sentenced to life sentences for the murder of their school's band teacher, I was truck by the pathetic quality of these boys. The "Lords of Chaos?" Are they kidding? As I listened to them reflect on what they had done in 1996, it seemed to me that even the boys themselves could appreciate how silly and pompous they were as they sought to compensate for the shame of being nobodies in their school. Listening to the interview of a group of their classmates and hearing the dismissive scorn in their voices as they laughed *at* the self-proclaimed "lords," I could see why shame was such an issue for the boys who ended their foray into the dark side with murder.

It is because of the central role of shame in instigating and sustaining violence that we must communicate *respect* in every facet of institutional life as a precondition for transformation of troubled and violent boys. This includes the language used by staff to communicate with youth—no dismissive terms like *knucklehead*. And it includes taking them seriously as participants in the management of their rehabilitation. Boys have real ideas, often good ideas, about how to manage things, and they should play a role, with guidance and supervision. It means providing them with opportunities for success—academic, vocational, and social. One of the finest experiences I've had in my work in youth prisons was attending an awards ceremony where boys who had completed their high school equivalency requirements were honored and the leaders in every academic subject taught in the prison school were acknowledged. There was genuine pride there—both in the voices of staff members who delivered the awards and in the faces of boys who received them. The goal is always to convey acceptance as an antidote for shame and to build a justifiable sense of pride and a responsible and appropriate self-esteem among boys who have been "looking for love in all the wrong places."

9. Youth violence is a boy's attempt to achieve justice as he perceives it.

The more we know about violent boys, the more we understand the role of frustrated justice in their violent behavior. Their sense of frustrated justice combines with their contracted web of caring to produce the stunted and distorted moral judgment and moral feelings they use to justify lethal violence. Therefore, the first step in moral reeducation is to acknowledge the boys' perception of the justice of their violent actions; by starting from a position of empathy, we can energize their moral feelings. When boys speak of their violent actions as "mistakes," an accepting but transformation-oriented adult response can be the beginning of the process of change. This adult response is the starting point for seeing the parallels between how they were hurt and how they have hurt others.

In his book *A Path with Heart,* psychologist and meditation teacher Jack Kornfield explains the spiritual practice of loving-kindness. The ultimate goal of this practice of meditation is to achieve a more caring attitude toward the world, a more ethical stance in relation to the community, and a more spiritually grounded experience of others. But the practice does not *start* with loving-kindness toward others, it starts with loving-kindness toward oneself. The ancient meditation is coupled with images of being cared for, being cradled in love: "May I be filled with loving-kindness. May I be well. May I be peaceful and at ease. May I be happy." This is wise: to love others we must first love ourselves. This self-love is not a matter of self-aggrandizement and egotistical self-congratulation. It is not the origin of what I identified in an earlier chapter as deadly petulance. It is, instead, a firm psychological foundation for being able to care for others. Everyone involved in dealing with troubled and violent youth can benefit from this practice of self-acceptance.

Having created a new emotional climate, the goal is to engage boys in a dialogue about moral issues. The purpose of such a dialogue is to help them reinterpret their perceptions of justice. Here the focus should be on addressing issues in a way that models higher levels of moral judgment and feelings as a basis for stimulating moral development in the boys. In pursuit of this goal, readings and videos that provide models of higher-order handling of moral dilemmas and that promote alternatives to aggression are recommended.

10. Violent boys often seem to feel they cannot afford empathy.

Troubled and violent boys have been so emotionally busy struggling with their own internal demons that they have had little psychic energy for others. A lost boy's own vulnerability leads him to develop strategies to depersonalize other people, so that he can remain strong enough to do what he believes he has to do to survive psychologically (and sometimes physically). Because we know that empathy is the enemy of aggression and that depersonalization is its ally, all efforts at moral rehabilitation of violent and troubled boys hinge upon cultivating empathy and fighting against their tendency to depersonalize others.

Programming and institutional management should promote the development of empathy as a goal for day-to-day interaction among staff and youth. But to model empathy, staff need to be treated empathetically themselves by supervisors and administrators. Here, as elsewhere, the starting point lies with Mahatma Gandhi's guiding principle: "You must be the change you wish to see in the world." I hear this in the pained voices of junior staff members who confide to me that they often feel caught between their desire to help the boys and their duty to respond to the demands of administrators that they remain always in control.

When staff feel depersonalized by administrators, they hardly feel encouraged to be empathetic with the boys in their charge. I can think of few more difficult tasks in the current political and cultural climate than to adopt and maintain an empathetic stance toward violent and troubled boys. I do not think it is too strong a statement to say that society, for the most part, hates and fears these boys. The inner demons these boys carry with them militate against the likelihood that adults will feel emotionally connected to them.

All teenagers in groups are programmed to distinguish themselves from adults in public settings. The same teenager who with his friends in the mall seems cold and scornful toward an adult may be warm and friendly to that same adult when they talk one-on-one in private. Violent and troubled boys are still teenagers. This fact adds to the emotional burden of adult staff who work with them. And it suggests that institutions serving violent boys would do well to seek ways to promote one-on-one time between adults and teenagers. This innovation is possible, once conventional thinking is put aside.

In one facility I visited, the staff was bemoaning the fact that they did not have the time to have one-on-one sessions with the resident boys. I asked them, "What is the total number of staff at this facility?" "Sixty," replied a member of the group. "How many kids are there in this facility?" I asked. "Fifty-two," someone responded. I smiled and said, "That means that if once or twice a week you could have everyone in the building stop what they are doing for one hour—everyone, including the maintenance and kitchen staff, the secretaries and the counselors, stop what they are doing—you *could* for that one hour have each adult be with one boy, one-on-one. Wouldn't that be an interesting mentor program?" There was silence as they thought about the implications of what I had said. Then a few of the staff nodded and smiled. Perhaps a seed was planted.

FROM BOOT CAMP TO MONASTERY

In recent years there has been a lot of public and professional interest in the use of "boot camps" as placements for delinquent, violent, and troubled boys. These programs usually mimic military basic training: a lot of shouting, a lot of threats, powerful leaders who dominate new recruits through the force of their personality, and implicit (and sometimes explicit) violence. Even those of us who have not been through basic training most likely have some concrete ideas of the experience from watching movies or television.

Here I use the term *boot camp* to represent the model of power assertion, didactic lecturing, and shaming that is common in youth prisons. I reject it as a model, because I think it is most *unsuited* to violent boys, given where they come from psychologically and who they are developmentally and spiritually. The boot camp model typically violates many, if not most, of the ten principles I have just presented. It violates much of what we know about the developmental histories of violent boys. Psychiatrist Bruce Perry was one of the first to point this out. For starters, he directed our attention to the fact that the very last thing a boy with a traumatic psychological history needs is someone getting in his face and screaming at him (Principles 2 and 3).

While I certainly understand some of the impulse to create boot camp programs—and acknowledge that while they may be all wrong on some accounts, they *can* offer some positive experiences of structure and reward for positive behavior, for some boys—I think there is a better way to get those advantages, and without the disadvantages. I believe the little evidence that is available evaluating the impact of the boot camp concept is consistent with this suspicion on my part. For example, a review of these programs conducted for the federal government's Office of

Juvenile Justice and Delinquency Prevention found that boot camp programs overall had no higher rate of success than conventional youth detention programs.

I do not think that programs and institutions based on a boot camp model will be successful in promoting the kinds of profound transformations needed to reclaim lost boys once they have committed acts of lethal violence. These programs lack too many of the crucial spiritual, psychological, and social anchors violent and troubled boys need. Instead, as an alternative to the boot camp, I propose the model of a monastery.

A monastery emphasizes contemplation, reflection, service, cooperation, meditation, and peace, instead of confrontation, dominance, and power assertion. I recall offering this analysis to a friend who had spent the early years of her vocation as a nun in a convent to prepare her for later saintly work "in the world," healing the sick and working for social justice in the United States and abroad. "Of course," she said with a smile, "these boys need the vows of poverty, chastity, and obedience." She gave it her blessing.

Violent and troubled boys need these vows in the safety of a secure setting, within a caring community, and with the therapeutic support of cognitive–behavioral programs to teach them new social skills. They need the deeply spiritual practice that a monastery-like setting can provide. I think of my saintly friend as I develop the monastery model implicit in the ten principles for programming that I have just outlined, and I am always grateful for her blessing.

Where does my concept of the monastery model for youth detention facilities come from? In part it comes from my interviews with boys and a strong sense that peace proceeds when adults practice peace with kids, not declare war on them. It comes from my own spiritual development and my efforts to make sense of myself and my relationships with the world. It comes from Claire. I found inspiration for the monastery model in her study of Buddhist and Christian contemplative practices and in a passage from *Peace Is Every Step* by world-renowned Zen Buddhist master and Nobel Peace Prize nominee Thich Nhat Hanh. The following passage is entitled *Blaming Never Helps*:

When you plant lettuce, if it does not grow well, you don't blame the lettuce. You look into the reasons it is not doing well. It may need fertilizer, or more water, or less sun. You never blame the lettuce. Yet if we have problems with our friends or our family, we blame the other person. But if we know how to take care of them, they will grow well, like lettuce. Blaming has no positive effect at all, nor does trying to persuade using reason and arguments. That is my experience. No blame, no reasoning, no argument, just understanding. If you understand, and you show that you understand, you can love, and the situation will change.

In many ways it is as simple and as hard as that. "Love thy neighbor as thyself."

"Judge not lest ye be judged."

"The unexamined life is not worth living."

"If you begin a journey of revenge, start by digging two graves, one for your enemy and one for yourself."

Like all the great wisdom of the ages, the simplicity of Thich Nhat Hanh's words is as awesome as the challenge of living by them in our efforts to reclaim violent and troubled boys. Knowing what we know about the lives of these lost boys, I think we can find ways to embrace this wisdom and translate it into day-to-day reality in the institutions we support to reclaim them. Martin Luther King Jr. spoke often of the power of "soul force" in meeting the challenge of dealing with violence. We need to harness that soul force in the transformation of violent and troubled boys, and there are efforts to do so. I am part of one such effort.

LEADERSHIP IS CRUCIAL

The climate in any institution reflects the leadership, who they are and what they value. The atmosphere at Louis Gossett Center is due in large measure to the leadership provided by Director Joe Impiccatore. I first met Joe when he was director of the MacCormick Center, where he and his colleague, Assistant Director Alvin Lollie, had engineered a major turnaround, bringing it from a period when it was regularly criticized for being brutal and "out of control" to being recognized as a "model" facility throughout the OCFS system. Both Joe and Alvin welcomed me warmly when I began to visit MacCormick with my colleague Claire Bedard. They were proud of the positive changes they had made to the program, were eager for further improvement, and became advocates for us in the larger

OCFS system. Joe was named "Administrator of the Year" in 1996 in recognition of his success in turning around MacCormick (and in recognition of Joe's and Alvin's success, in 1998 Joe was asked to become director of the Gossett Center—which is three times the size of MacCormick—and Alvin was offered the directorship of OCFS's Goshen Center).

Gosset is Joe's facility now, and it reflects his decency and his skill. One proof of Joe's success in establishing his leadership is that Malcolm once referred to Joe as "the owner." From the very beginning, Joe was supportive and helpful. Having visited many institutions of one sort or another over the years, I was quite aware of the fact that we could do our work there only because of the support we received from the leadership.

In early 1998, Joe asked us to provide four half-day seminars to bring together the key staff at the facility so we could share with them what we had learned in the previous year's interviews with the boys and from our review of the available research. It was an opportunity to see how what we thought we were learning would sit with the people who were responsible for the boys day and night. It was a chance to bring to the front line staff our application of the research on trauma, violence, attachment, and social development that I have shared throughout this book.

We knew that this group of staff were exposed to "training" every month, and they were quite jaded, since much of what they heard was boring and not very useful. But scary as it was, this opportunity to speak with the staff was a very important event for me. I had spoken in general terms about the issues and content of our project with psychologists, psychiatrists, educators, probation officers, lawyers, and social workers on the *outside* before, but this was my first experience with staff on the *inside*.

What to do? If the answer was easy, the recidivism rate would not be as high as it is. If the path was clear, staff would not be frustrated and skeptical. If someone knew exactly how to do this effectively, those who argue that society should "lock them up and throw away the key" would not be succeeding in more and more state legislatures. It's a hard, hard question, certainly the hardest I have dealt with in my professional career.

HOPE AGAIN

In the months following the presentation, and encouraged by Assistant Director Brenda Aulbach, Joe Impiccatore made a commitment to try the monastery model at the Gossett Center. A task force of staff members at Gossett was created to make the transition in one of the facility's five units on an experimental basis. And this is what Claire and I started doing in February of 1999, working with Joe, Brenda, the facility's psychologist Puck Wullenweber, Supervisor Rit Gallucci, and other staff members to implement the boot camp to monastery model in one small place, with one small group of troubled and violent boys. These are people who have worked for many years in the youth correctional system. They entered that system because they wanted to help kids. Their frustration with "business as usual" motivated them to take on the risky challenge of changing to the monastery model. I salute them.

It will take years to discover how well the monastery model works, and how to make it work better. But it feels very good to know these fine brave people are making a go of it. They have refused to give in to cynicism and defeatism. Despite the challenges of going to work day after day to face troubled and violent boys, despite the defeats and the disappointments, Joe and his colleagues continue to hope. They continue to struggle against the dark side. They continue to do their best to reclaim lost boys. We all owe them a debt of gratitude.

WHO IS RESPONSIBLE FOR YOUTH VIOLENCE?

Violent boys in prison have it drilled into their heads that they are personally responsible. They mouth the words they have been taught by "the system." Indeed, to the extent that there is a reward structure in this system, it is predicated on a boy's willingness to take on this personal responsibility for his actions. Decision-making skills. Victim awareness. Personal accountability. And a boy often does take on this rhetoric, even retroactively, as he speaks about the bad decisions he made at age eight to get involved in dealing drugs or carrying a weapon to school.

But sometimes boys choke on these concepts as they spit out their resentment at having been abandoned to their own fate. They cry out for empathy. Malcolm says, "You place any one of them people outside, you put them in that predicament, and they going to do the same thing."

What are we to do for and about violent boys after they are released? I hope that we can continue the process of personal transformation, beginning with community-based programs that seek to hold on to the boys that have benefitted from the monastery program and claim them from the social poisons around them and the negativity inside. California's "Street Soldiers" program, developed by Joe Marshall and his colleagues, provides a working model. This program combines mentoring, spiritual development, skills training, political education, and education.

In some case, a "perpetrator relocation" program can help. Some violent boys are released into new, less socially toxic environments in which they can start fresh with whatever newfound skills, beliefs, and social maps they acquired during incarceration. But even this would not be enough to solve the problem we face. The change must begin inside violent boys. That is why I focus my attention on promoting personal transformation (what in Chapter Seven I refer to as "positive functional autonomy") so powerful that it develops enough positive momentum to sustain boys once they return home.

Conventional prison models are based on power assertion, which means ramming changed rhetoric and behavior down a boy's throat. Violent boys need to make connections with higher powers and realities, to connect with something untouchable by the social toxicity they come from and to which they will likely return. They need to harness their own soul force.

The monastery model is not a new idea, of course. Quakers in Philadelphia in the nineteenth century sought to create just such asylums for the troubled of their time. The Lionheart Foundation, created by Robin Casarjian, seeks similarly to make the spiritual connection for the incarcerated of our time. Her book *Houses of Healing* is a guide for adult prisoners. Bo Lozoff has developed this same line of insight in his book *We're All Doing Time*, which he promotes through the Prison Ashram Project. Jarvis Masters's *Finding Freedom* is a memoir of one man who did so after, and chronicles his path to discovery, enlightenment, and redemption. In his case the gateway led to Buddhism and redemptive nonviolence. Malcolm X found his redemption though Islam. For others, the opportunity comes through Christianity. The point is that violent and troubled boys can achieve redemptive transformation if they cultivate the life of the spirit, if they tend to their souls.

I've seen this in adult men myself. More than a decade ago I visited an adult prison in Pennsylvania to spend time with a group of men serving life sentences without possibility of parole, life terms that often had begun in adolescence ten, fifteen, or twenty years earlier. Each of these men had found the spiritual gateway and walked through it. Sometimes it had taken a decade of resistance and false starts to find that gateway and to gather up the courage to walk through it. But walk through it they had. This is what I hope for in the lives of the lost boys—but through the monastery model my hope is that they can do it *now*, rather than wait years. This short cut to redemption and rehabilitation is my hope and my prayer.

In one sense, the monastery program we have envisioned is simply an attempt to bring boys back to the developmental path I have outlined throughout this book as the alternative to violence. That path starts with positive attachment based on the spiritual character of the human child. It continues with the skillful management and guidance of boys who are temperamentally at risk and who are abused and neglected psychologically and physically. It focuses on making the social environment around these boys—family, school, and community—more competent in meeting their special needs. It anchors these boys in empathy and socially engaged moral thinking. In short, it organizes the daily life experiences of boys around opportunities to learn positive lessons about how to be a man—a strong man who does not succumb to the cultural stereotypes of a socially toxic society that defines manhood in terms of aggression, power, and material acquisition. If offers hope, to the lost boys and to the society as a whole. Amen to hope.

Appendix

WHERE TO GET HELP

Prevention and Intervention Resources

Boston Gun Project

The Boston Gun Project, started in 1994, has also been called Cease-fire. The project was developed by David M. Kennedy, a researcher at Harvard University's John F. Kennedy School of Government, in reaction to the increase in the number of kids killing kids in Boston during the early 1990s. The program combined tracking down and arresting illegal gun suppliers and tracing the ownership of popular handgun models. The results have been astounding: no juveniles under eighteen died from handgun fire in all of 1996 in Boston. Additionally, the homicide rate for those under twenty-five, the age category of most gang members, dropped by two-thirds from 1995 to 1996. To learn more, visit the National Rifle Association's Web site at http://www.nra.org/politics96/1197tar.html.

Center for the Study and Prevention of Violence

Under the direction of Delbert Elliott, this University of Colorado center has exhaustively researched "what works" when it comes to violence prevention and reduction programs. For information, contact

Center for the Study and Prevention of Violence
University of Colorado
Campus Box 442
Boulder, CO 80309
(303) 492-8465

Family Life Development Center

The Family Life Development Center's mission is to improve professional and public efforts to understand and deal with risk factors—in the lives of children, youth, families, and communities—that lead to family violence and neglect. It focuses on strategies and programs to help vulnerable children and youth by strengthening families and communities. Operating out of Cornell University, the center accomplishes its mission through research, training, outreach, and education. It carries out its mandate through program development and implementation and through evaluation projects serving New York State and the nation, in addition to the international community. The current areas of special interest are the role of emerging technologies in training professionals, childhood violence prevention, and programs to guarantee children's rights. For additional information, call (607) 255-7794 or send E-mail to jg38@cornell.edu.

Good Behavior Game

The Good Behavior Game is a positive behavior management program for the first grade classroom. The program was first tested in 1969 and has since been confirmed as an effective means of increasing the rate of on-task behaviors in children while reducing disruptions in the classroom. This program is an approach to the management of classroom behavior that rewards children for displaying appropriate on-task behavior during instructional times. To receive more information on the game or on putting the game into effect in your classroom, visit the following web site: http:/twww.scsd.k12.ny.us/sbit/dirhtml/intfile/intpackg/pkggbg.htm.

Just "For Kids!"

The mission of the Just "For Kids!" program is to make a difference in the lives of children by assisting adults in the prevention, early identification, and intervention of psychological battering of children. A curriculum has been recently developed to supplement the training of child protection workers who are forced to recognize and address cases of psychological maltreatment. Just "For Kids!" also generates and disseminates empirical information pertaining to prevention, intervention, and the long-term effects of psychological abuse. For additional information about program activities, contact

> Just "For Kids!"
> Family Life Development Center
> Cornell University
> N210 Martha Van Rensselaer Hall
> Ithaca, New York 14853-4401
> (888) 594-KIDS

Or send E-mail to just4kids@cornell.edu.

Let's Talk About Living in a World with Violence

This violence prevention program for school-age children was designed by the Erikson Institute to be used by teachers and other professionals who work with children. The program's purpose is to begin a discussion with children and their parents on the meaning and effects of violence on their day-to-day lives. The goal is to help children learn to cope with violence and to find alternatives to aggression. To find out more information about the training program, or to order program materials, contact

> The Family Life Development Center
> Cornell University
> MVR Hall
> Ithaca, NY 14853
> (607) 255-7794
> E-mail: mjh19@cornell.edu

Men and Women Against Domestic Violence

MADV is an Internet-based coalition of men and women working to address the issue of domestic violence. They stress that domestic violence is not just a women's issue. Therefore, they have taken the responsibility of launching an initiative to educate the public and advocate against physical, mental, emotional, and sexual violence of all kinds. They offer advocacy, information, and statistics, but not clinical consultation. They can be found at their Web site http://www.silcom.com/~paladin/madv/ or reached by E-mail at jrm@silcom.com.

National Association for the Education of Young Children

NAEYC is the nation's largest organization of early childhood professionals and others dedicated to improving the quality of early childhood education programs for children from birth through age eight. NAEYC exists for the purpose of leading and consolidating the efforts of individuals and groups working to achieve healthy development and constructive education for young children. Their primary attention is devoted to assuring high-quality early childhood programs for young children. For more information, contact

National Association for the Education of Young Children
1509 16th Street, NW
Washington, DC 20036
E-mail: pubaff@naeyc.org

National Birth to Three Center

Birth to Three is a Washington, DC, program that assists children with developmental delays in reaching their full potential through developmental home activities and referral to community resources. The purpose of the program, which involves both professionals and parents, is to give these children the opportunity to reach their full potential and become integrated as fully as possible into their community. To find out more about this initiative, call Julie Scott, Director of Family Services, at (309) 786-9861.

National Committee to Prevent Child Abuse: Healthy Families America

Healthy Families America is a program developed by the National Committee to Prevent Child Abuse that assists parents by assessing a family's needs before and immediately after their baby's birth and offering the services of a home visitor. Home visitors are volunteers who are selected for their ability to develop trusting, nonjudgmental, and supportive relationships with parents. They work with families to identify their strengths and specific needs, to link them to health and social services, and to provide support and parenting education. Today, there are over three hundred programs in forty states and the District of Columbia. To learn more about the initiative or to request material on how you can establish a Healthy Families America site in your community, call 1-800-CHILDREN or send E-mail to ncpca@childabuse.org.

Pathways: A Boys Town Training Program

The goal of the Pathways program, designed by Thomas J. Everson of Boys Town, Nebraska, is to foster spiritual development among at-risk youth. Available in training manual form, this program aims to nurture spiritual values in hope of helping troubled youth discover meaning in the suffering they have experienced in their lives. Moral reasoning and faith development are integrated throughout the program. To learn more, contact

Boys Town National Resource and Training Center
Father Flanagan's Boys' Home
14100 Crawford Street
Boys Town, NE 68010

Parents as Teachers

Parents as Teachers (PAT) is a primary prevention program designed to maximize children's overall development in their early years by laying a foundation for school success, minimizing developmental problems, and preventing child abuse. The program covers early childhood development and suggests parenting activities that encourage a child's language and intellectual growth, curiosity, and social skills. For more information about this national program, contact

Parents as Teachers National Center, Inc.
10176 Corporate Square Drive, Suite 230
St. Louis, Missouri 63132
(314) 432-4330
Fax: (314) 432-8963
Web site: http://www.patnc.org/

The Perry Preschool Program

The Perry Preschool Program, sponsored by the National Crime Prevention Council, is one of a small number of programs that have considered the connection between preschool education and delinquency. The program demonstrates the benefits of high-quality early education programs for disadvantaged children. It emphasizes the ability of a sound preschool education to (1) increase the proportion of young people who at age nineteen are literate, employed, and enrolled in postsecondary education; (2) reduce the number of children who drop out of school; and (3) reduce the probability of a child's being labeled mentally challenged or arrested or growing up to become dependent on public assistance. The program also offers significant benefits to the parents of at-risk children. For additional information and detailed results of the program, visit the National Crime Prevention Council's Web site at http://www.crime-prevention.org.

Safe Havens Training Project

Witnessing violence changes a child almost overnight. In the Safe Havens training package, parents, teachers, and others who care for children are introduced to the effects on a child's development of witnessing community violence and are given steps to take in order to counteract the negative effects of being exposed to violence. All children need safe havens, that is, places where they can feel safe from the chaos of modern American life. For more information on creating safe havens (home, school, church, clinic, etc.) for the children in your community visit the following Web site: http://www.misterrogers.org

Educators for Social Responsibility

The mission of ESR is to help young children develop the skills necessary to lead safe, successful lives. ESR is nationally recognized for its programs to foster social development and accomplishes its goals through programming in conflict resolution, violence prevention, intergroup relations, and character education. The instructional materials that ESR offers are geared toward children as well as parents. Programs include "Teaching Conflict Resolution Through Children's Literature," "Who's Calling the Shots? How to Respond Effectively to Children's Fascination with War Play and War Toys," and "Changing Channels: Preschoolers, TV, and Media Violence." To receive more information about ESR programming or to order a catalog of resources, contact

Larry Dieringer, Acting Executive Director
Educators for Social Responsibility
23 Garden Street
Cambridge, MA 02138
(800) 370-2515
Web site: http://eric-web.tc.columbia.edu/directories/anti-
    bias/esrnb.html

The following additional resources were not mentioned in the text. They are designed to claim youth before they become lost.

Family Focus: Parenting the Adolescent

Family Focus, a training curriculum put out by the University of New Hampshire Cooperative Extension, stresses the idea that parents are a child's most influential teachers. The program teaches parents adaptive problem-solving skills to use with their adolescents and also demonstrates how to access community support when they find themselves struggling to parent a difficult teen. Parents are taught how to look for early warning signs of "risky behaviors" and how to address such behaviors as they arise. This parenting course touches on difficult-to-address topics such as values, drug use, and sexuality. For more information, contact

Dr. Mary Temke
University of New Hampshire
214C Pettee Hall
55 College Road
Durham, NH 03824
(603) 862-2493

Managing Your Child's Behavior: Ages Birth Through Four

This program, originally geared for use in military settings, focuses on proactive parenting through skill building and prevention. This eight-hour training program is designed to increase parents' ability to anticipate and prevent child behavior problems in a nonphysical disciplinary manner. The highly structured nature of the program makes it potentially effective with either large or small groups of parents, although groups of eight to twelve parents are ideal for purposes of group discussion and active involvement. The coordinators recommend that both parents, if possible, participate in the program, because parental tasks are not gender specific. For more information, contact

Behavioral Science Associates, Inc.
PO Box 87
Stony Brook, NY 11790
(516) 689-6114

National Network of Violence Prevention Practitioners

NNVPP is an interdisciplinary organization consisting of members from the fields of education, criminal justice, and public health and from youth and community organizations. This group stresses the importance of arming frontline practitioners with research-based approaches and knowledge to better serve our communities by preventing youth violence and strengthening families. Additionally, the experience, perspective, and wisdom of network members has been collected and integrated by Education

Development Corporation (EDC) staff in order to provide information to policymakers, government agencies, organizations, foundations, national advocacy organizations, and practitioners throughout the United States. To join the National Network or learn more about the information they offer, visit their Web site at http://www.edc.org/HHD/NNVPP/ or contact Gaea Honeycutt at (617) 969-7101, ext. 2380.

Prevent Violence on Your Campus: Create a Positive Environment for School Safety and Student Success (PVOYC)

PVOYC is a series of training packets for principals, school safety officers, counselors who work with at-risk children, and teachers. These packets deal with various school issues, from school safety to positive classroom management. The producers of this material understand that violence is a concern for all of us and that school safety begins with discipline and good classroom management. The training packets are designed as an empowerment tool for at-risk students and present these students with decisions and positive alternatives to choose from. To order the Prevent Violence on Your Campus training packets, contact

Corwin Press
2455 Teller Road
Thousand Oaks, CA 91320-2218
(805) 499-9774
E-mail: order@corwinpress.com

Resolving Conflict Creatively Program

RCCP is an initiative put forth by the aforementioned Educators for Social Responsibility (ESR), a nonprofit organization with a mission to maintain the schools of our nation as caring and nonviolent environments. RCCP is currently operating in over 325 schools nationwide, reaching over 150,000 young people. Through curriculum development, training, and consultation, this program teaches and advocates peer mediation, conflict resolution, prejudice reduction, appreciation of cultural diversity, and positive group relations. RCCP is a multifaceted program for teachers, students, trainers, school administrators, and parents. For more information, contact

Mariana Gaston
163 3rd Avenue, Room 239
New York, NY 10003
(212) 260-6290

Responding in Peaceful and Positive Ways

Responding in Peaceful and Positive Ways is part of the Richmond Youth Against Violence Project. This program offers middle school children the information they need to reduce their involvement in violence and helps them develop the necessary attitudes and skills. The program's goals are to promote peaceful and positive alternatives to situational violence by creating an environment that encourages health-enhancing behaviors and weakens health-compromising behaviors. The program incorporates a sixth grade curriculum and a peer mediation component directed mainly at high-risk African American middle school children.

Strong at the Broken Places: Turning Trauma into Recovery

Strong at the Broken Places is a documentary that reinforces and portrays true heroism. The 38-minute film is both inspirational and instructional. People devastated by trauma and loss who were able to find common ground for recovery teach us the meaning of the word *hero*. This documentary shows how personal loss and suffering can be turned into a powerful tool for restoring hope and changing society. To obtain a copy of this documentary or to view other titles available, visit the Cambridge Documentary Films Web site at http://www.shore.net/~cdf or call (617) 484-3993.

Teen Challenge

The Teen Challenge program strives to educate adolescents about the harmful effects of drugs. Teen Challenge is the oldest, largest, and most successful program of its type. Other educational programs are also offered to the community free of charge. Additionally, Teen Challenge volunteers reach out to people in juvenile halls, jails, and prisons. Teen Challenge believes that education will help the community correct the drug epidemic. For information on Teen Challenge's curriculum, either visit their Web site at http://www.teenchallenge.com, E-mail them at tcusa@ncsi.net, or call them at (800) 814-5729.

Therapeutic Crisis Intervention

Therapeutic Crisis Intervention (TCI) is a "train the trainer" program developed by Cornell University's Family Life Development Center, for child and youth care workers. It is designed as a crisis prevention and intervention model to assist those who work in residential facilities help children deal with crisis. It gives staff the skills and knowledge necessary to help children and youth when they are at their most destructive, and it stresses the importance of adult responsibility for the treatment and protection of troubled youth in crisis situations. TCI successfully increases a staff's ability to manage and prevent crisis while decreasing the number of physical restrains used and the number of bodily injuries inflicted on the children and staff. To establish TCI at your organization, visit http://www.child.cornell.edu or contact

Michael Nunno
Family Life Development Center
MVR Hall
Ithaca, NY 14853
(607) 255-5210

Violence Prevention Curriculum for Adolescents

The Violence Prevention Curriculum for Adolescents is a program that addresses the growing epidemic of homicide and violence in general among young people. This school-based curriculum acknowledges anger as a normal and natural emotion; alerts students to the risks of being involved in an act of violence, as either victim or perpetrator; and offers alternatives to fighting through anger management and improved conflict resolution skills. This curriculum has been proven to be effective in high school health, sociology, and psychology classes. For more information, contact

Millie LeBlanc
EDC Publishing Center
555 Chapel St., Suite 24
Newton, MA 02160
(800) 225-4276

Newsletter for Parents of Children with Very "Difficult" Temperaments

A new electronic newsletter called *Behavior-Development-Individuality* is under the editorial direction of Dr. Kate Anderson. It can be reached at B-DI@temperament.com with the message "subscribe newsletter."

References

Chapter 1

Page

4 *Given our society's history:* Dowdy, Z. (1998, July 5). Racial Bias in Coverage by Media of Kids Who Kill. *Sacramento Bee*, Metro Final, p. F01.

4 *In 1995, 84 percent of the counties:* Office of Juvenile Justice and Delinquency Prevention (1997). *Juvenile Offenders and Victims: 1997 Update on Violence*. Washington, DC: U.S. Department of Justice.

6 *The FBI reports that:* U.S. Federal Bureau of Investigation (1995). *1994 Uniform Crime Report: Supplemental Homicide Reports*. Washington, DC: U.S. Department of Justice.

7 *An example of the change:* Garbarino, J., Dubrow, N., Kostelny, K., & Pardo, C. (1992). *Children in Danger: Coping with the Consequences of Community Violence*. San Francisco: Jossey-Bass.

7 *American homicide data:* Bronfenbrenner, U., McClelland, P., Wethington, E., Moen, P., & Ceci, S. (1996). *The State of Americans: This Generation and the Next*. New York: Free Press.

7 *while the overall homicide rate:* Ibid.

7 *The period of greatest growth:* Ibid.

7 *Much has been made:* Heide, K. M. (1998). *Young Killers: The Challenge of Juvenile Homicide*. Thousand Oaks, CA: Sage.

8 *Similarly, after more than a decade:* Ibid.

8 *our juvenile homicide in particular:* Fox, J. A. (1996). *Trends in Juvenile Violence*. Washington, DC: U.S. Department of Justice, Bureau of Justice Statistics.

8 *In the mid-1990s:* Metaksa, T. K. (1997, November). *Attacking Gangs Not Civil Rights*. Available online at http://www.nra.org/politics/1197tar.html

8 *According to the FBI:* U.S. Federal Bureau of Investigation (1997). *1996 Uniform Crime Report*. Washington, DC: U.S. Department of Justice.

8 *But perhaps the most disturbing:* Fields, G., & Overberg, P. (1998, March 26). Juvenile Homicide Arrest Rate on Rise in Rural USA. *USA Today*, sec. A, p. 11.

9 *15 percent of high school boys:* Centers for Disease Control and Prevention (1998). *Youth Risk Behavior Surveillance – United States, 1997*. Washington, DC: U.S. Department of Health and Human Services.

9 *acts of self-destruction:* Gilligan, J. (1996). *Violence: Our Deadly Epidemic and its Causes.* New York: Putnam.

10 *the federal government's Office of Juvenile Justice:* Office of Juvenile Justice and Delinquency Prevention (1997). *Juvenile Offenders and Victims: 1997 Update on Violence.* Washington, DC: U.S. Department of Justice.

10 *Think about the characteristics:* Zagar, R., Arbit, J., Sylvies, R., & Busch, K. G. (1991). Homicidal Adolescents: A Replication. *Psychological Reports, 67*(3), 1235–1242.

11 *Interestingly, the U. S. populations:* Butterfield, F. (1995). *All God's Children: The Basket Family and the American Tradition of Violence.* New York: Knopf.

11 *until the 1960s:* Lane, R. (1997). *Murder in America: A History.* Columbus: Ohio State University Press.

11 *Connection between Southern culture:* Butterfield, F. (1998, July 26). Southern Curse: Why America's Murder Rate Is So High. *The New York Times,* sec. 4, pp 1, 16.

11 *But religious tradition is important as well:* Ibid.

12 *code of honor:* Nisbett, R. E., & Cohen, D. (1996). *Culture of honor: The Psychology of Violence in the South.* Boulder, CO: Westview Press.

12 *In 1994 the African American:* Fox, J. A. (1996). *Trends in Juvenile Violence.* Washington, DC: U.S. Department of Justice, Bureau of Justice Statistics.

12 *homicide rates of blacks living in Africa:* Gilligan, J. (1996). *Violence: Our Deadly Epidemic and Its Causes.* New York: Putnam.

13 • Child abuse: Sedlak, A. J., & Broadhurst, D. D. (1996). *The Third National Incidence Study of Child Abuse and Neglect (NIS-3): Final report.* Washington, DC: U.S. Department of Health and Human Services, National Center on Child Abuse and Neglect.

13 • Gangs: Gangs: Violence on the Rise in U.S. Schools (1998, April 13). *The Minneapolis Star Tribune,* sec. A, p. 5.

13 • Substance abuse: Centers for Disease Control and Prevention (1998). Youth Risk Behavior Surveillance – United States, 1997. Washington, DC: U.S. Department of Health and Human Services.

14 • Arrests: Fox, J. A. (1996). Trends in Juvenile Violence. Washington, DC: U.S. Department of Justice, Bureau of Justice Statistics.

15 • Difficulties at school: Bronfenbrenner, U., McClelland, P., Wethington, E., Moen, P., & Ceci, S. (1996). *The State of Americans: This Generation and the Next.* New York: Free Press.

15 *Since 1969 the percentage of :* Ibid.

15 *According to the 1997 CDC survey:* Centers for Disease Control and Prevention (1998). *Youth Risk Behavior Surveillance—United States, 1997.* Washington, DC: U.S. Department of Health and Human Services.

15 *The first wave of lethal youth violence:* Fox, J. A. (1996). *Trends in Juvenile Violence.* Washington, DC: U.S. Department of Justice, Bureau of Justice Statistics.

16 *tipping point in the social decline of neighborhoods:* Crane, J. (1991). The Epidemic Theory of Ghettos and Neighborhood Effects on Dropping Out and Teenage Childbearing. *American Journal of Sociology, 96,* 1226–1259.

17 *Harvard University sociologist:* Wilson, W. J. (1993). *The Ghetto Underclass: Social Science Perspectives.* Newbury Park, CA: Sage.

17 *War zone neighborhoods are places:* Garbarino, J., Dubrow, N., Kostelny, K., & Pardo, C. (1992). *Children in Danger: Coping with the Consequences of Community Violence.* San Francisco: Jossey-Bass.

19 *Bronfenbrenner was there to talk:* Bronfenbrenner, U. (1970). *Two Worlds of Childhood: U.S. and U.S.S.R.* New York: Russell Sage Foundation.

19 *I was there to talk about my book:* Garbarino, J. (1995). *Raising Children in a Socially Toxic Environment.* San Francisco: Jossey-Bass.

23 *with two-thirds of our teenagers:* Fields, G., & Overberg, P. (1998, March 26). Juvenile Homicide Arrest Rate on Rise in Rural USA. *USA Today,* sec A, p. 11.

25 *As I noted earlier:* Centers for Disease Control and Prevention (1998). *Youth Risk Behavior Surveillance—United States, 1997.* Washington, DC: U.S. Department of Health and Human Services.

25 *Recent research suggests:* Cornell, D. G., Benedek, E. P., & Benedek, D. M. (1989). A Typology of Juvenile Homicide Offenders. In E. P. Benedek & E. G. Cornell (Eds.), *Juvenile Homicide.* Washington, DC: American Psychiatric Press.

Chapter 2

34 *Psychiatrist Leonard Shengold:* Shengold, L. (1989). *Soul Murder: The Effects of Childhood Abuse and Deprivation.* New Haven, CT: Yale University Press.

35 *I find inspiration in the life:* Casarjian, R. (1995). *Houses of Healing: A Prisoner's Guide to Inner Power and Freedom.* Boston: The Lionheart Foundation.

35 *I side with:* Prejean, Sister Helen (1993). *Dead Man Walking: An Eyewitness Account of the Death Penalty in the United States.* New York: Random House.

37 *Psychologists Patrick Tolan and Nancy Guerra:* Tolan, P., & Guerra, N. (1996). Youth Violence Prevention: Descriptions of Baseline Data from Thirteen Evaluation Projects. *American Journal of Preventative Medicine, Supplement to 12*(5), 1–134.

38 *Working in Israel:* Gewirtz, J. (1966). The Course of Infant Smiling in Four Child-Rearing Environments. *Megamot, 14*(4), 281–311.

38 *Gewirtz's results:* Vygotsky, L. (1978). Thought and Language. Cambridge, MA: MIT Press.

39 *Exploring varieties of attachment:* Bowlby, J. (1979). *The Making and Breaking of Affectional Bonds.* London: Tavistock.

39 *In a project conducted by psychologist:* Van den Boom, D. (1994). The Influence of Temperament and Mothering on Attachment and Exploration: An Experimental Manipulation of Sensitive Responsiveness Among Lower-Class Mothers with Irritable Infants. *Child Development, 65*(5), 1457–1477.

39 *"Not all anxiously attached children:* Sroufe, A. (1981, October). Infant-caregiver Attachment and Patterns of Adaptation in Preschool: The Roots of Maladaptation and Competence. Paper presented at the Minnesota Symposium, University of Minnesota, p. 15.

40   *In her book:* Harris, J. R. (1998). *The Nurture Assumption: Why Children Turn Out the Way They Do.* New York: Free Press.

40   *Parental behavior plays a critical role:* National Research Counsel (1993). *Understanding Child Abuse and Neglect.* Washington, DC: National Academy Press.

41   *Psychiatrist Rene Spitz carried out:* Spitz, R. (1945). Hospitalism: An Inquiry into the Genesis of Psychiatric Conditions in Early Childhood. *The Psychoanalytic Study of the Child, 1,* 53–74.

41   *Research by psychologist Ronald Kessler:* Kessler, R. cited in M. Elias, (1998, August 13), Rich or Poor, More Kids Struggle with Symptoms. *USA Today,* sec. D, p. 1.

42   *high rates of depression are being found:* Luthar, S. cited in M. Elias, (1998, August 13), Rich or Poor, More Kids Struggle with Symptoms. *USA Today,* sec. D, p. 1.

42   *In his book:* Real, T. (1997). *I Don't Want to Talk About It: Overcoming the Secret Legacy of Male Depression.* New York: Scribner.

46   *Research shows that:* Weintraub, K. J., & Gold, M. (1992). Monitoring and Delinquency. *Criminal Behaviour and Mental Health, 1*(3), 268–281.

47   *British psychiatrist Michael Rutter:* Rutter, M. (1989). Pathways from Childhood to Adult Life. *Journal of Psychology and Psychiatry, 30,* 25–51.

48   *While not denying that:* Daly, M., & Wilson, M. (1997). Violence Against Stepchildren. *Current Directions in Psychological Science, 5*(3), 77–81.

50   *"Do You Know Me?":* Farley, C., & Willwerth, J. (1997, January). Dead Teen Walking. *Time.* 151(2), 33ff.

50   *Anthropologist Ronald Rohner:* Rohner, R. (1975). *They Love Me, They Love Me Not.* New Haven, CT: Human Relations Area Files Press.

53   *Accurately seeing and hearing:* Goleman, D. (1995). *Emotional Intelligence: Why It Can Matter More Than IQ.* New York: Bantam.

58   *In his book* Homecoming: Bradshaw, J. (1990). *Homecoming: Reclaiming and Championing Your Inner Child.* New York: Bantam.

Chapter 3

66   *According to the results:* Kellam, S. G., Ling, X., Merisca, R., Brown, C. H., & Ialongo, N. (1998). The Effect of Level of Aggression in the First Grade Classroom on the Course and Malleability of Aggressive Behavior into Middle School. *Development and Psychopathology, 10,* 165–185.

66   *Research by psychologist Leonard Eron:* Eron, L. D., Gentry, J. H., & Schlegel, P. (Eds.). (1994). *Reason to Hope: A Psychosocial Perspective on Violence and Youth.* Washington, DC: American Psychological Association.

66   *There is a formal name:* American Psychiatric Association (1994). *Diagnostic and Statistical Manual of Mental Disorders* (4th ed.). Washington, DC: Author.

67   *That is not surprising:* Edens, J. F., & Otto, R. K. (1997, Spring). Prevalence of Mental Disorders Among Youth in the Juvenile System. In *Focal Point: A National Bulletin on Family Support and Children's Mental Health.* pp. 1, 6–7. Portland, OR: Portland State University.

67   *British criminologists Farrington and Hawkins:* Farrington, D. P., & Hawkins, J. D.

(1991). Predicting Participation, Early Onset, and Later Persistence in Officially Recorded Offending. *Criminal Behavior and Mental Health, 1*, 1–33.

67 *Other investigators:* Kazdin, A. E. (1997). Conduct Disorder Across the Life-Span. In S. S. Luthar & E. Zigler (Eds.), *Developmental Psychopathology: Perspectives on Adjustment, Risk, and Disorder*. Cambridge, MA: Cambridge University Press.

67 *Indeed, surveys show:* Loeber, R., & Farrington, D. P. (1998). Serious and Violent Juvenile Offenders. In R. Loeber & D. Farrington (Eds.), *Serious and Violent Juvenile Offenders: Risk Factors and Successful Interventions*. Thousand Oaks, CA: Sage.

68 *According to Kazdin's research:* Kazdin, A. E. (1994). Interventions for Aggressive and Antisocial Children. In L. D. Eron, J. H. Gentry, & P. Schlegel (Eds.), *Reason to Hope: A Psychosocial Perspective on Violence and Youth* (pp 341–381). Washington DC: American Psychological Association.

70 *Child analyst Anna Freud:* Freud, A. (1958). Psychoanalytical Study of the Child. *Adolescence, 13*, 255–278.

70 *In her book:* Winn, M. (1983). *Children Without Childhood*. New York: Pantheon.

70 *But research conducted:* Offer, D., & Offer, J. D. (1975). *From Teenager to Young Manhood; A Psychological Study*. New York: Basic Books.

71 *Psychologist Aaron Ebata:* Ebata, A. T. (1987, October). A Longitudinal Study of Psychological Distress During Early Adolescence. Dissertation Abstracts International 48(4–A): 1027.

71 *A report compiled:* Eron, L. D., Gentry, J. H., & Schlegel, P. (Eds.). (1994). *Reason to Hope: a Psychosocial Perspective on Violence and Youth*. Washington, DC: American Psychological Association.

71 *most teenagers who assault their parents:* Gelles, R. (1978). Violence Toward Children in the United States. *American Journal of Orthopsychiatry, 48*, 580–592.

71 *Some people are tempted:* Sleek, S. (1998, August). The Basis for Aggression May Start in the Womb: Is There Really Such a Thing As a Natural Born Killer? *American Psychological Association Monitor, 29*(8), 37.

72 In contrast: *Pasamanick, B.* (1987, Winter). Social Biology and AIDS. *Division 37 Newsletter*. Washington, DC: American Psychological Association.

72 *So when all is said and done:* Bronfenbrenner, U. (1979). *The Ecology of Human Development: Experiments by Nature and Design*. Cambridge, MA: Harvard University Press.

73 *Sarnoff Mednick and Elizabeth Kandel:* Mednick, S. A., & Kandel, E. (1998). Genetic and Perinatal Factors in Violence. In S. A Mednick & T. Moffit (Eds.), *Biological Contributions to Crime Causation* (pp 121–134). Dordrecht, the Netherlands: Martinus Nijhoff.

76 *As threats accumulate:* Sameroff, A., Seifer, R., Barocas, R., Zax, M., & Greenspan, S. (1987). Intelligence Quotient Scores of 4-Year-Old Children. Social Environmental Risk Factors. *Pediatrics, 79*, 343–350.

76 *Psychologist Alan Kazdin:* Kazdin, A. E. (1994). Interventions for Aggressive and Antisocial Children. In L. D. Eron, J. H. Gentry, & P. Schlegel (Eds.), *Rea-*

son to Hope: A Psychosocial Perspective on Violence and Youth (pp 341–381). Washington, DC: American Psychological Association.

76 Psychologists Carl Dunst and Carol Trivette: Dunst, C., & Trivette, C. M. (1992) Risk and Opportunity Factors Influencing Parent and Child Functioning. Paper based upon presentations made at the Ninth Annual Smoky Mountain Winter Institute, Asheville, NC.

77 In her book: Harris, J. (1998). The Nurture Assumption: Why Children Turn Out the Way They Do. New York: Free Press.

77 In a study by child psychologists: Erickson, S. F., Egeland, B., & Pianta, R. (1989). The Effects of Maltreatment on the Development of Young Children. In V. Carlson & D. Cicchetti (Eds.), Child Maltreatment: Theory and Research on the Causes and Consequences of Child Abuse and Neglect (pp 647–684). Cambridge, MA: Cambridge University Press.

78 But in her classic study: Maccoby, E. E., & Martin, J. A. (1983). Socialization in the Context of the Family: Parent-Child Interaction. In P. H. Mussen (Series Ed.) & E M. Hetherington (Vol. Ed.), Handbook of Child Psychology: Vol. 4. Socialization, Personality, and Social Development (4th ed., p 1–101). New York: Wiley.

78 But psychiatrist Stanley Greenspan: Greenspan, S. I. (1992). Infancy and Early Childhood: The Practice of Clinical Assesments and Intervention with Emotional and Developmental Challenges. Madison, CT: International Universities Press.

78 University of Oregon researcher: Patterson, G. R., & Stouthamer-Loeber, M. (1984). The Correlation of Family Management Practices and Delinquency. Child Development, 55, 1299–1307.

79 Psychologist Byron Egeland and his colleagues: Egeland, B., & Vaughn, B. (1981). Failure of "Bond Formation" as a Cause of Abuse, Neglect, and Maltreatment. American Journal of Orthopsychiatry, 51, 78–84.

80 problems with early attachment: Egeland, B., & Stroufe, A. (1981). Developmental Sequelae of Maltreatment in Infancy. In R. Rizley & D. Cicchetti (Eds.), Developmental Perspectives on Child Maltreatment (pp. 77–93). San Francisco: Jossey-Bass.

80 Nothing tells us more about: Dodge, K. A., Pettit, G. S., & Bates, J. E. (1997). How the Experience of Early Physical Abuse Leads Children to Become Chronically Aggressive. In C. Cicchetti & S. L. Toth (Eds.), Developmental Psychopathalogy: Developmental Perspectives on Trauma: Vol. 9. Theory, Research, and Intervention (pp 263–288). Rochester, NY: University of Rochester Press.

82 4 to 7 percent of kids: Kazdin, A. E. (1994). Interventions for Aggressive and Antisocial Children. In L. D. Eron, J. H. Gentry & P. Schlegel (Eds.), Reason to Hope: A Psychosocial Perspective on Violence and Youth (pp. 341–381). Washington, DC: American Psychological Association.

83 Some at-risk children are saved: Patterson, G. R. (1982). A Social Learning Approach to Family Intervention: III. Coercive Family Process. Eugene, OR: Castalia.

83 There is of course, another question: Polansky, N. A., Borgman, R. D., & De Saix, C. (1972). Roots of Futility. San Francisco: Jossey-Bass.

84 *In fact, neglect is more common than abuse:* Sedlak, A. J., & Broadhurst, D. D. (1996, September). *Third National Incidence Study of Child Abuse and Neglect: Final Report.* Washington, DC: U.S. Department of Health and Human Services.

84 *There is more to the link:* Perry, B., Pollard, R., Blakley, T., Baker, W., & Vigilante, D. (1995). Childhood Trauma, the Neurobiology of Adaptation, and "Use-Dependent" Development of the Brain: How "States" Become "Traits." *Infant Mental Health Journal, 16,* 271–289.

85 *There is a third explanation:* Ibid.

87 *As I watch Sharnell rock:* Perry, B. (1994, March.). *Children of Waco.* Presentation to the Chicago Association for Child and Adolescent Psychiatry.

87 *for some it reflects a biological predisposition:* Losel, F., Bender, D., & Bliesener, T. (1998, July). Biosocial Risk and Protective Factors for Antisocial Behavior in Juveniles. Paper presented to the 15th Bi-ennial Conference of The International Society for the Study of Behavioral Development, Bern, Switzerland.

90 *Terrence Real provides a road map:* Real, T. (1997). *I Don't Want to Talk About It: Overcoming the Secret Legacy of Male Depression.* New York: Scribners.

91 *These boys need someone:* Ibid.

91 *These boys need someone:* Casarjian, R. (1995). *Houses of Healing: A Prisoner's Guide to Inner Power and Freedom.* Boston: The Lionheart Foundation.

Chapter 4

94 *Working in the 1950s:* Sullivan, H. S. (1953). *The Interpersonal Theory of Psychiatry.* New York: Norton.

94 *We can see this in:* Egan, T. (1998, May 22). Oregon Student Held in 3 Killings: One Dead, 26 Hurt at His School. *The New York Times,* sec. A, pp. 1, 20.

95 *In Edinboro:* Hampson, R. (1998, April 27). Another Small Town Struggles for Answers. *USA Today,* sec. A, P. 3.

95 *within months of these violent assaults:* Dwyer, K., Osher, D., & Warger, C. (1998). *Early Warning, Timely Response: A Guide to Safe Schools.* Washington, DC: U.S. Department of Education.

100 *It pains me greatly to recognize:* Garbarino, J. (1995). *Raising Children in a Socially Toxic Environment.* San Francisco: Jossey-Bass.

101 *Bronfenbrenner's 1970 book:* Bronfenbrenner, U. (1970). *Two Worlds of Childhood: U.S. and U.S.S.R.* New York: Russell Sage Foundation.

101 *His most recent book:* Bronfenbrenner, U., McClelland, P., Wethington, E., Moen, P., & Ceci, S. (1996). *The State of Americans: This Generation and the Next.* New York: Free Press.

102 *Social poisons affect us all:* Harris, J. (1998). *The Nurture Assumption: Why Children Turn Out the Way They Do.* New York: Free Press.

102 *Surveys consistently report:* Fields, G., & Overberg, P. (1998, March 26). Juvenile Homicide Arrest Rate on Rise in Rural USA. *USA Today,* sec. A, p.11.

103 *A study by psychologist Jeremy Shapiro:* Shapiro, J. P., Dorman, R. L., Burkey, W. M., & Welker, C. J. (1997). Development and Factor analysis of a Measure of

Youth Attitudes Toward Guns and Violence. *Journal of Clinical Child Psychology*, *26*(3), 311–320.

104 *It is often easy to recognize:* Hart, S. (1998 August 9). Residents of Quiet Community Wonder: Why Here? Why Now? *The Post-Standard Herald American (Syracuse, NY)*, sec. A, pp. 1, 10.

104 *Some of the small-town:* Helmore, E. (1997, November 18). Murder at Pearl High. *The Guardian Newspaper Limited (London)*, p. 6.

105 *In Paducah, Kentucky:* Malone, J. (1998, June 24). Carneal Wanted to Feel Powerful, Two Mental Health Experts Report. *The Courier-Journal (Louisville, KY)*, sec. A, p. 5.

106 *Trauma occurs when:* Herman, J. (1992). *Trauma and Recovery.* New York: Basic Books.

107 *When I visited Kuwait:* Nader, K., & Pynoos, R. S. (1993). *The Psychological Effects of War and Violence on Children.* Hillsdale, NJ: Lawrence Erlbaum.

108 *Analyses of television content:* Murray, B. (1998, June). Study Says TV Violence Still Seen as Heroic, Glamorous. *American Psychological Association Monitor*, p. 16.

108 *Psychologist Leonard Eron:* Eron, L. D., Gentry, J. H., & Schlegel, P. (Eds.). (1994) *Reason to Hope: A Psychosocial Perspective on Violence and Youth.* Washington, DC: American Psychological Association.

109 *Psychologist Victor Papanek:* Papanek, V. J. (1972). *Design for the Real World: Human Ecology and Social Change.* New York: Pantheon.

111 *According to the National Survey of Youth:* University of Michigan (1993). *Monitoring the future 1975–1992.* Ann Arbor.

112 *Yale University psychologist Stanley Milgram:* Milgram, S. (1965). Some Conditions of Obedience and Disobedience to Authority. *Human Relations. 18*, 57–75.

113 *We made a film at Cornell: I Still Can't Say It: A Documentary About Preventing Child Abuse* [Video]. (1986). Cornell University: Gordon/Fraser Productions.

114 *Desensitization is another:* Grossman, D., & Siddle, P. (1999). Combat. In L. Kurtz (Ed.), *The Encyclopedia of Violence, Peace, and Conflict.* San Diego: Academic Press.

114 *Grossman sees it this way:* Ibid.

115 *Those 98 percent:* Ibid.

115 *What percent of kids are resilient:* Tolan, P. (1996, October). How Resilient Is the Concept of Resilience? *Community Psychologist, 4*, 12–15.

116 *most boys feel an intense pressure:* Real, T. (1997). *I Don't Want to Talk About It: Overcoming the Secret Legacy of Male Depression.* New York: Scribner.

117 *Michael Carneal in Kentucky:* Malone, J. (1998, June 24). Carneal Wanted to Feel Powerful, Two Mental Health Experts Report. *The Courier-Journal (Louisville, KY)*, sec. A, p. 5.

117 *The truth is:* Loeber, R., & Farrington, D. P. (1998). Serious and Violent Juvenile Offenders. In R. Loeber & D. Farrington (Eds.), *Serious and Violent Juvenile Offenders: Risk Factors and Successful Interventions.* Thousand Oaks, CA: Sage.

117 *Overall, more and more kids:* Achenbach, T., & Howell, C. (1993). Are Ameri-

can Children's Problems Getting Worse? A Thriteen-Year Comparison. *Journal of the American Academy of Child and Adolescent Psychiatry. 32*(6), 1145–1154.

118 *Psychitrist Lenore Terr:* Terr, L. (1983). Chowchilla Revisited. The Effects of Psychic Trauma Four Years After a School-Bus Kidnapping. *American Journal of Psychiatry. 140* , 1543–1550.

Chapter 5

121 *Regardless of its origins:* Helmore, E. (1997, November 18). Murder at Pearl High. *The Guardian Newspaper Limited (London)*, p. 6.

121 *Luke Woodham:* Ibid.

121 *Michael Carneal:* Malone, J. (1998, June 24). Carneal Wanted to Feel Powerful, Two Mental Health Experts Report. *The Courier-Journal (Louisville, KY)*, sec A, p. 5.

121 *Mitchell Johnson:* Kifner, J. (1998, March 29). From Wild Talk and Friendship to Five Deaths in a Schoolyard. *The New York Times*, sec. A, p. 1.

121 *Andrew Wurst:* Hampson, R. (1998, April 27). Another Small Town Struggles for Answers. *USA Today*, sec. A, p. 3.

126 *There are individuals:* Otnow-Lewis, D. (1998). *Guilty by Reason of Insanity: A Psychiatrist Probes the Minds of Killers.* New York: Fawcett Columbine.

127 *Their psychopathy is chilling.* Hare, B. (1996). Psychopathy—A Clinical Construct Whose Time Has Come. *Criminal Justice and Behavior 23*, 25–54.

127 *nearly 10 percent of juvenile offenders:* Damphousse, K. R., & Crouch, B. (1993). Did the Devil Make Them Do It? An Examination of the Etiology of Satanism Among Juvenile Delinquents. *Youth and Society, 24*(2), 204–227.

127 *The fourteen-year-old shooter:* Hampson, R. (1998, April 27). Another Small Town Struggles for Answers. *USA Today*, sec A, p. 3.

127 *Kip Kinkel in Springfield:* Reed, C. (1998, May 23). Classroom: How 'Schizoid' Kid from Good Home Turned Murderer at Oregon School. *The Guardian Newspaper Limited (London)*, p. 21.

127 *Luke Woodham:* Helmore, E. (1997, November 18). Murder at Pearl High. *The Guardian Newspaper Limited (London)*, p. 6.

128 *I learned this lesson:* Gilligan, J. (1996). *Violence: Our Deadly Epidemic and Its Causes.* New York: Putnam.

129 *Boys do commit parricide:* Mones, P. (1991). *When a Child Kills: Abused Children Who Kill Their Parents.* New York: Pocket Books.

130 *In Paducah, Kentucky:* Malone, J. (1998, June 24). Carneal Wanted to Feel Powerful, Two Mental Health Experts Report. *The Courier-Journal (Louisville, KY)*, sec. A, p. 5.

131 *His note said:* Pressley, S. A. (1997, October 24). Bible Belt Town Hunts for Answer to Killings. *The Guardian Newspaper Limited (London)*, p. 15.

131 *According to the classmate:* Hewitt, B. (1997, December 22). Marching On: Stunned by Tragedy, the People of Paducah Search Their Hearts and Find the Healing Grace of Compassion. *Time Magazine*, p. 42.

133 *Ethologist Desmond Morris:* Morris, D. (1967). *The Illustrated Naked Ape: A Zoologist's Study of the Human Animal.* New York: Crown.

134 *A rapist will say:* Quoted in Mary Sykes Wylie (1998). Public Enemies *Family Therapy Networker, 22*(3), 24ff.

134 *As character education expert:* Lickona, T. (1991). *Educating for Character: How Our Schools Can Teach Respect and Responsibility.* New York: Bantam.

134 *The standard for efforts to assess:* Kohlberg, L. (1981–1984). *Essays in Moral Development: Vol. 1. The Philosophy of Moral Development. Vol. 2. The Psychology of Moral Development.* New York: Harper & Row.

135 *Juvenile delinquents in general tend:* Nelson, J., Smith, D., & Dodd, J. (1990). The Moral Reasoning of Juvenile Delinquents. *Journal of Abnormal Psychology, 18,* 231–239.

136 *Another way of looking at moral development:* Stilwell, B. M., Galvin, M., & Kopta, S. (1991). Conceptualization of Conscience in Normal Children and Adolescents. *Journal of American Academy of Child and Adolescent Psychiatry, 30,* 16–21.

137 *When it comes to the feeling part:* Real, T. (1997). *I Don't Want to Talk About It: Overcoming the Secret Legacy of Male Depression.* New York: Scribner.

138 *Twenty years ago:* Jurkovic, G. J., & Prentice, N. M. (1997). Relation of Moral and Cognitive Development to Dimensions of Juvenile Delinquency. *Journal of Abnormal Psychology, 86*(4), 414–420.

138 *In his widely read book:* Goleman, D. (1995). *Emotional Intelligence: Why It Can Matter More Than IQ.* New York: Bantam.

139 *He reportedly said:* Tuohy, L. (1998, May 22). The Reaction Once Again Was 'Oh, God.' Now It Is 'Not Again': Eighth Shooting Has Americans Shaking Heads. *The Hartford Courant,* sec. A, p. 1.

141 *Sociologist Erving Goffman:* Goffman, E. (1969). *Strategic Interaction.* Philadelphia: University of Pennsylvania Press.

142 • *Third, adults can:* Weaver, A. J., Flannelly, L. T., Flannelly, K. J., Koenig, H. G., & Larson, D. B. (1998). An Analysis of Research on Religious and Spiritual Variables in Three Major Mental Health Nursing Journals, 1991–1995. *Issues in Mental Health Nursing, 19*(3), 263–276.

Chapter 6

152 *Right there in front of me:* Erikson, E. (1963). *Childhood and Society* (2nd ed.). New York: Norton.

152 *Like the epidemic of youth violence:* Harris & Associates (1994). *Metropolitan Life Surveys of the American Teacher: Violence in America's Public Schools: Part II.* New York: Metropolitan Life Insurance.

153 *psychoanalyst Carl Jung wrote:* Jung, C. (1933). *Modern Man in Search of a Soul.* New York: Harcourt Brace, p. 260.

153 *Psychologist Viktor Frankl:* Frankl, V. (1962). *Man's Search for Meaning: An Introduction to Logotherapy.* Boston: Beacon Press.

153 *having a coherent and meaningful:* Cohler, B. J. (1991). The Life Story and the Study of Resilience and Response to Adversity. *Journal of Narrative and Life History, 1*(2–3), 169–200.

156 *Religion can be much more:* Wright, L. S., Frost, C. J., & Wisecarver, S. J. (1993). Church Attendance, Meaningfulness of Religion, and Depressive Symptomatology Among Adolescents. *Journal of Youth and Adolescence, 22*(5), 559–568.

156 *When spiritually grounded:* Weaver, A. J., Flannelly, L. T., Flannelly, K. J., Koenig, H. G., & Larson, D. B. (1998). An Analysis of Research on Religious and Spiritual Variables in Three Major Mental Health Nursing Journals, 1991–1995. *Issues in Mental Health Nursing, 19*(3), 263–276.

157 *Psychiatrist Bessel van der Kolk:* van der Kolk, B. (1994, October). *Meaning and Trauma.* Paper presented at the Rochester Symposium on Developmental Psychopathology, University of Rochester, Rochester, NY.

159 *Psychologists Johathan Davidson and Rebecca Smith report:* Davidson, J., & Smith, R. (1990). Traumatic Experiences in Psychiatric Outpatients. *Journal of Traumatic Stress Studies, 3,*459–475.

159 *Psychiatrist Robert Coles:* Coles, R. (1990). *The Spiritual Life of Children.* Boston: Houghton Mifflin.

160 *As Terrance Real points out:* Real, T. (1997). *I Don't Want to Talk About It: Overcoming the Secret Legacy of Male Depression.* New York: Scribner.

160 *For example, psychologist Joianne Shortz:* Shortz, J. (1994). Young Adults' Recall of Religiosity, Attributions, and Coping in Parental Divorce. *Journal for the Scientific Study of Religion, 33*(2), 172–179.

160 *When a boy's need for something:* Douglas, J., & Olshaker, M. (1995). *Mindhunter.* New York: Scribner.

161 *"It may seem remarkable":* R. Janoff-Bulman (1992). *Shattered Assumptions-Towards a New Psychology of Trauma.* New York: Free Press.

162 *True, research shows:* Edens, J. F., & Otto, R. K. (1997, Spring). Prevalence of Mental Disorders Among Youth in the Juvenile System. In *Focal Point: A National Bulletin on Family Support and Children's Mental Health.* Portland, OR. Portland State University, pp 1, 6–7.

166 *We must be careful:* Goleman, D. (1995). *Emotional Intelligence: Why It Can Matter More Than IQ.* New York: Bantam.

166 *The inability to be emotionally smart:* Nowicki, S., & Duke, M. (1992). *Helping the Child Who Doesn't Fit In.* Atlanta: Peachtree.

166 *As psychiatrist Dorothy Otnow-Lewis reports:* Otnow-Lewis, D. (1998). *Guilty by Reason of Insanity: A Psychiatrist Probes the Minds of Killers.* New York: Fawcett Columbine.

167 *So many boys seem:* Real, T. (1997). *I Don't Want to Talk About It: Overcoming the Secret Legacy of Male Depression.* New York: Scribner.

169 *Psychologist Emmy Werner's:* Werner, E. E. (1982). *Vulnerable but Invincible: A Longitudinal Study of Resilient Children and Youth.* New York: McGraw-Hill.

170 *How do we measure:* Miringoff, M. (1993). *The Index of Social Health.* New York: Fordham University, Institute for Innovation in Social Policy.

170 *A Study by sociologists:* Blyth, D. A., & Leffert, N. (1995). Communities as Contexts for Adolescent Development: an Empirical Analysis. *Journal of Adolescent Research, 10*(1), 64–87.

171 *Children are fundamentally:* Lancaster, J. B., Altmann, J., Rossi, A. S., & Sherrod, L. R. (1987). *Parenting Across the Life Span: Biosocial Dimensions.* New York: A. de Gruyter.

171 *Affirmation means receiving:* Comer, J. P. (1988). *Maggie's American Dream: The Life and Times of a Black Family.* New York: New American Library.

172 *In a study conducted in Toledo:* Price, J., & Desmond, S. (1987). The Missing Children Issue: A Preliminary Examination of 5th Grade Students' Perceptions. *American Journal of Diseases of Children, 141,* 811–815.

172 *Lee May's book:* May, L. (1995). *In My Father's Garden.* Atlanta: Longstreet Press.

174 *Data from the Luxembourg:* Rainwater, L., & Smeeding, T. (1995). U.S. Doing Poorly Compared to Others. National Center for Children in Poverty, *News and Issues, 5*(3), 4ff.

Chapter 7

181 *British psychiatrist Michael Rutter:* Rutter, M. (1989). Pathways from Childhood to Adult Life. *Journal of Psychology and Psychiatry, 30,* 23–51.

181 *Community Psychologist Rudolf Moos:* Moos, R. (1979). *Evaluation of Educational Environments: Procedures, Measures, Findings and Policy Implications.* San Francisco: Jossey-Bass.

183 *The premier researcher:* Olds, D., Eckenrode, J., Henderson, Jr., C. R., Kotzman, H., Powers, J., Cole, R., Sidora, K., Morris, P., Pettit, L., & Luckey, D. (1997). Long-Term Effects of Home Visitation on Maternal Life Course and Child Abuse and Neglect: 15-Year Follow-up of a Randomized Trial. *Journal of the American Medical Association, 278,* 637–643.

183 *Babies in a comparison:* Ibid.

184 *In her book:* Harris, J. R. (1998). *The Nurture Assumption: Why Children Turn Out the Way They Do.* New York: Free Press.

184 *Commenting on Harris's view:* Quoted in S. Begley (1998). The Parent Trap. *Newsweek,* September 7, 53ff.

185 *Programs like Parents as Teachers:* Vygotsky, L. (1986). *Thought and Language.* Cambridge, MA: MIT Press.

186 *What is more, psychological maltreatment:* Garbarino, J., Guttman, E., & Seeley, J. W. (1986). *The Psychologically Battered Child.* San Francisco: Jossey-Bass.

187 *When parents or other adults:* Greenspan, S. I. (1992). *Infancy and Earl Childhood: The Practice of Clinical Assessments and Intervention with Emotional and Developmental Challenges.* Madison, CT: International Universities Press.

191 *Many child protection agencies:* Garbarino, J., Guttman, E., & Seeley, J. W. (1986). *The Psychologically Battered Child.* San Francisco: Jossey-Bass.

192 *After analyzing violence prevention:* Tolan, P., & Guerra, N. (1993). *What Works in Reducing Adolescent Violence: An Empirical Review of the Field.* Chicago: University of Chicago Press.

192 *Sheppard Kellam's program:* Kellam, S. G., Rebok, G. W., Ialongo, N., & Mayer, L. S. (1994). The Course and Malleability of Aggressive Behavior from Early First Grade into Middle School: Results of a Developmental Epidemiology-

Based Preventive Trial. *Journal of Child Psychology and Psychiatry and Allied Disciplines. 35*(2), 259–281.

193 *A related effort:* Fried, S., & Fried, P. (1996). *Bullies and Victims: Helping Your Child Through the Schoolyard Battlefield.* New York: M. Evans.

194 *The seventh line:* Hartshorne, H., & May, M. (1928). *Studies in the Nature of Character: Vol. 1. Studies in Deceit.* New York: Macmillan.

197 *Suburban, small-town, and rural schools:* Lantieri, L & Patti, J. (1996). *Waging Peace in Our Schools.* Boston: Beacon Press.

198 *In the early 1960s:* Bronfenbrenner, U., McClelland, P., Wethington, E., Moen, P., & Ceci, S. (1996). *The State of Americans: This Generation and the Next.* New York: Free Press.

198 *After reviewing the evidence:* American Psychological Association (1993). *Summary Report of the American Psychological Association Commission on Violence and Youth: Vol. 1. Violence and Youth: Psychology's Response.* Washington, DC.

199 *Military psychologist David Grossman:* Grossman, D., & Siddle, P. (1999). Combat. In L. Kurtz (Ed.), *The Encyclopedia of Violence, Peace and Conflict.* San Diego: Academic Press.

203 *Research dating back to the 1950s:* Barker, R., & Gump, P. (1964). *Big School, Small School.* Stanford, CA: Stanford University Press.

204 *Research on school size:* Garbarino, J. (1995). *Raising Children in a Socially Toxic Environment.* San Francisco: Jossey-Bass.

204 *On one side of this debate:* Ibid.

Chapter 8

207 *the case of three Fort Meyers, Florida, seniors:* The Lords of Chaos [TV broadcast] (1998, September 25). *Dateline News Magazine.* New York: National Broadcasting Company.

208 *surveys of adolescents reveal:* Loeber, R., & Farrington, D. P. (1998). Serious and Violent Juvenile Offenders. In R. Loeber & D. Farrington (Eds.), *Serious and Violent Juvenile Offenders; Risk Factors and Successful Interventions.* Thousand Oaks, CA: Sage.

209 *Numerous youth advocates:* Rotenberg, S. (1997, Spring). Responding to the Mental Health Needs of Youth in the Juvenile System. In *Focal Point: A National Bulletin on Family Support and Children's Mental Health.* Portland, OR: Portland State University, pp. 1, 3–5.

209 *Among the treatment options most favored:* Henggeler, S. W., & Borduin, C. M. (1990). *Family Therapy and Beyond: A Multisystemic Approach to Treating the Behavior Problems of Children and Adolescents.* Pacific Grove, CA: Brooks/Cole.

209 *most evaluation studies give high grades:* Henggler, S. W., & Blaske, D. M. (1990). An Investigation of Systemic Conceptualizations of Parent-Child Coalitions and Symptom Change. *Journal of Consulting and Clinical Psychology, 58,* 336–344

210 *In their review of the evidence:* Krisberg, B., & Howell, J. C. (1998). The Impact of the Juvenile Justice System and Prospects for Graduated Sanctions in a Comprehensive Strategy. In R. Loeber & D. Farrington (Eds.), *Serious and Vio-*

lent Juvenile Offenders: Risk Factors and Successful Interventions. Thousand Oaks, CA: Sage.

211 *Surveys reported by psychologist Rolf Loeber:* Loeber, R., & Farrington, D. P. (1998). Serious and Violent Juvenile Offenders. In R. Loeber & D. Farrington (Eds.), *Serious and Violent Juvenile Offenders: Risk Factors and Successful Interventions*. Thousand Oaks, CA: Sage.

211 *The California study:* Krisberg, B., & Howell, J. C. (1998). The Impact of the Juvenile Justice System and Prospects for Graduated Sanctions in a Comprehensive Strategy. In R. Loeber & D. Farrington (Eds.), *Serious and Violent Juvenile Offenders: Risk Factors and Successful Interventions*. Thousand Oaks, CA: Sage.

212 *A study conducted:* Goldstein, A. P., & Gluck, B. (1994). *The Prosocial Gang: Implementing Aggression Replacement Therapy*. Thousand Oaks, CA: Sage.

213 *Theraputic Crisis Intervention:* Budlong, M., Holden, M., & Mooney, A. (1993). *Theraputic Crisis Intervention: A Train the Trainer Curriculum* (3rd ed.). Ithaca, NY: Family Life Development Center.

214 *Goldstein calls this package:* Goldstein, A. P., Sprafkin, R. P., Gershaw, N. J., & Klein, P. (1980). *Skillstreaming the Adolescent*. Champaign, IL: Research Press.

215 *treatment approach for violent boys:* Goldstein, A. P., & Glick, B. (1987). *Aggression Replacement Training: A Comprehensive Intervention for Aggressive Youth*. Champaign, IL: Research Press.

215 *ART was used with gang members:* Goldstein, A. P., & Glick, B. (1994). *The Prosocial Gang: Implementing Aggression Replacement Therapy*. Thousand Oaks, CA: Sage.

218 *kids often assume:* Hershberger, S. (1996). *Violence Within the Family: Social Psychological Perspectives*. Boulder, CO: Westview Press.

219 *The experience of trauma:* Perry, B., Pollard, R., Blakley, T., Baker, W., & Vigilante, D. (1995). Childhood trauma, the Neurobiology of Adaptation, and "Use-Dependent" Development of the Brain: How "States" Become "Traits." *Infant Mental Health Journal. 16,* 271–289.

221 *One interesting innovation:* The Samaya Foundation (Producer). (1996). *Healing the Causes of Violence* [Video]. (Available from the Samaya Foundation, 75 Leonard Street, New York, NY 10013)

221 *Vipassana meditation:* Menahemi, A., & Ariel, E. (Producers). (1997). *Doing Time, Doing Vipassana* [Video]. (Available from Karuna Films Ltd.)

223 *psychiatrist James Gilligan:* Gilligan, J. (1996). *Violence: Our Deadly Epidemic and Its Causes*. New York: Putnam.

224 *Biographies of boys who seem mired:* Masters, J. J. (1997). *Finding Freedom: Writings from Death Row*. Junction City, CA: Padma.

224 *The Autobiography of Malcolm X:* Haley, A., & Malcolm X (1995). *The Autobiography of Malcolm X*. New York: Chelsea House.

226 *psychologist Lev Vygotsky's:* Vygotsky, L. (1978). *Thought and Language*. Cambridge, MA: MIT Press.

227 *theologian Reinhold Niebuhr:* Niebuhr, R. (1972). *The Children of Light and the Children of Darkness: A Vindication of Democracy and a Critique of Its Traditional Defense*. New York: Scribner.

227 *psychologist James Pennebaker:* Pennebaker, J. W. (1982). *The Psychology of Physical Symptoms.* New York: Springer-Verlag.

227 *Watching the Lords of Chaos:* The Lords of Chaos [TV Broadcast] (1998, September 25). *Dateline News Magazine.* New York: National Broadcasting Company.

230 *A Path with Heart:* Kornfield, J. (1993). *A Path with Heart.* New York: Bantam.

232 *a review of these programs:* Peters, M., Thomas, D., & Zamberlan, C. (1997, September). *Boot Camps for Juvenile Offenders.* Washington, DC: U.S. Department of Justice, Office of Justice Programs, Office of Juvenile Justice and Delinquency Prevention.

233 *Peace Is Every Step:* Thich Nhat Hanh (1991). *Peace Is Every Step: The Path of Mindfulness in Everyday Life.* New York: Bantam.

237 *California's "Street Soldiers" program:* Marshall, J. (1996). *Street Soldier: One Man's Struggle to Save a Generation, One Life at a Time.* New York: Delacorte Press.

237 *The Lionheart Foundation:* The Lionheart Foundation, Box 194 Back Bay, Boston, MA 02117.

237 *Houses of Healing:* Casarjian, R. (1996). *Houses of Healing: A Prisoner's Guide to Inner Power and Freedom.* Boston, MA: The Lionheart Foundation.

237 *We're All Doing Time:* Lozoff, B. (1997). *We're All Doing Time: A Guide for Getting Free.* Durham, NC: The Human Kindness Foundation.

237 *Finding Freedom:* Masters, J. J. (1997). *Finding Freedom: Writings from Death Row.* Junction City, CA: Padma.

Index